Praise for *Tell...*

"Bader and Pearson, in this sensible, us...
that 'truthfulness is the beating heart of...
explain that telling the truth compassiona...
truth compassionately may be harder still. What a profound observation! I
enormously value this book and its subtle, wise message."

— Frank Pittman, M.D., author of *Private Lies: Infidelity and the Betrayal of Intimacy*
and *Grow Up!: How Taking Responsibility Can Make You a Happy Adult*

"Everybody lies, but few people really look at the lies they tell one another to
decipher their impact on those intimate connections. Drs. Bader and Pearson
shine light on what lies mean and what deception may be masking for both people in a marriage."

— Ellen Wachtel, Ph.D., author of *We Love Each Other, But . . .*

"Along with anniversary flowers and candy, partners should exchange copies
of Bader and Pearson's new book, *Tell Me No Lies*. Two of the world's leading experts on couple relationships, the authors show us how to revive the vital
connection that is the reason people get married in the first place. *Tell Me No
Lies* offers candid exploration of the consequences of dishonesty and deceit—
and, even more important, it presents ways out of the betrayal trap."

— Jeffrey K. Zeig, Ph.D., director of the Milton H. Erickson Foundation

...ll Me No Lies is a serious, funny, beautiful, and compelling book that
...onstrates the importance of truthfulness in relationships. From seemingly
...cent courtship lies through what Bader and Pearson call 'the shocking
...e of anything goes,' they delineate how couples can use honesty to achieve
...acy. This book is the best wedding present any couple could receive. I
...mmend its use in any stage of a relationship, and to all mental health pro-
...onals."

— Mary Goulding, M.S.W., internationally recognized teacher
of psychotherapy and author of *Changing Lives*

...! Me No Lies is a breakthrough, flat-out fabulous book. The premise is
...le and clear: everybody lies and lying causes trouble for couples. . . .
...ugh their own revealing experiences, and countless familiar case exam-
...the authors beautifully describe how to build a close, intimate relationship
...ie radical foundation of telling the truth. This book will challenge much of
...conventional thinking and wisdom about what is a good, and what is a
...e, relationship. It's a shock and a welcome breath of honesty."

— Stephanie Brown, Ph.D., director of the Addictions Institute, Menlo
Park, California, and coauthor of *The Alcoholic Family in Recovery*

Also by Ellyn Bader, Ph.D.
and Peter Pearson, Ph.D.

IN QUEST OF THE MYTHICAL MATE

Also by Judith D. Schwartz

THE MOTHER PUZZLE

THE WELL-INFORMED PATIENT'S GUIDE TO CAESAREAN BIRTHS
(WITH KATHRYN COX, M.D.)

THE WELL-INFORMED PATIENT'S GUIDE TO HYSTERECTOMY
(WITH KATHRYN COX, M.D.)

Tell Me No Lies

How to Stop Lying to Your Partner—and Yourself—in the 4 Stages of Marriage

Ellyn Bader, Ph.D., and Peter T. Pearson, Ph.D., with Judith D. Schwartz

A SKYLIGHT PRESS BOOK

ST. MARTIN'S PRESS ⚘ NEW YORK

www.stmartins.com

Designed by Kathryn Parise

Library of Congress Cataloging-in-Publication Data

Bader, Ellyn.
    Tell me no lies : how to stop lying to your partner—
and yourself—in the 4 stages of marriage / Ellyn Bader and
Peter T. Pearson.
        p. cm.

    1. Marriage—United States—Psychological aspects.
2. Communication in marriage—United States. 3. Truthfulness
and falsehood. I. Pearson, Peter T. II. Title.

HQ734.B212 2000
306.85—dc21   00-029684

ISBN 978-0-312-28062-8

D 30 29 28 27 26 25 24

We dedicate this book to the many clients with whom we have worked over the years. Your quests for authenticity have inspired, accelerated, and deepened our knowledge about the joys and struggles of the human condition.

Contents ✻

Contents

Your way of saying things is strange,
Your fluent phrases twist and change
As wind-bewildered waters do,
And half is false and half is true.
How shall I find out what you mean
With true and false to choose between?
Or how remember to be wise,
Hating your truth and loving your lies?
                    —AUTHOR UNKNOWN

Tell Me No Lies

1 ✿

Truth . . .
and Consequences

*E*verybody lies. Friends lie to friends. Children lie to their parents. Politicians lie to constituents. And, certainly, husbands and wives lie to each other.

That any given marriage has its deceptions doesn't mean that anything's "wrong." Certain lies allow loving partners to be sensitive, reassuring, even giving to each other. They can help couples reserve their energy for the more important conversations. Marital lies may be playful when harping on the truth would spoil the fun. A comment like, "You're the best lover on the whole planet" may not pass double-blind testing, but it does convey emotional truth.

Lies between lovers, however, can be highly electric: they have tremendous potential to both nurture and destroy a relationship. Unfortunately, lies usually undermine a relationship because, when unchecked by compassion and honest introspection, they tend to feed on each other. Most couples underestimate the power that lies—even seemingly harmless lies—wield in their marriage.

As codirectors of The Couples Institute, we have devoted more than fifteen years to studying marital communication. We've been privy to the intimate dramas of couples in various phases of discord and distress. We've seen marriages virtually implode after a major betrayal. We've also seen couples hold onto what's true for them despite fierce disagreement and, in the process, manage to strengthen their trust.

We do believe that most people want to be honest with those they love. But the nature of marriage, with its infinite number of interdependencies and huge emotional stakes, guarantees that spouses will lie to each other and fool themselves. Being honest with another person, particularly one you're dealing with all the time, can be dicey. The impetus for most marital lies does not stem from a wish to deceive the other, but rather from the wish to keep the relationship *as it is.* That's the incredible irony: *Couples lie to preserve their relationships, but it's those very lies that create dissent and leave the partners feeling stagnant, isolated, and alone.*

Why do we lie in marriage? We want to look good—so we lie. We want to avoid hurting or disappointing a partner—so we lie. We fear that the truth will unleash conflict that will endanger the relationship—so we lie. We feel foolish about something that we said or did—so we lie. We have trouble putting the whole truth into words—so we manipulate it. We're reluctant to admit the darker sides of ourselves, our greed, envy, and selfishness—so we try to hide them. We lie because lies come with being human, and we are probably never so exposed in our humanness as we are with our mates.

This book is a wake-up call. At our clinic, The Couples Institute in Menlo Park, California, our focus is helping couples create extraordinary relationships. Through our workshops, individual cases, and the clinical work of therapists we supervise, we have seen literally thousands of couples. Through our experience, we have gained a unique perspective on the trials upon which marriages succeed or fail. We have found that at the heart of most couples' problems is some form of deception or withheld truth. We've seen deception sabotage marriages when one or both partners

> tell furtive lies and allow chronic dishonesty to turn good feeling into bad,
>
> lie themselves into corners because they lack the nerve to tell a partner what they feel,
>
> sense a mate would be uncomfortable with the truth so they soothe him or her with a lie,

fool themselves so that they're blinded to realities that are visible to everyone else.

But we've also seen those very same lies—once reckoned with—push relationships towards growth. We know there are powerful reasons to address the truth. We also know that there are powerful emotional reasons to avoid it. No one wants to give up the deceptions that they believe keep their marriage together.

Lie Patterns

Over the years, we've found that long-term relationships follow a predictable pattern of growth, involving four marital "stages."

1. The Honeymoon
2. Emerging Differences
3. Freedom
4. Together as Two

Certain types of lies arise at different points in a marriage in response to the specific challenges of each stage. Deception will stunt development in each stage, creating an emotional gridlock that leaves both partners stuck. We call these stalled points "Detours and Dead Ends." From the Honeymoon, you can veer into The Dark Side of the Honeymoon. When deceit obscures your Emerging Differences, you can end up in the Seething Stalemate. The failure to negotiate independence can thrust you into Freedom Unhinged. The only way to get on track is to confront the truth.

Intimate relationships are difficult, despite what cultural myths would have us believe, and every couple will encounter some tough situations. The grit to withstand those challenges—and to keep your marriage growing and alive—requires that you find the courage to voice the truth. And the resolve to listen to it.

Honesty: A Solid Foundation

Truthfulness bases a marriage in reality and trust. The failure to deal with truth—the all-too-common tendency to fall into expedient truth bending or lulled complacency—may be the first fumbling steps towards disaster. Don't follow in the footsteps of John and Sarah, whose story we recount in the book. You'll see that so-called white lies can lose their pearly innocence with blinding speed.

No one wants to think of himself as a liar, and we generally don't see our lies as lies. What happens in marriage, then, is that we lie and call it something else: protecting a partner, looking on the bright side of things, waiting until the right time to speak, keeping the peace. Through the day-to-day, give-and-take of a long-term relationship, we seek cover in many forms of deception. In this book, we make the case that becoming conscious of those lies—and understanding when, how, and why you lie—will help you make your marriage stronger.

Through our work, as well as our own marriage, we've learned that the way to inoculate your marriage against real stressors is to know that you can handle the tough stuff. And when you can speak truthfully about difficult things and find the truth in strong disagreements, you will feel more confident that you can handle just about anything. This is the substance of extraordinary, enduring marriages: the passion, tenderness, and generosity that can only emerge when two people have achieved a high level of mutual honesty. Honesty with compassion can spark the growth that keeps a marriage vibrant.

Lying isn't something we can or necessarily should relinquish altogether, but in marriage it must serve a useful purpose. It must promote the good feeling at the core of your relationship, not just the semblance of it.

Beware of Dormant Grenades

People typically hope that downplaying something or leaving out a detail isn't lying. Beware of the little lie, for fibs that start with benign intent may develop into open invitations to subterfuge.

For instance, little lies about how much someone spends for a fall suit can stay little. Or, before you know it, a partner can compound that little lie by falsifying how much money is spent on travel, all the way up the dishonesty scale to hoarding funds in hidden accounts. But at many milemarkers along this road, simple changes, or even small conversations about how to handle money, divvy up tasks, or talk about things, could have averted catastrophe.

Or, say a man wants his wife to wear a sexy nightgown. He doesn't say anything to her because he's afraid she'll think he's reducing her to a sex object, and so he keeps his fantasy private. As a result, their sex life becomes boring. If other parts of the marriage are less than terrific, he starts to justify flirting with other women. From there it's just a short hop, skip, and jump to sharing his sexual fantasies online or secretly visiting a pornography site. He may go on to have an affair. Or he may just bear with a tolerable but passionless relationship.

Throughout your marriage you will have lots of opportunities either to be more truthful with your partner or to sink deeper into deception. This happens not only in key moments (the credit-card bill arrives with dubious charges; a lover's lacy bra shows up in the laundry) but also in *everyday* events.

Here's an example from our own marriage:

ELLYN: Pete left town for a conference on Sunday and wasn't due back until Friday. By chance, the conference was cancelled and on Monday evening Pete walked in shouting, "Honey, I'm home!" I raced to the door and hugged him and said, "What a great surprise!"

Well, it was a nice surprise . . . but it was also a bit disappointing because I had been looking forward to the special plans our daughter, Molly, and I had made together. We had talked about going to our favorite restaurant and seeing a sappy movie. The energy around the house is different when it's only Molly and me. So I was both happy and *un*happy to see Pete.

On Tuesday night I was really crabby. Everything Pete did irritated me. I decided to tell him what was on my mind. "You know," I confessed, "part of me didn't really want you to come home so soon." I explained to him a bit about our "girl" plans and he understood. Once I said it, I could get on with the week that I now had before me—a week that included and, because I didn't want to give up those plans, excluded Pete.

Many people assume that it means something bad if they don't always want to see their partner around the house, but it's common to want more time alone—that simple kind of puttering-around time. If I hadn't been able to tell Pete that I liked aspects of his being away, I probably would have been irritable all week, especially at night. Being around the house wouldn't have been terribly pleasant for anyone. Or let's say that, rather than understanding where I was coming from, Pete said, "Okay, Ellyn, you won't see me till Friday night, if that's what you want!" and stormed out, slamming the door. That would have sent a pretty clear message, and I probably would avoid being truthful like that again.

Several times each day you're faced with these choices: (1) to pursue a path of honesty or deception; and (2) as a listener, to encourage more truthfulness or to close down the avenues that could lead you to truth.

Learning to ground your relationship on a foundation of truth involves resilience, fortitude, and the ability to hold on to and describe what's important to you. It's also about the courage to change old patterns and the capacity to weather disagreement. You can learn a lot about each other *if* you're willing to know. You can laugh about many things together *if* you're willing to face your own flaws and those of the relationship with humor. We want to help you recognize moments that offer an opening for truth. The more you work with the truth, the less you have to be afraid of it.

Hard-Won Honesty

We know that we can't ask couples to be more honest in their marriages unless we're willing to take those risks ourselves. The couples we've worked with have inspired us many times with their courage in telling the truth. They've also kept *us* honest, forcing us to practice what we preach.

PETE: Several years ago, we were on a vacation in the Southwest. I was in a major funk, moping around a lot, rejecting every activity Ellyn suggested and, basically, being an all-around drag. I had been ruminating over things about our relationship that bugged me, stuff we'd been over many times. Essentially, Ellyn wasn't living up to my vision of the ideal mate. Compared to the mental picture of the partner I wanted, Ellyn wasn't attractive enough, humorous enough, or high-voltage enough. Without work and other day-to-day distractions, that disappointment really hit me on the trip. But how could I ever express that?

Here's a fragment of the conversation that followed:

ELLYN: "What's wrong?"

PETE: "Nothing."

ELLYN: (*Blurted out on a wild intuitive hunch*): "Are you thinking of getting rid of me?"

PETE: "As a matter of fact, I am."

ELLYN: "What did you have in mind?"

PETE: "Well, I was thinking we would go to the Grand Canyon, and you'd peer over the edge and whoops—"

ELLYN: "Oh, I see. Bye, bye, Sweetie. So why wouldn't you do that?"

PETE: "You might end up only getting seriously hurt, and I don't want you to suffer."

ELLYN: "Were you thinking about anything else?"

PETE: "Yes, I was thinking about those really nasty-looking mushrooms in the backyard. I would fry up a batch and then that would be the end of you."

ELLYN: "What's wrong with that plan?"

PETE: "Well, I was afraid I would go to prison for homicide and then Molly would really be out of luck."

ELLYN: "Anything else?"

PETE: "I thought that maybe I'd go to Alaska, and every few months I would send you a postcard saying that I'm alive."

ELLYN: "Have you thought about just getting a divorce?"

PETE: "No, I don't want to go through that."

ELLYN: "One more question. Is there anything I should be seriously worrying about?"

PETE: "Actually, now that you ask it, the answer is no."

What happened here was that while we were half-kidding (and the black humor definitely helped) we were also quite serious. There was a dark side to our relationship, with Pete's chronic disappointment and the tension that arose from holding back those feelings. In talking, we confronted the shadowy underbelly of our marriage and found that we could live with it and even laugh at it. Here's how each of us experienced that exchange:

PETE: That series of questions was like lancing a boil for me. The fact that I could talk about what I was thinking allowed me to stop obsessing about it. I learned that I could express the most reprehensible things and share my darkest feelings, and Ellyn wouldn't drop me.

At the same time, my respect for Ellyn skyrocketed. When I said I was thinking of getting rid of her, her knees didn't buckle. She could ask me questions without folding or flinching. As we spoke, she had no idea what was going on with me; I wasn't sure what was going on myself. Her ability to listen to me impressed me enough to adjust the mental blueprint I had of my ideal mate. That created a shift. I saw other aspects of who she is and realized that the mate I have is more dimensional than what I had conjured up in a fantasy. Amazingly, I saw that there was room for all of me, even parts of me that weren't so pleasant, in this marriage.

ELLYN: It was simply an intuitive flash that made me ask if Pete was thinking of ending things with me. I trusted my intuition and went with the question. Once I opened that door, all I could do was step back and see where the discussion would lead. I continued to ask questions that seemed like they needed to be asked, even though I didn't think I was going to like what would come back to me. I still don't know what got me through that conversation. I remember saying to myself, "You really need to know what's wrong." Pete's gloom was severely hanging over the marriage and our vacation. Once I knew how bad things were, instead of merely guessing what Pete's feelings were and tiptoeing around him, I actually felt stronger. I knew I could hear the worst and survive. I didn't like it, but ignoring his unhappiness wasn't doing me any good either. Since then, we've certainly had our share of ups and downs and difficult discussions, but we've never had to have that particular talk again.

As this dialogue demonstrates, there are always two sides to every truth moment: (1) Eliciting the truth and (2) telling the truth. And not only is each situation a moment of truth, but so is each exchange within the discussion. Each person will have his or her own behind-the-curtain inquest: *Do I hold steadfast? Do I turn away? What's going on with him that he's not unstrung by now?* These thoughts whirl by at breakneck speed. You can never know what the other person is thinking. You'll hear what they say, but you won't know what they're censoring.

Often the truths we need to hear or to tell are not easy ones, but rather are the kind that make your palms sweat and your stomach clench. When you start, you won't know where it will take you. But that doesn't mean that what you hear will destroy you or that you will never recover from it. Take heart. You can withstand more than you think.

Going through it ourselves has enabled us to help couples through similar discussions. Having survived it, we can't so easily dismiss the pain of telling and hearing marital truths. Having come through stronger on the other side gives us the conviction that we have something to say about honesty in marriage.

Acknowledging truths may expose significant differences within a relationship. But in our experience, few differences prove insurmountable. We find that what topples relationships and leaves little choice but divorce are not problems but *rigidities* in one or both partners. It's not the size of the problem that determines whether a couple holds together or splits, but rather their ability to stay open to the situation and each other.

We've had the privilege of sitting with couples as they tested the boundaries of truth, as the following examples demonstrate:

James, a successful stockbroker, had a serious heart condition and had come perilously close to dying. Since recovering from that episode, he and his wife fought nonstop. In a session, his wife, stammering through tears, said to him, "I'm afraid of you dying. That's why I push you away. You can't do anything right because I don't want you to do anything right. I don't want to get so close to you only to have you leave me heartbroken." Visibly touched, James replied, "I had no idea that you cared that much."

Marion and Don attended one of our intensive workshops and had a discussion that will forever remain vivid in our memories. As they were sitting almost knee-to-knee, Marion asked, "Don, do you really want to know how I feel? I mean, how I *really* feel?" Don slowly nodded his head, and Marion replied, "I pray for your death." Don was able to remember key points we had been teaching about how to contain himself when things get tense. Breathe deeply, remember that most things aren't personal, and ask questions about what your partner is saying. After his deep breath he asked "Just how long have you been praying?" Her response, about ten years."

In the conversation that followed, Marion went on to explain how her belief in the sanctity of marriage precluded any consideration of divorce, leaving her no way to get out of the psychological black hole of their marriage other than to wish him dead. This couple had been so terrified of conflict that they had avoided any expression of bad feeling. As a result, each was filled with tension and despair. Marion, in particular, couldn't imagine saying what she really felt. Now she began to describe the thoughts and feelings she had kept mute over the years. She spoke the worst, and it wasn't as volcanic as she feared.

Two days later they were walking down the highway and an eighteen-wheel truck was traveling toward them, Don said, "Well, now's your chance." Marion later said, "At that moment the hourglass of our marriage was turned upside down. I knew then that I could tell Don what was in my heart and both of us could handle it."

Truths behind the Lies

Behind many marital lies is the inability of men and women to trust that their partner will understand them and that they'll be heard. This uncertainty is often rumbling beneath a man's stoicism or withdrawal, and beneath a woman's pleas for more engagement.

You are about to read a declaration of raw truths that have been boiling beneath the polite surface of an archetypal married couple.

He says, "You say you are a woman and therefore understand feelings. You say you are relationship oriented. You may understand tens, hundreds, even thousands of people, but you don't understand one very important person in your life, me. As much as I want to blame you for that, as much as I want to shove your hypocritical 'understanding' down your throat, as much as I want to throttle you for all those barbs you throw at me, I know deep in my heart that it is not all your fault.

"I feel (yes, there is that dreaded word I am accused of not appreciating) unequal to the task of explaining myself. I search for words to describe those tender areas that I rarely investigate in myself, let alone describe to you. Here's what I find so impossibly hard to express: No matter how clever I am, no matter how responsive I am to you or the world, it is never enough. There it is. What I don't want to say aloud is this: I feel a chronic sense of inadequacy.

"So I stonewall. I defend myself when I feel another verbal attack from you. It really pisses me off when you say you can talk to your women friends so much more easily. Great. Tell me one more time that you wish I were like a woman. What an extraordinary slap coming from someone who has staked such a claim on being 'understanding.'

"What you don't know, and what I struggle in my own fumbling way to tell you, is that indeed I want to be your hero. I want to be a good provider and feel the deep satisfaction of providing well. I also want to tell you that I really want to do just about all the things you are so hungry for me to do. But I don't. So what I do is become secretive. I lie to you. I lie to myself. I drink. I have affairs. I lust after money. I strive for recognition. I hide out with the television, the newspaper, sports, and hobbies because the truth is that too often I want to get away from how I feel when I'm around you. I hate that I don't have the courage to be honest with you—or with myself.

"When I feel attacked, my choices are to either blame you and defend myself (and believe me, I've learned the severe limits of doing that) or stonewall and feel like a wimp. I know you think I have all the power when I stonewall, but I feel anything but powerful. The irony is that if I tell you about my powerlessness, I feel more like a wimp while you, dear wife, think I am doing great by expressing my feelings. Your emotional health is my psychological poison."

And she responds: "As long as we are in the truth-telling mode, let me tell you a few things. I want to look up to you and admire you.

Instead, I don't respect you. You want to be my hero. Well, I would admire you for a whole lot less than you imagine. You think I'm so complicated. I'm really a lot simpler than you think. I want to count on your involvement, count on you to coparent, and count on you to come through when you say you'll do something. And, yes, to even occasionally ask me what I feel.

"I really don't expect of you what you expect of yourself. What I really want is a partner to share my life with. A partner who can sometimes be romantic. A partner who cleans up his own messes. A partner who sometimes gets a baby-sitter and takes me out. A partner who can anticipate problems at home so I don't have to think of everything first.

"Unlike you, I do try to tell you about my struggle. I must admit, though, when you feel the sting of the verbal lash, I think to myself, *Good, maybe I finally got his attention, and he'll wake up from his sleepwalking.* I lie not out of self-protection like you do but out of helplessness and resignation. I give up and then you don't get the best parts of who I am or the potential of who I could become."

What do you imagine would happen to a couple who actually had this exchange? Would it be the fatal blow to their relationship? Suppose they could each step back and realize that they had just spoken from the darkest and most starkly truthful corners of their being. And suppose they could each accept that they had delivered and received some very caustic hits from one another in the past. And out of that acceptance, they developed compassion for themselves and each other. And they realized how few people in the world could listen openly to such expressions of pain and then grow from them. Might each one recognize how unusual, precious, and rare his or her partner is? Could they conclude that this is a relationship worth further investment? Would they realize the special gift they had given to each other—and to themselves? Might they even use this confrontation as a turning point and let it serve as a springboard to greater understanding between them?

At the truth-telling moment, both partners are at their best. The person speaking is at his most expressive, describing his interior life as precisely as he can. The person listening isn't collapsing or scrambling to send up a decoy. Don't underestimate the transformation that can take place when two people speak to each other in this way and manage this level of honesty. When you can confront a huge fear and get through it, there's a shift in how you exist in the world. The ground beneath you feels firmer; there's less to tip you off-balance.

The Lying Partnership

An honest marriage is not something you can do alone. Both partners have to be willing to face the truth, and *hearing* the truth is as important as *telling* it. It's easy to fall into the trap of focusing on the lie and the liar and forget the person on the receiving end of the lie. This is a mistake because he or she plays a critical role in the creation of lies. We call this person the "Lie Invitee."

The Lie Invitee in some way encourages the partner to lie. For example, there are people who lament that they're always being lied to and betrayed. They may seem like innocent bystanders who simply have the bum luck of pairing off repeatedly with liars and cheats. However, they may respond to honesty by ignoring it, deflecting it, or railing against it—ultimately pushing the other person toward deception.

Were it not for Lie Invitee behavior, we believe, many destructive marital lies would not occur. We want to alert readers to common Lie Invitee patterns and offer tools to counteract them so that no one need keep the truth at arm's length.

The Marital Stages and the Lies that Stall Them

In this book, we introduce you to a new way of thinking about marriage that takes as its premise the intrinsic need for a marriage to grow. We have created a model for how marriages naturally evolve. As we noted, a relationship will go through stages of development, which can be subverted by deception. The way to alleviate the resulting distress, and to get the marriage back on its proper path to growth, is to work through those deceptions.

At the same time, we have learned that couples will find themselves at common impasses on this journey through the stages. No couple skates through the stages without stumbling. Each impasse could be either a detour or a dead end on the footpath to growth. If you reckon with the lies that hold you back, even if it takes a long time, you move on. If not, you remain stuck and marriage becomes an exercise in endurance. No one walks into a marriage equipped to deal with everything. So when tension heats up, what do people do? They lie.

You can think about the passage through the marital stages this way: When two people get together, they imagine two halves joining to make a whole. After the marriage has matured, it becomes more than the sum of its parts. In other words, in new relationships two people are often looking to complete themselves. It is only after significant growth, however, that they can be two separate but deeply connected individuals, secure in themselves and the relationship.

A brief discussion of the light and dark sides of each of the marital stages will introduce you to the lies and challenges of each stage. Later we will acquaint you with two couples and the knots of deception that will either liberate or destroy them.

STAGE ONE: THE HONEYMOON

When a couple first gets together, along with the glow of new love comes a blissful feeling of togetherness. This is crucial in establishing a loving bond, but no one can stay at this stage forever without squelching each person's uniqueness.

Classic Honeymoon Lies: "I like everything about you." "We like all the same things."

In the Honeymoon, it all seems simple. You have gotten a taste of Nirvana and you want this to work. You dismiss with lies any inkling you may have that this person or the relationship is anything less than utter perfection and harmony.

DETOUR OR DEAD END:
THE DARK SIDE OF THE HONEYMOON

Couples get caught down this blind alley when they won't let go of the Honeymoon. They insist, despite all signs to the contrary, that everything remains "perfect." They are so afraid of tension or dissension that they avoid significant truths and hide more and more in the deceptions they tell themselves and each other.

Classic Dark Side of the Honeymoon Lies: "No, nothing's wrong. Why do you ask?" "Sure it's okay with me if we spend every holiday with your family."

Couples who spin off on this byway are pretending to themselves and the world that they're still in the Honeymoon Stage. They lie away their discontent and use deception to cushion themselves from conflict.

STAGE TWO: EMERGING DIFFERENCES

At some point, partners begin to assert their individual desires. Differences are then inevitable. Vital relationships do more than tolerate difference; they are enriched by it. Each person discovers new strengths and beliefs, which are then brought back into the relationship. As people traverse this stage, they can be torn between revealing themselves and discovering a renewed sense of integrity or wanting to retreat, hide out, and enjoy happy coupledom.

Classic Emerging Differences Lies: "I'm glad to raise our kids according to your religion." "It doesn't matter to me if I'm the sole supporter."

By this stage, the gap between what you feel and what you admit has become untenable. When you choose to confront your own truths, you begin to reap some of the rewards of honesty. When you continue to bluff, you'll find yourself at a standstill.

DETOUR OR DEAD END: SEETHING STALEMATE

People get detained here when they can't abide the fact that they have differences. They bicker, intimidate, yell, attack, and engage in passive-aggressive sniping in an effort to coerce each other into agreement, even as their behavior drives away any remaining good will.

Classic Stalemate Lies: "You never listen to me." "All our problems would be solved if you would change."

This is guerrilla warfare. Still unwilling to take responsibility for your own truths and embrace differences within the relationship, you use lies as manipulative tools while ostensibly holding the higher ground. The desire is to browbeat the other person into accepting your version of the truth.

STAGE THREE: FREEDOM

As each partner makes forays out of the "we-ness" of the relationship, interests and satisfactions outside the marriage may take center stage. These include careers, hobbies, friendships, travel, and just plain solitude. The couple has to negotiate space and distance, time together and time apart. With a firm foundation and a willingness to accept truth, the marriage can find a balance.

Classic Freedom Lies: "I didn't think you wanted to take yoga (but in truth it means something to me to try this on my own)." "I'm only going back to school for this one class (but I'm really thinking about changing careers)."

The couple at this stage has grappled with differences and now must address the next challenge: reconciling the two partners' conflicting interests. When they can address their desires truthfully and with regard to the other, they will enjoy independence within the security of a loving relationship. When they get sneaky, however, they may land in serious trouble.

DETOUR OR DEAD END: FREEDOM UNHINGED

Here the yearning for independence turns into a power struggle, or one partner checks out rather than be truthful with the other. The effects on the marriage can be devastating. This is when huge "felony" lies occur, such as infidelity and misrepresenting finances.

Classic Freedom Unhinged Lies: "I'm working late at the office again." "Those extra charges on the phone bill? Oh, those were to an old friend from college."

At this point, one or both partners has strayed well off the morality map, taking liberties without concern for how it affects the other. People lie recklessly so that they can do what they want or get away with what they've already done.

STAGE FOUR: TOGETHER AS TWO

As the partners become emotionally more distinct, they are more accepting of themselves and each other. The marriage deepens as a result. The two know themselves and each other so well that there's little need for lying. They are likely to respond to differences with humor and compassion rather than with deceptions.

Classic Together as Two Lie: "I don't mind taking the kids for the weekend."

Well, maybe he does mind—a bit. But the inconvenience is scant compared with the pleasure his wife will receive from going away with her friends without feeling guilty that she's putting him out. Couples at this stage lie out of love, not out of fear.

Every couple starts at the Honeymoon. Then there are essentially two courses: towards increased honesty or increased deception. Increased deception taken to its logical extreme is Freedom Unhinged; steadily building up honesty will steer a couple towards the happy sanctuary of Together as Two.

This framework helps organize the passages most couples experience. Knowing the basic sequence and the common sticking points can reassure you that snags and growing pains in marriage are perfectly normal. Of course, few paths take a straight line, and there are plenty of offshoots and intersections along the way. Every marriage is continually evolving in an ongoing process of testing one another and calculating risks. It's also unusual for any two people to go through the developmental sequence at the same speed. This creates a dynamic tension and helps push a marriage towards growth—or crisis.

When you can brave the trials that mark the ascent through the stages, you will increase your self-esteem and strengthen your marriage. In order to master the skills necessary to keep the marriage moving, you will need to venture into unknown emotional terrain and take the risk of voicing unfocused truths and putting elusive dreams into words. The alternative is to hide your truths and to lie. In *Tell Me No Lies*, we want to help you recognize the lies that are hampering your marriage so that you can begin to shift in the direction of truthfulness.

What This Book Will Do

Tell Me No Lies will show you a new way of thinking about truth and deception. It will help you understand the dynamics of your marriage within the context of the marital stages. You'll be able to pinpoint where you are in your marriage and then interpret any barriers to honesty accordingly.

Starting with Chapter 4 we will present a guide to truths and lies. We will follow two couples—John and Sarah and Paul and Mary—through the four stages and examine deception's impact on their marriages. We will watch how one pair is able to enhance their marriage through a series of difficult revelations while the other, through continued deceit, makes the descent toward Freedom Unhinged.

An important theme throughout will be *distinguishing between lies that bear watching and lies that needn't worry you*. Not all lies are dangerous. Some lies are constructive, and some are even an expression of love. For example, when you say, "Reprogramming the computer is no problem right now" you may really mean, "It might be inconvient, but I will do it anyway because I know it will help you." Or you might humor your partner and say, "Sure, I'd be happy to eat Hungarian food" even if you don't like Hungarian food, because you're pretty sure you're not going to run into the situation very often.

Nor is everything that sounds false a lie. Someone may be testing out an idea or struggling to find the right words to express their feelings.

But the lies you *assume* to be benign aren't always so. Going along with whom your mate wants to socialize with may set up a dangerous pattern of abdicating what you want. Also, a matter of taste—like choosing furniture or art—may not seem like a big deal, but if you pay attention to your own reaction you may be more invested in your preference than you thought.

Another important theme in this book is *decoding the lie*. Deceptions act as a kind of emotional code for the problems in a relationship. Somewhere within the lie are the issues the two of you have to face. People typically lie about things that touch on their vulnerabilities. You think that once the truth is out your partner will either reject you outright or will lack the fortitude to stick by you while you work things out. The lie, then, is a cover for your own growth issues.

An example would be lies about money. Some people may keep funds stashed away out of a fear of being too dependent on their partner. Others may rely on impulse purchases to cheer themselves up, and then try to conceal them rather than dealing directly with sadness or depression.

Another theme is *heeding signals*. Most people have some form of radar to detect when someone's being dishonest. But that intuitive sense is greatly swayed by our own psychological needs. If, for instance, I really want to depend on someone, I may not pay attention to clues that he is drinking on the sly, hyping up his achievements, or otherwise being crooked with me. My emotional needs will override all evidence; my truth-testing apparatus goes on the blink.

In this book, we want to help you build the courage to keep that radar plugged in. The signals rarely arrive in big letters saying, "DON'T BELIEVE IT!" You're more likely to feel a vague uneasiness, a clutch in the stomach, or a sense of "did I hear that?" when stories don't quite add up. This is how you intercept lies.

We want to consistently remind you to follow up on your hunches. This means being honest with yourself, and being honest with your partner in areas where you know you've been deceptive. This can be scary because such truths may cast doubt on what you've believed up to now. But it's these transient glimpses into reality that set the stage for psychological, emotional, and marital growth. And with that, the likelihood of lying or being lied to diminishes.

Through both our own experience and case histories from our practice, we will address questions such as how to:

avoid falling into lying as a coping mechanism from the very beginning of your relationship

listen to your partner's truths without taking them personally

anticipate and brace yourself for strong reactions from your partner

love your partner through disappointment or disillusionment and continue to love your partner

call your partner on a lie without resorting to attack

address fragile intuitions or tentative truths and not shove them underground for fear of what your partner will say

overcome the desire to please others and smooth things over at the expense of the truth

own up to a lie gracefully

above all, to overcome the fear that runaway honesty will topple your marriage

This is your chance to enjoy a more honest relationship. People too often think the route to deeper connection is marked by seamless accord. In fact, it must be peppered with difficult feelings and dilemmas because finding their way through such challenges is what propels couples forward together.

It is our hope that this book will encourage you to push your own honesty threshold, that it will inspire you to be more honest with yourself and your partner, and that you will be able to tolerate more truthfulness from one another. We hope that you will become more fluent in the language of emotional truth. We hope that you will be able to laugh at what you've been afraid to share, for there can be a comical side to how we lie to conceal what may be obvious. In sum, we hope you won't be terrified of an outbreak of candor between you and your mate.

Tell Me No Lies is a book for couples who might otherwise hold on to their deceptions under the mistaken notion that to act differently is to break the spell. It's for everyone who wants a more honest, more satisfying relationship, not merely for those already tangled up in lies. It's for everyone who has wondered if their lover is on the up-and-up with them, or who is trying to gather the gumption to speak up about something that may be unknown by a mate.

The reality is that the romantic spell is already broken—as it should be. Giving up illusion is necessary to create a rich, passionate bond. Lying in marriage drains energy, breeds distrust, and prevents you from being the couple you want and have every right to be. Honesty dissolves the barriers, frees you up, and most definitely feels better.

Don't let your truths, hopes, and longings die on the vine. Don't fritter away your married life wondering what would happen if you revealed what's on your mind and in your heart. Above all else, truthfulness is about courage. Do you have the confidence to show your mate who you are? Do you have the courage to hear your mate's truths?

It's up to you.

2 ❀

The Complex
Lies of Husbands
and Wives

*I*f only lying were simple. If only you could catch yourself every time you lie. If only you could answer in one sentence exactly why it's hard to speak the truth. If only you could see that the two of you have fallen into falsehood before you got mired in it.

But when it comes to intimate relationships, lies are rarely simple. Behind the false front is a lot of pain, fear, and resistance to dealing with the truth. Often you're second-guessing each other. In this chapter, we explain why marital lies are so complicated in nature. And why they're tough to recognize, tricky to unravel, and seemingly impossible to stop.

We want to raise your consciousness of how deception may operate in your marriage, for we believe that at any point in your relationship you can become more attuned to deception. With this understanding, you can learn to prevent destructive lies before they gather enough momentum to inflict damage.

Lies in Motion

When married people lie to one another, it's not a discrete event. Each lie sets a precedent. Every false claim becomes the statement of record, the benchmark response for whenever that subject comes up again. Every time one person winks at a lie, it becomes that much easier for his mate to lie next time. Every time a lie is uncovered, trust is eroded. A lie travels through a marriage, becoming part of the way a couple interacts.

Lies can take over the most unsuspecting marriage in numerous ways. For one, lies can *infect* a relationship. The bad feelings engendered by a single lie can seep into every corner. One lie—one moment of cowardly evasion, one incriminating detail conveniently "forgotten"—can gather increasing significance in a marriage until it halts communication altogether. The deceiving partner may not have any idea of how it may have affected his or her mate. The lie acts like a virus, invisible to the eye but with huge destructive potential.

Lies can also *infest* a relationship. Lies of all sizes and import can swarm around a couple constantly, provoking and distracting them. A couple can quickly succumb to the habit of lying and distorting even the most mundane things. The lies can be so automatic that neither partner notices that the honest core—the spark of connection that brought them together—has been buried beneath the heap.

When people get married, there's an assumption of blanket trust. There's a belief that you know the other person and can count on that person to act and react as you expect. That's an illusion. You're going to find yourself at crossroads all the time. With each new awareness, you will confront the question: Will I face the truth or will I lie?

We think of marriage as a romance, but it's more like a drama—one that you're writing together. You don't just happen into your marriage at a set level of honesty. You determine how truthful you are with each other. You're continually establishing patterns, revising the rules, subtly influencing, inspiring, and inhibiting each other.

The ground is ever shifting because each of you is getting to know each other better as you get to know yourself, and thereby gaining insight and wisdom. And each exchange between you holds within it the possibility of either triggering your mate's defenses or encouraging forthrightness.

Despite divorce statistics, there is a great deal of societal pressure to be married and stay married. People also have a fundamental desire to belong. Strong forces operate on a marriage. Fortunately, this means people will work hard to make their marriages successful and to use marriage as a place to mature. However, people are highly reluctant to cut ties when they are in a bad relationship because they dread dating again or or being alone. This makes people hesitant to confront deception and leads them to linger in compromised relationships.

For many couples we've encountered through the years, the price paid to keep their marriage license is misery. What makes them miserable are the accommodations they make to maintain the status quo—unexpressed misgivings, grudging acquiescence, or feigned approval. People lie to make it possible to be together; then they lie to deal with the misery that these accommodations have created. People twist their psyches into pretzels to avoid revealing who they are. We don't think it needs to be this way.

Lies Reflect History

A critical lie or perceived disloyalty can put a marriage on ice for years. What one partner sees as a trivial event may be deemed high treason by the other. With issues of trust, each person's psychological history comes into play. It may be hard to grasp the significance of a lie, but that lie may conjure up some weighty emotional baggage. Dean and Annie are a powerful illustration of this point.

By the time we met them, their decade-long marriage was already reeling from years of disaffection. Each was very dissatisfied; each felt misunderstood. They made love maybe once or twice *a year*—in a *good* year. In treatment, it took a lot of wading through old grudges and grievances to determine that underneath all this woe was a lie.

Dean and Annie met when Annie was coming out of a relationship with a man named Bert—whom Dean knew and disliked because he had had a bad experience doing business with Bert. When Dean started dating Annie, he said, "Please, I need to know that you won't see this man again." Annie said, "I promise. I won't." About a year after their wedding, Dean heard from a friend that he had seen Annie having cocktails with Bert at a local inn. Dean was furious and told Annie as much. "It's *my* life," she replied. "I'm not running off with the guy. We just had a drink."

To Annie, the incident was no big deal. The fact that she swore not to see Bert was immaterial; she had agreed without giving it much thought. However, her feeling was that she wasn't "choosing" Bert over Dean, so she thought Dean was silly to be upset.

To Dean, however, this was a betrayal. In his view, Annie had made a vow and had broken it. From that moment on, he regarded Annie as untrustworthy and began to guard himself. "I would look at her and think, 'She's a liar. I can't trust her,' " he said later. "I just couldn't get that image of her out of my mind." Essentially, a lot of emotional scar tissue had built up around that single instance of disloyalty. And it required some exploratory surgery for us to locate and resolve the original deception.

It turned out that Dean grew up in an unstable family, and felt that he couldn't count on anyone. As an adult, Dean was often accused of being "remote" or "cold." It wasn't until he met Annie, who had a warm manner and an easy, infectious laugh, that he felt he could open up to someone. Then he heard about Annie seeing Bert. He knew it wasn't an actual threat to their marriage, but, he recalled, he felt like he "got kicked in the stomach" and felt nauseated for days. "It felt like the way I was treated when I was a kid, that I was invisible," he said. "I didn't want that again, so I decided I could never count on Annie, either."

In their marriage, however, there were plenty of reasons they needed to "count on" each other. Annie was laid off at work, and Dean had to carry them financially for a while. He privately resented this. She picked up on his frustration and was annoyed that he wasn't more sympathetic about her work situation. Dean knew that Annie's professional insecurity would affect their retirement plans but wasn't sure how. He had trouble bringing this up, however, because he thought Annie would get defensive. Tension smoldered beneath every substantive conversation about their finances or the future of their relationship.

When, in our office, the earlier betrayal got hauled out of Dean's silence, he was able to articulate just how hurt he had been and how that hurt was still with him. Annie was stunned. "I had no idea," she said. "If I had known how much it would hurt you, I would never have been so cavalier about seeing Bert."

In our session together, Dean recalled the lies, deceit, and affairs plaguing his family when he was a child. The notion of a broken promise was highly charged for him, awakening memories of the ugly suspicion that invaded his house in his youth. His parents not only shut down around each other, but they shut him out too. When Annie recognized what a traumatic effect Dean's past had on him, she decided that claiming her freedom to do what she wanted wasn't worth stirring up his bad memories.

For Dean and Annie to mend that breach, we had to take him to where he felt tender and raw and hold him there. This was precisely the place where Dean never wanted to go. In our experience, when you help a person gain access to the original pain, the partner generally shows compassion, more so than the person suffering would have guessed. Dean had hid the pain of his upbringing for so long. Once he opened up, he saw that he didn't have to carry it alone, and that the episode with Bert represented a misunderstanding rather than a betrayal. For Annie, seeing the depth of Dean's pain prompted her to confront some of her own behavior. Difficult as it was, she was able to acknowledge her deception.

Lies Become Routine

Lies can erode a relationship without there being a specific malignant cause. Sometimes a couple stumbles into the habit of deception, with lots of small lies of convenience that add up to a marital pattern of pretense. When this happens, it's difficult to pinpoint lies because lying has become second nature.

Let's duck into Charlie and Jane's house and see how a marriage can get ground down by the sheer inertia of deception. We first find Charlie on a Sunday afternoon watching TV while Jane is running errands. He's half napping, dipping in and out of sleep in a state of blissful indolence. The house is cluttered with books, newspapers, and empty glasses here and there. From the depths of napland Charlie hears Jane's car pull into the driveway. He reluctantly rouses himself and starts picking things up so that he doesn't have to hear Jane say, "What were you doing all day?" He's annoyed that he feels like he's ten years old again, scrambling to look productive now that "Mom" is home. Just like that ten-year-old he wants to stay on the couch, but he can't bear the thought of Jane's disapproving look.

One day not long after, Charlie wants to visit his brother George. He hasn't seen much of George or his close friends since his marriage, and he misses male comradery. He says, "Honey, I'm thinking about going and spending a weekend with George." Jane's disappointed because she likes George, too. She asks, "Why don't you want me to go?" Here, Jane has shifted the focus to herself rather than asking, "Why is it important to you?"

Now Charlie's in a dilemma, struggling to answer a question that doesn't even fit the situation. It's not that he doesn't *want* her to go, it's just that he was *hoping* to go alone.

"I guess you could come with me," he says, but it's not quite what Charlie had in mind. Jane raised her question in such a way that he doesn't know how to say anything else.

After dinner at his house, George says, "Hey, Charlie, want to go pheasant hunting tomorrow?" Charlie says, "My wife can't handle my killing a spider. I don't even want to bring it up. It's a no-win situation." He feels disappointed but doesn't say anything to Jane.

About a year later, Charlie and Jane are in bed. Jane has had a good day, and she starts to feel sexy. She reaches out to Charlie and touches him. They both know what that touch means. Charlie tightens up; he's not feeling amorous. His annual performance review is the next day, and he's worried about how it will turn out. He also doesn't want Jane to know how nervous he has been feeling on the job lately.

Jane can sense that her advances aren't going anywhere. She drops them, turns away from Charlie, and resigns herself to sleep. Charlie thinks, *It would be nice if I could tell her why I'm not in the mood tonight*, but he doesn't know where that discussion would lead. It doesn't seem worth the trouble. Jane is frustrated and wonders, *Why doesn't Charlie respond?* She knows that if he doesn't respond to her advances, she's less likely to be assertive the next time.

Another year passes, with multiple opportunities for significant discussions avoided, and Charlie goes to an office party. He has a drink and observes how easily he can talk to Joanne, a new coworker. He notices that there isn't the kind of tension or need to cover up that he often experiences with Jane. He also notices that Joanne finds him charming and witty. He likes that. Later on he finds himself thinking about Joanne. They go to lunch the next week, and three hours zip by.

Now Charlie feels like a crumb. He knows what's happening and feels guilty about it. He wonders if he can say to Jane, "Something's missing between us." But how can he say this when he couldn't even say he wanted to laze around on the couch? By this point Charlie is pretty far along on a different trajectory from Jane, one that started with their very first excuses, evasions, and moments of grudging acquiescence. The next time Charlie has a drink with Joanne he utters the classic line, "My wife doesn't understand me."

He's right. His wife doesn't understand him. But he also doesn't understand himself. Nor does he understand the part he's played in their marital malaise through all that he's concealed over the years. It will take difficult retroactive self-disclosure to rekindle a vital connection between them.

Wars Between the Sexes

When people think of deception between men and women, they often think in terms of stereotypes: A woman will lie to lure a man into commitment, and a man will lie to get a woman into bed. In our experience, however, the tone and tenor of men's and women's deceptions are more alike than different.

At root all lies are either self-protective (intended to avoid or alleviate emotional distress and/or painful self-reflection) or self-serving (designed to gain advantage). Both types of lies cut across genders. Neither men nor women have a monopoly on being self-protective or self-serving.

We often see this play out in marriages. The woman wants the man to give more to her emotionally, and the man feels attacked. Given the way he responds, you wouldn't imagine in a million years that he's harboring any tender feelings. But the truth is that he often wants to be giving to his wife. The problem is that he can't give to someone who's beating up on him, and expressing his desire to give to her then feels like a capitulation.

The irony is this: Often what the man hides—his tender-hearted affection—is the very thing the woman wants. The man wants gentleness and warmth, too, but his defensive style is such that it doesn't appear that way. The woman tries to extract endearments out of him, which is the approach least likely to get them. In cases like this the "truths" match, but the divergent way of expressing them keep men and women at cross-purposes.

While we've seen men and women run the gamut of lies, men are more likely to lie to serve their ego, and women are more likely to lie about matters related to attractiveness. For instance, a man might lie to bolster others' impressions of how he's doing financially. We've known men who haven't informed their wives that they've been fired until they've pinned down a new job. However, a woman will lie about her weight ("Oh, maybe I weigh five pounds more than when we were married.") or will lie about how much clothing purchases cost, which a man would be unlikely to do.

In traditional marriages, where women feel less powerful, women are more likely to lie from the standpoint of self-protection. This could mean buttering up their partner after an argument. She might conceal something he disapproves of, like spending time with her mother or sister because he thinks they're too close. In such pairs, a man might lie to get what he wants, like saying a financial expert is handling his money while he's taking big financial risks, or lie about his work schedule to give himself more freedom.

Once a Lie, Not Always a Lie

The style and content of marital deceptions depend partly on the stage of the relationship. One lie will have a different meaning at different stages. For example, your mate got busy and forgot your parents' anniversary, even though he promised to send them something. You say, "Well, all right."

In the early stage of a relationship, you could be starting a pattern of suppressing yourself and not speaking up about things that bother you. You say "Well, all right" while you think, *I'm disappointed, but I don't want to say anything because if I make too many waves, I may be putting our relationship in jeopardy.*

Let's consider the dead end called "Seething Stalemate." You say, "Well, all right. Make my family insignificant; see if I care," with a resignation that suggests you didn't expect anything better from him anyway. You want him to know you're displeased—you think, *Let him sit with that*—and you file the incident away to be brought out as ammunition the next time the two of you have an argument.

Now skip a few steps ahead to Together as Two. This time, when you say "Well, all right," you're not really lying. Here the implication is, "I know from experience that you care about my parents and that you really intended to follow through on your promise. I can take up the slack. In the scheme of things, this isn't all that important."

The context will shape the harmfulness of the lie. If the intent of the statement is to deceive, protect, or offer gain, then a lie is a lie. If the intent shows acceptance and a deeper understanding of who the partner is and the concern for the other is genuine, then the lie will not result in any harm.

But the intent may not be as it appears on the surface, and thus it can be hard to discern. However, when you have the ability to self-appraise and can ask yourself, "Why am I saying this?" you will be able to monitor your level of honesty and ensure that you don't slide into deceit.

Rules and Presumptions: Magnets for Lies

The route to deception in a marriage is mainly found within routine exchanges. Couples make demands upon each other and often expect things to be a certain way (their way). When you react in the moment, speaking off the top of your head, you don't realize that you're asking your partner to start lying. But by laying down the law, you may inadvertently set the stage for deception. It can take only a few snippets of conversation to cue your mate to be more open or to shut up and shut down.

This situation can be hard to spot because, at first glance, it looks like everyone's in agreement. Also, a rule might not be articulated until it's been violated. But let's look in on a few ordinary moments in the lives of some couples we've worked with.

When Sam comes home at night, he doesn't want to hear *anything* until he's had a solid hour of peace and quiet. "Don't tell me that you need any help with the kids," he tells Jeanette. "I need to decompress." Jeanette, who's put in several hours as sibling referee, bites her lip and fumes. The message she takes from his attitude is, "I don't care what's going on with you." She closes down, pushing her dissatisfaction underground.

In another instance, Marissa says to Jim, "I don't like pornography. I don't want it in the house." End of subject. Jim isn't going to protest because he already feels guilty about his penchant for raunchy magazines. The message is, "If you're into this stuff, I don't want to know about it. This is not a discussion. This is a mandate." Jim is either going to be sneaky about his X-rated tastes or feel bulldozed into giving up his magazines.

The operating word here is "don't." "Don't" is a strong word. A marriage needs to have room for each person's complex truths. You want it to be possible to express complicated, even conflicting parts of yourselves and tolerate the uncertainty that results.

Sometimes truths are revealed through the very measures taken to preclude them. For example, when one person sends the signal, "Don't ever do *X*" there's usually an issue underneath the action that the person doesn't want to face.

For example, Sam wouldn't listen to Jeanette or consider what she needed because he feared that commiserating with her distress meant he would have to give up his desire for down time. In order to get what he wanted, he would have to shut off. Or, Marissa may have had bad sexual experiences or may believe that pornography is degrading to women. But her proclamation shuts down all dialogue.

Or take a woman who says to her husband, "I don't want to discuss investments." This request may cover the part of herself that wants to be a little girl forever.

Accepting a "don't" laid down as a decree in your marriage puts a fence around a sensitive area. It prevents you from exploring difficult truths about each other. Truths often have some kind of vulnerability to them. The word "don't" often means, "I don't want to be exposed as vulnerable." If you come into the marriage with a need for your partner to be strong, you're not going to want to explore anything that may suggest otherwise. The message you send will be: "Don't let me see any part of you that demonstrates weakness." You're also fooling yourself by assuming that a rule is akin to a guarantee.

There's a constant interplay between what you demand from your partner and what your partner can give in return; what you reveal about yourself and what you're willing to know about your partner.

We Don't Lie. . . . Do We?

With many couples, it's often not the big issues that bog down a marriage in lies but rather the little ones. Most people have a sense of when the chance to tell the truth is presented to them. Each time this happens there's a surge of tension: *Should I say something or let it ride?* Each time you opt away from candor, your self-esteem takes a little hit. After fifty or so scenes like that, you start to armor yourself so that you don't even feel the impact. You just get a quick blip of awareness: *Oh no, here's another one of those experiences.* You deaden yourself to the consequences. After a while, you forget that speaking the truth is even a possibility.

One factor that helps determine the relative ease of truthfulness in a marriage is how situations and questions are framed. Recall Jane's earlier response to Charlie, "Why do you want to be away from me?" This question carries with it a vast constellation of doubts and anxieties. It also does a giant leapfrog over the immediate situation, loading it with negative presumptions. That's just the kind of question that would cause Charlie to flinch and lead him to shade the truth.

If we catch this type of behavior early in a relationship, we can help clarify whatever concerns lie beneath the automatic response: Charlie's desire to go to see George on his own, the anxiety this may cause Jane, his fear that if he is direct Jane will cry and he'll feel awful. It's hard for Charlie to say, "Hey, what I really want is to see my brother alone. Can you deal with that?" It's hard for Jane to say, "Sometimes I get sad when

I see that what's fun for you may not always include me" or for Charlie to say, "I can see you are sad and disappointed, and I can listen compassionately without changing my plans."

Truth is about meaning, not just facts. It's about what's important to each person at the core. Annie knew Dean was disappointed when she saw Bert, but she was clueless as to how deep those feelings went. The very depth of that pain—how it struck an unbearably raw nerve—*that* was the important truth that the two needed to grasp in order to find their way back to each other.

Truth telling at this level isn't something you can do according to formula. People generally have a vague idea of what it means to have integrity in their marriage but lack training or role models for how to get there. It requires a great deal of fortitude. Even when people pride themselves on being honest, the commitment to personal integrity is tested all the time. It's the ability to think, calm, comfort, and encourage yourself during those times that enables you to be open and speak the truth.

Raising Consciousness

At any moment, you have the choice whether or not to be more honest with your partner. You have plenty of opportunities to pay attention to your own cues and ask, *Do I want to be honest with myself?* and *Do I want to be honest with my partner?*

Rather than allowing himself to feel belittled, for example, Charlie could have said, "Sprawling out on the couch is my regeneration for the coming week. I'm sure I don't look productive, but I know myself and loafing does for me what a massage or trip to the spa does for you." Or, "Hunting with George would really be a treat for me." Or, "When I'm nervous about something, my libido is the first thing to disappear."

At different junctures Jane could have said, "Seeing you lounging around frustrates me because I want to do something like that, too, but feel guilty when I do." Or, "I'm sad when I realize that I never make you laugh the way George can." Or, "You used to want to make love all the time and I don't understand what's changed." Either Jane or Charlie could have spoken up before, during, or after, at anyone of the count-less tense moments or freighted silences.

But be aware that *one* person will always make that choice. Couples simply don't come to a significant intersection at the *same* time with the *same* desire to be honest over the *same* situation. So whoever speaks up is already ahead of the other. That person has thought about it, played the scenario over in her mind, surveyed the terrain. When you break the moratorium on truth, don't expect your mate to be where you are. Jane, for instance, might not be thrilled to learn that Charlie thrives on lots of down time; it may be hard for Charlie to hear that Jane envies his spe-cial relationship with George. But don't conclude that you're wrong just because your partner struggles with it.

The longer you wait to straighten out a lie, the harder it is. As time goes on, a deception gets entrenched in your history; smaller accessory lies start clinging to it like burrs to clothing. For instance, rather than letting his anger burn a hole in his gut, Dean could have told Annie right from the start that breaking a vow was out of bounds and that he couldn't trust her unless she honored that. It's never easy. But the sooner you can address something, the less repair work will need to be done later. As it was, Dean and Annie had plenty of bad feeling to address.

No Truth Too Small

Like lies, the truths in a marriage can be complex, even contradic-tory. We now know that problems with dishonesty can start with the small stuff. Honesty in a marriage can start with the small stuff, too. And the easiest way to get truthfulness rolling is to begin at ground zero.

Had a couple like Adam and Cathy exercised honesty early on, they might have made it. The pair showed up at my office after Cathy told Adam that she was leaving him. "I'm done with this marriage, Adam, DONE," she repeated in the session, very nearly spelling out the words for him. "I don't get it," Adam said. "You can't go. You'll never find someone who loves you as much as I do." "Be real," she said. "I checked out of this relationship long ago." Adam kept shaking his head. "But no one will love you like I do." Did Cathy feel loved? No. And if she had emotionally quit the marriage a few years back as she said, you'd have to wonder exactly what version of Cathy Adam had been loving.

In the session, I (Ellyn) learned that, though they had been "tight" when they met, Cathy had started feeling estranged from Adam after only a year of marriage. As she explained, she then began to psychologically extricate herself from it. Adam said that he had noticed her distance but had never spoken up about it. Whenever he felt that pang of loneliness when he was with her, it was more convenient to just bury his head in his work than to ask Cathy what was bothering her—and risk finding out that it was him.

This is the most difficult kind of case to see, the kind where instinct tells us that if we had met them sooner, their marriage could have survived. As Cathy and Adam talked, it became clear that they went off on differing tangents *not* for lack of love but from fear. Adam, in particular, would tuck away different aspects of himself into remote emotional pockets, sharing very little with his wife.

For example, they used to disagree in the video store. Cathy would want a comedy when Adam was in the mood for drama. Each time Adam would think, *"Is this video worth having a fight about? Is it worth losing the marriage?"* He'd say to himself, "of course not" and go along with Cathy.

Of course no video is worth a marriage, but Adam had it exactly wrong: A couple needs to learn how to have different wants and how to disagree. By dodging these discussions, he wasn't protecting the marriage but rather was putting it at risk. Adam's rationalizations meant very few things would be worth fighting for. Arguing, however, was about more than the video. It was about the process of how they handled disagreement.

Adam might have recognized, "If I give in now, I'm setting a dangerous precedent." It's not that you have to hassle over every issue, but a pattern of evading all conflicts can spell danger. Every couple who finds a means of disagreement that takes each person into account will build a stronger foundation. Adam needed practice with the little issues because when Cathy came to him with the big issues ("I'm out of here") he tried to finesse that one too.

People think that liars are sneaky. But the lies or withheld truths themselves can be sneaky, too. As we've seen, they may lie dormant for years and then catch a couple unaware.

Let's look at another hidden aspect of deception—the person who's responsible may not be the one you'd expect.

3 ✳

The Lie
Invitee

*E*verybody knows about the liar: the person who lies through his teeth, covers his tracks, or acts evasively. But few are aware of the person working behind the scenes, orchestrating the deception even as they're demanding to hear the truth. We call this individual the "Lie Invitee," the forgotten partner in marital deception. For indeed, it often takes two to lie.

The Lie Invitee is unwilling to handle the truth. This may be a person who's afraid that any truth will mean another jab at his self-esteem. Or this may be someone who wants to run the show and refuses to allow anything—like what the other person wants—to interfere with her plans. Or this may be someone who fears having holes poked in the ideal fantasy of his partner (or of himself). He or she is often thin-skinned by temperament, with many sensitive areas that need guarding. This tendency may derive in part from personal history. Frequently, someone who tempts lies grew up in a family that tolerated manipulation and evasion and neither sought nor encouraged the full truth.

Some people are completely unaware of the fact that they're invoking lies, while others understand what they're doing but feel helpless to do otherwise. On the unconscious end, someone may say, "I'm only expressing my feelings as a reaction to what my partner is telling me" with the implication that this doesn't affect the other partner at all. Someone more aware may think, *I know I overreact to things I don't want to hear* or *I know this is a leading question.*

The Lie Invitee isn't commonly recognized because in part the defining behavior can be subtle or difficult to explain. (It's hard to describe "the Look," but you sure know it when you see it.) The concept also goes unnoticed because the person often isn't aware of what he's doing. Just as people want to think they speak truthfully, people want to believe they elicit truth. The lie-inviting behavior is a reflexive response. Feeding the Lie Invitee lies can become automatic as well. We want to raise your awareness of what may trigger deception in your marriage so that you can identify and interrupt the cycle.

Tell Me, Tell Me Not

Meet the typical Lie Invitee. This is a person who claims to want the truth but who, through tone of voice, expression, and posture, is doing everything he/she can to drive a mate underground. She says she wants an honest answer, but she really wants her mate to give back to her what's in her script. The Lie Invitee will say, "Tell me again, where were you last night?" Judging by words alone, this could be a request for further clarification, but nonverbal cues will suggest the implicit meaning: "I'm giving you another chance to come up with an explanation that I can accept and handle."

When the Lie Invitee gets a dose of the truth—that is, when incriminating facts seep out before anyone has a chance to insert the stopper—he'll demonstrate his disapproval in several ways: sarcasm, glares, and escalating defensive behavior which then prod the partner into future evasions.

We worked with one woman who would lie down in the middle of the driveway and outright dare her boyfriend to run her over if he really wanted to leave the house. Usually her tantrums were milder, with mere crying and whining when he told her he wanted more time alone or to be with his friends. But just knowing that she was capable of serious emotional outbursts made him very cautious about speaking up when he wanted time alone.

More subtle but almost as potent is withdrawal: pouting, not speaking, and refusing to acknowledge the other person until he takes back or atones for what he said. Never underestimate the power of the silent treatment; it's a sure way to encourage your partner to deceive you. No one likes being shut out, so people will hedge about the truth and recant things they said that were honest so they don't have to suffer the indignity of having that door slammed in their face again. People will do a lot to avoid being met with icy glares.

The irony is that it's not the truth itself that causes the problem, but rather the partner's emotional response to it. The Lie Invitee's reaction can set up a whole new series of lies.

Terry didn't want to lie to her husband, Cal, but in the end she decided a little fibbing would save her a lot of grief. Terry is an avid bridge player, and she wanted to play with Neil, an old friend. Cal always got upset about her teaming up with a man, and all day he would be hypercritical of Terry and make ridiculous demands—everything he asked of her *suddenly* became urgent—as if to punish her for going.

Finally, Terry simply started telling Cal she was going somewhere else. On Sunday afternoons, bridge day, she would announce that she was going "shopping with girlfriends." It worked; she didn't have to face his griping and moping around. But after a while, Terry grew disgusted with herself. Here she was, slinking around when she wasn't doing anything wrong in the first place. She was a good bridge player and wanted a partner of her caliber, that was all.

In our experience, women more typically overdo the emotionality, while men more often withdraw. But we've seen all kinds of variations on these behaviors through the years. People can become pretty crafty when it comes to avoiding the truth. Whatever the lie-inviting style, it becomes a clear deterrent to honesty. The other partner merely anticipates the cold shoulder or a conniption fit, and that's enough to scare them away from candor.

A Folie à Deux

The Liar/Lie-Invitee pattern is universal in intimate relationships. Everybody lies. Likewise, everybody steps into the Lie Invitee role from time to time. There is not a person alive who willingly peers into every dark corner of his partner's psyche or looks unflinchingly at himself. No one wants total truth.

Multiply these exchanges a hundred times over, and you may have a marriage in trouble without knowing exactly why.

Juanita and Marco go to a party one night, and she becomes justifiably annoyed because Marco continually interrupts her, corrects her version of stories, and spoils the punch lines of her jokes. The next morning over breakfast she says, "It seems to me that you were kind of childish last night." Maybe childish is only the best word she can come up with at the moment, but Marco doesn't like it. He says, "There you go again, getting parental with me."

What Juanita receives is the verbal equivalent of a brick wall: no passage. At that moment she has two choices: keep charging the brick wall and hope to break through, or drop her point. If Marco is successful at stonewalling, he wins the battle. But then they're in a war. Juanita will clam up and disengage yet another part of herself.

Time passes. Juanita seems quiet, and Marco asks if anything is bothering her. She says nothing is bothering her. He starts probing, and finally she tells him to back off. He complains that she won't be honest with him, little realizing that the tension stemmed from him not creating space for an honest exchange.

These interactions occur repeatedly in many marriages, and they happen so quickly it's hard to see the bigger picture of cause and effect. If Juanita and Marco run through this kind of dialogue often enough, Juanita is going to think, *I can't talk to Marco about his behavior.* So she shuts down. Marco will sense that she's distant and will feel slighted. His sensitivity to what she says climbs up another notch. Juanita gets the message and, next time, stops yet shorter of the truth. Marco either doesn't notice or pretends not to. He's just glad to escape the criticism.

This dynamic is at the heart of much dishonesty in marriage. Sometimes one partner does most of the lying and the other most of the inviting. Sometimes the two alternate positions, like two players switching offense and defense. But nobody is locked into either position. Both can make the opportunity to step outside and blow the whistle—once they understand what this psychological duet is doing to their marriage.

Tell Me No Truths

The Tell Me/Don't Tell Me dance can become deeply ingrained into the way two people interact. The process becomes almost mechanical. For years, someone may continually flick the truth away like a crumb at the table and deny that her mate has been trying to get through to her, and will remain oblivious to his growing frustration.

Janie's husband, Will, is a football junkie, and she doesn't like it. She wouldn't speak to him before and after games, and if he tried to include her—"Really, honey, you gotta see this play"—she acted as if he were invisible. When Will told her he was coming home late and it didn't suit her, she whined.

Janie longed for a bigger house, but Will wanted to invest in the stock market rather than spend heavily on a move. She called him insensitive and controlling. Will caved in and they bought a larger house. But Will resented it. And he knew he would resent it. Had he been totally honest, he would have said, "I don't want to be bullied into this. If I give in, I'll resent it and pout. If you can stand my pouting, let's go ahead and buy the big house. But if you want me to be with you, let's try to figure out something else." Even though he knew what was coming, he went along with Janie.

Ultimately inviting lies will backfire. When someone is repeatedly pressed into lying, a lot of accumulated bad feeling gets bound up with the truth.

Once Will and Janie had their large, sprawling house, Janie launched into decorating it and choosing the basic style, color scheme, and fabrics. Will was not wild about it. When he told her he didn't like the effect, Janie exploded, "You never like anything I do. You always find something wrong with it." Will backed off and said, "Okay. *Fine.*" But he winced every time he walked through the main hallway, which had peach-colored wallpaper that made him think of a doctor's waiting room.

After a long time, he told her he couldn't stand to look at it anymore. Janie said, "It's easy for you to complain. I did all the work." Finally, with more than half the house done, Will said, "That's it. I'm taking over the decorating decisions from here on in."

Against all evidence, Janie had convinced herself that Will liked the way she did the house. Will had to go on the attack in order to be heard, and they lost any hope of having a collaboration.

Janie begged to be pandered to in every way short of outright saying, "Lie to me, please." With the Lie Invitee, it's often not the words but the *subtext* to them that sends the partner scurrying to camouflage his or her intentions.

Here are some classic Lie Invitee statements (innuendo included):

"I want you to tell me how you feel (but watch out if you tell me something I don't want to hear)."

"Tell me again why (but this time tell me what I want to hear)."

"I want the truth (but you know I'm going to suffer for it)."

"I want the truth (but *you're* going to have to suffer for it)."

"I don't want to hear it (and if that's the truth, I don't want to know)."

"How can you be so insensitive (and have an opinion that's so hard for me to hear)?"

Lie Invitees can't handle the disillusionment that the truth is bound to deliver. Some unlit corner of reality is making itself visible, and they don't want to look. They have the feeling: "I don't want to know the truth because I don't know what I'll do if I know it."

Often a self-serving element comes into play: "If I just sit tight, then I can remain blameless and hold the high moral ground." The partner says, "I'm not happy about your being rude to my sister." The Lie Invitee then says, "I just can't handle your talking about this. It's too much for me," and culpability shifts to the partner who's talking. The partner gets a double whammy: (1) He or she is attacked for raising the issue, and then (2) is forced to deal with it alone. And he or she gets the message that his or her concerns are not welcome in the relationship.

The Many Faces of the Lie Invitee

Depending on their own personalities and what has worked in the past, people have different gambits for getting their spouses to lie. Let's run down some of these tactics.

The scenario: Sally takes her friend Jenny out for a birthday dinner. Before she leaves the house, she says to her husband, Ed, "Look, when I'm gone will you give the kids a bath?" Nine o'clock finds Ed and the kids engrossed in a TV program about elephants. He hands each of them a washcloth and after a thirty-second scrubdown whisks them off to bed.

Sally comes home just as the first snores are audible from the kids' bedrooms. "You did give the kids a bath, didn't you?"

For a split second Ed thinks, *Do I fib or do I tell her?* He says, "Well, no."

Following are rough sketches of several ways Sally could play the Lie Invitee. Any one of these responses is likely to make Ed think, *The heck with this. Next time I'll just say, "Yes, it was taken care of."*

1. **The Fury:** "Ed, I don't believe it! I told you as clearly as I could that they needed a bath. Don't you know anything about taking care of the kids?"
2. **The Martyr:** Sally's eyes start misting. "Oh, if I were a better mother, I wouldn't leave the house until everything got done. I shouldn't have gone out. Next time I should just bake Jenny a cake and stay home."
3. **The Crybaby:** With tears streaming down her face, Sally says, "I thought it was such a simple thing." She continues crying and saying, "I can't say another thing."
4. **The Blamer:** "If you didn't do so much traveling, you would have more time with the kids so you wouldn't have to make a big party of it every time I leave the house. If you were around more often, you would know what it takes to get the kids ready for bed, which obviously you don't."
5. **Plugged Ears:** Ed starts to explain that they got involved in this documentary and . . . "I'm just not interested in

another one of your excuses," Sally says. "I'm going to bed."

6. **The Attack:** "What is the matter with you, Ed? Is it really that hard to get the kids to bed on time?"

7. **The Character Assassin:** "You know, you've always been unreliable. You never come through. You'll never get anywhere in life because no one can ever count on you."

8. **The Look:** Sally just stands there, glaring and saying nothing while Ed explains himself and squirms.

9. **Confusion:** Sally: "I just don't get it. The kids need a bath. I don't understand why you do things the way you do." (The message is: "I disapprove of what you do." "I don't understand" means "I don't agree.")

10. **Too Busy to Talk:** "I don't want to hear about it right now. I've got too much to do to get ready for tomorrow."

11. **The Drill Sergeant:** Before leaving, Sally says, "Here's what I want you to do. By 7:30, I want the dishes cleaned up and put away. At 8:00, I want the kids in the bath. Use no more than one-half capful of bubble soap so it doesn't get in their eyes. They can play with the plastic sailboat but not the wind-up whale because they always fight over it. By 8:25, I want them in pajamas with teeth brushed and flossed."

    Here Sally has set things up so that it's almost impossible for Ed to do as she asks without feeling like an underling taking orders. Sally asks, "Did the kids get their bath?"

    Ed says, "Yeah."

12. **Desperately Seeking Reassurance:** Before leaving, Sally says, "It's really okay that I'm going out, right? You will give the kids a bath? I told you where the bubble bath is, right?"

    Ed says, "Yeah, yeah, yeah."

13. **Pretending to Listen:** Ed says, "Sally, we've got to talk about the bedtime routine. It's just not working. Here's what—"

    Sally looks straight at him but doesn't blink. She says, "Okay" and goes into the kitchen to busy herself and then starts talking about the funny noise the car is making that she thinks should be checked out.

14. **Laying Down the Law:** Before leaving Sally says, "I have this rule that the kids always need a bath."

Ed thinks, *Oh, another of her rules. I'd better just say I did it.*

Each of these maneuvers hits Ed in vulnerable spots. They play on guilt, ensuring that he feels bad about things he probably already feels bad about. Why wouldn't Ed sidestep that extra layer of chagrin?

Forced into Deception

A relentless Lie Invitee can push even fairly honest people to the far side of truth. Here's an example from our practice:

Carl and Karen had known each other since childhood and had a bond based largely on shared friends and similar intellectual interests. Carl was exceedingly sensitive and would plunge into gloom at the slightest cause. This was fine when Karen was Carl's confidant before their marriage, but it proved more difficult afterwards.

Carl refused to have sex with Karen for years. She would try to talk to him about it by asking, "What's bothering you? Is there something about me that turns you off? Is there a way I can turn you *on?*" He reacted as though she had violated his privacy by even speaking about it. After several years of this behavior, Karen went on a university-sponsored tour abroad, but Carl declined the trip because he was afraid of getting sick in a third-world country. Karen went on the trip without Carl, and she met a man and had an affair. Under normal circumstances, Karen would never imagine herself having an affair; she was quite shaken up by it. But this came after several years of trying to get Carl to talk to her. His spurning her honest appeals left her vulnerable to temptation.

Sometimes when one partner has a strict agenda, the other person feels compelled to lie. For example, one woman told her boyfriend, "I could never be with someone who drinks. My father drank, and that's something I won't stand for." Her boyfriend happened to like an occasional drink, but he didn't drink in her presence; he said it wasn't a big deal. And, at first, it wasn't. He preferred to keep the relationship and give up his periodic drink. Finally, however, he grew tired of the stringent rules, so he would sneak off and drink without telling her, at first feeling guilty and later feeling entitled.

In this situation, the Lie Invitee would argue, "I'm just saying what I want." The other person becomes the liar by default. He would make the point, "But you weren't interested in what I wanted or thought." At times the Lie Invitee is so adamant about her desires that she unilaterally blocks out what her partner wants. Sooner or later this behavior will backfire, with very unpleasant consequences.

Lies about drinking, gambling, and other potentially addictive behaviors put both parties in a bind. The "addict" is torn between being straight about the desire to engage in the forbidden activity and the desire not to upset the partner. Lying obviates the need to choose: You can have your drink and keep your partner happy, too.

As for the "addict's" partner, he knows that by forcing the truth, he runs the risk of annoying and even alienating his mate. He's also aware that if he pushes what he wants, the partner may choose the addiction over him. The lie keeps things at status quo. Similarly, since the partner knows that the behavior is unlikely to disappear, playing the Lie Invitee may seem preferable to starting an argument. It's a kind of collusion where the message is, "Give me the answer I want, and I'll drop the subject (and ignore the smell of whiskey on your breath)." By delaying a confrontation, the partner hopes that the problem will magically disappear.

Stopping Truths Before They Start

It's easy both to squelch the truth and to allow it to be squelched, especially when it's inconvenient or barely breaking into one's consciousness. Truths rarely spring fully formed into awareness. Rather, they dawn slowly into one's realization, get tested, subside, and resurface.

There's generally a time when you have some intuition about the truth, but the words aren't yet there to describe it. It's at this point that emerging truths are most vulnerable. Juanita says, "Marco, there was something that upset me when we were together last night." Marco grumbles, "Oh, not *this* again." So Juanita pauses, wondering how she could possibly say what she wants to say. Because she's struggling to express new sentiments, she's susceptible to letting the discussion get cut short prematurely.

She can rationalize shelving the truth in twenty different ways, "Maybe I was in a bad mood . . . I know Marco had a tough day . . . etc." But then two things never happen: (1) Marco doesn't hear what Juanita experienced, which holds the deeper truth about her reaction, and (2) he misses the chance to learn something potentially important about himself.

Can't You Take a Joke?

People often use humor, especially sarcasm, to stifle another person's truths. Few will risk being ridiculed. When your partner makes light of something heartfelt, you'll pull back.

Typical examples are so-called jests about friends or family members.

The weekend is approaching, and Stella says to Hugh, "I'd like to have Todd and Beth over for a cookout." Hugh says, "Oh, so it doesn't bother you that Beth is an angry loudmouth?" Stella says, "Beth has a good sense of humor." Hugh retorts, "A feminist with a sense of humor is an oxymoron." It's hard, then, for Stella to say, "Actually I care deeply about this person whose personality you've just torn to shreds." Instead she says, "Hugh, that's not fair." Hugh responds, "Where's your sense of humor?" The conversation basically dies right there, but the feelings remain raw, and Stella is discouraged from speaking honestly about her friendship with Beth.

Some people routinely turn a partner's concerns into a joke. When the partner protests, such a person will say, "Don't take things so seriously." The response, then, may be to force a laugh and drive the truth back inside. Even if a comment is funny, sarcastic humor alters the tone of the exchange so that it's hard to express what you're feeling.

Even Inviting Tiny Lies Can Be Trouble

A few lie-inviting episodes aren't so bad. Everybody does it. You want to hear that you look terrific to psyche yourself up for an evening out: "Does this look great or what?" You want your partner to defer to your tastes: "You really want to go out for Chinese food tonight, don't you?"

Deception often starts with the small stuff. It can then develop into a persistent pattern. When that occurs the partner knows that should he dare broach a sensitive subject, he's going to receive an unpleasant response. So why even bother? The threat of tantrums, tears, or the silent treatment hangs heavily over the relationship and makes the free exchange of sentiment impossible.

Too often Lie Invitee behavior acts as a censor, constraining people from being honest. The Lie Invitee's mate fears a dramatic confrontation and is relieved to find that lying offers a way to avoid a big clash. This affords a clear way through the impasse of the moment but fails to lessen her resentment at having to remain silent. And every time you lie it goes on the record, and you have to work to maintain it. The lies invariably grow bigger, building on each other until one person becomes so fed up with the game that she's willing to blow the cover.

Being a Lie Invitee edges you towards the danger zone. It prevents you from catching important cues about what's happening in your significant relationship. As with Carl and Karen, it prohibits an important discussion, in their case concerning the lapse of sex in the marriage.

Remember, the truth itself is never the problem. It's the emotional response to the truth that causes mischief. Emotional reactions, as opposed to some abstract moral sense, are what govern truth telling and truth seeking in any close relationship.

The Lie Invitee deludes himself or herself with the belief "I can handle the truth," but the more accurate statement would be: "I can't handle how I feel when my partner tells me the truth."

The liar thinks, *My partner can't handle the truth*, but the reality is, *I can't tolerate how I feel when I speak the truth and see my partner's reaction.*

Truth Invitees

Forthright people will elicit more frankness; taciturn people, or those who don't like to express their feelings, will invite more guardedness. People who elicit truthfulness ask questions in a way that indicates that they can accept the truth. They don't ask for the truth and then "slap" their partner with a tone of voice or "the look."

If I (Pete) am working with rejection-sensitive people, for example, my bandwidth of responsiveness shrinks. In a sense, I am more limited in what I can give to them. I find that I have to move slower, water down my feedback, and backtrack a lot. Often by the time I get my message across, it is so diluted as to be almost meaningless. If I am more direct, I get a defensive response—like, "Why are you picking on me?"—that hinders how honest I can be. Even worse, the client will feel picked on and think *I don't need this*, cancel the next appointment, and never call back. If I move slowly I hear the lament, "Are we getting anywhere in this therapy?" Walking the tightrope with these clients is one of my toughest challenges.

Then there are truth-inviting people—those who have a greater capacity for involvement and engagement and call for more honest, more complete answers. They're not going to crumble if they hear something they don't like. I can be overt, I can be blunt, I can be direct. I have greater access to the full range of my skills and capacities because I'm not guarding myself and protecting them. The therapy crackles and moves ahead.

On some level, we're always registering how honest we can be with someone and adapting ourselves accordingly. This happens all the time with friendships, family members, and romantic partners. Often, without being conscious of it, we close off selective areas, like going through a large house and boarding up unused rooms. If you're in a marriage where there are a lot of blackout areas, the relationship is going to be in trouble.

One particular couple stands out as being willing to face difficult truths during difficult times.

Sandy and Clyde met in college, and after a few years with both of them working, they began to talk about marriage. Though he never gave any hints of being unhappy in the relationship, Clyde became panicky. A few of Sandy's friends told her to give him an ultimatum. She thought otherwise. She said to him, "Are you wishing you could have sex with some other women before getting married? Is that what's getting in your way?"

It was. He was antsy about commitment, afraid to be tied down while so young. They decided to spend time apart for a few months, and Clyde dated a few women. Getting a sense of what it was like "out there"—and the fact that Sandy wasn't threatened by his uncertainty—ultimately enhanced Clyde's devotion.

A lot of people bury the kinds of doubts Clyde had, but he was honest about his panic and wanted to get the dating bug out of his system. Sandy was able to listen and sustain herself through his unpredictability. Over the years we've seen plenty of couples where one will say, "You weren't ready to settle down with me," or "I know I pushed you into a commitment." Because Clyde and Sandy were able to face this directly, they were able to build their marriage on a stronger foundation.

The following quiz is designed to help you evaluate your ability to listen to and elicit truth from your partner.

Please check the column that most often applies.

When my partner begins to reveal a truth, emotion, or a disturbing aspect of himself or herself, I . . .

	Almost Never	*Occasionally*	*Very Frequently*
Look forward to the conversation			
Listen very carefully and nondefensively			
Ask for more information			
Coordinate with my partner and if necessary,			

	Almost Never	*Occasionally*	*Very Frequently*

negotiate a better time
to talk

Try to draw out a more
complete understanding
of his or her perspective

Tell myself to stay calm
and attentive

Tell myself not to take
personally what's being
said

Recognize and appreciate
the risk taken to self-
disclose

Compliment myself for
encouraging the truth

SCORING:

For each check in column 1–score 1 point
For each check in column 2–score 3 points
For each check in column 3–score 5 points

27–45	You facilitate unusual openness and honesty.
18–27	With more practice at managing your defensiveness, you will create the foundation for an honest relationship.
9–18	We applaud you for reading this book!

"When I hear my partner saying something I really don't want to hear, I . . ."

	Quite Often	*Occasionally*	*Almost Never*
Cry			
Believe it's mostly my fault			
Withdraw and pout			
Counterattack and blame			
Don't say much now but will dump on him or her later			
Use the silent treatment or cold shoulder			
Interrupt and change the subject			
Tell him/her why he or she is wrong			
Pretend to listen but tune out and don't remember a word that was said			

SCORING:

For each check in column 1—score 1 point

For each check in column 2—score 3 points

For each check in column 3—score 5 points

9–18	Congratulations for your honesty.
18–27	Watch out for your tendencies to discourage truth telling.
27–45	You're on a great track. You really know that eliciting the truth builds a stronger foundation.

Bolster Yourself for the Truth

Either partner can change the pattern. A Lie Invitee can continue his antics, and his partner need not be controlled by them. People can prepare themselves to hear uncomfortable truths, and committed partners can encourage each other to be increasingly more honest.

Under sufficient stress we all are potential liars *and* potential Lie Invitees. It takes guts to hear the truth. When faced with something unpleasant, some people might say, "I don't need to listen to this" because they don't recognize that it's important to be able to handle the truth.

In order not to be a Lie Invitee, you have to honor honesty as well as be able to manage your emotional state when you do hear the truth. Don't turn everything you find distasteful into a crisis, declaring "I'm outta here" or "You're a jerk." You'll wear each other out.

One basic rule for getting yourself in a position to hear the truth is to prepare yourself. Strengthen your resilience by anticipating difficult conversations and accepting that often you will not like what you're going to hear. People will study for a test, but with relationships there's a myth that you should just be able to deal with what comes up in the moment. In fact, preparation has a huge impact on how pleasant or difficult a revelatory exchange will be.

READY, SET, GO:
HANDY GUIDELINES TO PREPARE FOR
TOUGH DISCUSSIONS

- *Play out the worst-case scenario in your head.* Then think of five different ways you could manage this negative outcome. The more ways you have to manage the dreaded outcome, the less you will fear it and the more confidence you will generate during the discussion.
- *Try to imagine the situation from your partner's perspective.* This includes her concerns, interests, hopes, and frustrations. At some time early in the discussion, ask if you can summarize what you think her point of view is.
- *If you begin to feel overwhelmed, call for a time-out.* But not before you negotiate a set time to resume the discussion and then be the one

to restart the conversation. This keeps your partner from feeling like you are pulling a power play when you suddenly withdraw from the discussion.

- *Ask questions for clarification and then recap what you hear.* This is effective in slowing things down and ensuring that your partner feels listened to.

LEARN HOW TO INVITE TRUTHS

Shifting from encouraging lies to eliciting truths forces you to recognize that you play a role in the mischief-making patterns in your marriage. Try to understand how the two of you influence each other. The basic model to use is, "When he/she does X, I respond by doing Y."

Let's return to Sally and Ed, after the infamous bathing episode. (see pages 43–45.) Ed reflects mightily on whether or not to bring it up. His internal dialogue goes like this: *Aw, leave it alone. Every guy has to put up with his wife being difficult sometimes.* A different voice says, *You're nothing but a wimp if you put up with that.* Yet another pipes up, *Maybe there's another way. Maybe if I put my cards on the table . . ."*

ED: "Hey, Sally. Is this a good time to talk about last night?"

SALLY: "Sure."

ED: "Remember when you turned me into a human pincushion for not giving the kids a bath? Well, frankly, I don't like the way I react when I feel you're pouncing on me for not following through."

SALLY: "Well, if you'd just do what you say, I wouldn't blow up."

ED: "That's not the issue I want to talk about. Here's the deal: When you start firing with both six-guns, I have a strong desire to lie, bend the truth, mislead, misdirect, misinform, or otherwise do anything I can to avoid the inevitable avalanche that comes when you are upset and uptight."

SALLY: "Are you telling me you've been lying? On top of being undependable, you've been lying, too?"

Fortunately, Ed has mentally rehearsed a few responses according to the format described above. Initially, he feels like he's caught in a vise with no way out. But wait! Maybe there is a way: TELL THE TRUTH.

ED: "Well, to be honest, I have lied to you in the past. I'm not proud of it, but I did it to keep myself out of trouble with you."

Sally thinks to herself, *The creep. I knew it all along. But I have to give him points for being straight about this.*

SALLY: "Well, thanks, Ed, for owning up to the lie. I've rather suspected it, and frankly I was losing respect for you for being a weasel."
ED: "Well, thanks for being a little straight with me. Look, I don't want to weasel out when you're mad. If I don't do something, I want to be able to say so, explain why, and apologize, if appropriate. Then we deal with it. How about you? Would you rather that we had avoided a fight with a lie or had dealt with each other head-on?"
SALLY: "Ed!! My Hero!!!" *Fade out.*

(Okay, so this is a little exaggeration, but you can imagine how relieved Sally might feel.)

They could easily have reversed roles, with Sally saying to Ed, "You know, Ed, I think I come on too strong sometimes when I get mad. That's not how I want to be. The thing is that I'm afraid to tell you about the pain of feeling disappointed when I depend on you and then feel let down. It's hard for a part of me to want to depend on anyone, so I avoid it. How can we arrange things so that I don't feel disappointed, and you don't feel pushed?"

As our mythical Ed and Sally have done, use your awareness to try to break the circular discussion. Accept some hard truths about yourself and admit your own tendencies. When things are tense, you may feel compelled to fall back on your usual defenses. If you can own up to these patterns (saying, for example, "I know I can get rigid, and only give partial answers"), they won't become fuel for the next argument, and your partner won't be grinding on you to expose them.

Try to manage reactions that only escalate tension. Make an effort to complete a conversation without rushing to premature conclusions out of panic.

Resist the temptation to shift the topic to some tangential issue. For instance, if you leap in with the question, "How could you have waited this long to tell me?" you will derail your partner. When you're inclined to do this, tell yourself something like, "I want to communicate to my partner that I can handle the truth." Know that if you contain yourself and avoid becoming overly reactive, you will be able to ask better questions.

Recognize that the better your questions are, the better opportunity you will have to find out your partner's true position. Good questions invite truthfulness. They also help pinpoint what's bothering your partner when it's hard for him to say, or even to know.

STAY OPEN TO TRUTHS

Another important antidote to Lie Invitee behavior is holding on to information that you already know but may want to push out of your awareness. This is when you need to check in with yourself: *Why am I suddenly overcome by exhaustion? Might this, by any chance, have to do with my mate raising the subject of my spending habits?* Learn to recognize when you're suppressing information that you'd rather not hear. When you start to repress something that's really important to you or your relationship, you'll usually start to feel it as tension, a voice in the back of your head, or whatever your own signals are. Note what is threatening about the subject at hand and make an extra effort to deal with it.

Also recognize the symptoms of fending off information from others and yourself. Examples include zoning out, becoming easily distracted, avoiding eye contact, yawning, sarcasm, and interrupting your partner. Learn to tune into your own cues. Catch yourself pushing data away and make a conscious effort to reel it back in. Pay attention to any intuitions you have about yourself and your partner. Use questions to follow up on them. When an answer doesn't sound quite right to you, follow up on it rather than simply letting it go.

Congratulate yourself for each risk you take towards greater truthfulness. It's never too early to start.

4

The Honeymoon:
So Sweetly
Self-Deceived

*M*eet the two couples who will accompany you through the marital stages. We chose these two couples because they seemed so similar at the outset. Early in their relationships, it would have been impossible to predict the different paths the two pairs would take and which, if either, would collapse under the weight of their lies.

John and Sarah, who both work in the banking industry, met when he was twenty-seven and she was twenty-five. They each described falling in love at first sight. It was a storybook beginning, except, as Sarah put it, "Our eyes met across a conference table, not the palace dance floor." From the first date onward they were inseparable; sex was hot and "electric." They found they had a lot in common: Both were film buffs, both loved being outdoors, and they each maintained strong ties to their families.

Almost as an aside, John mentioned that he was "an old-fashioned kind of guy." "Even though I may not be politically correct, I believe a man should work while the woman stays at home with the kids," he said. Sarah's hopes soared. She not only wanted children, she wanted to stay home with them. Could this guy be for real? He seemed to be, but she didn't find out why a woman's staying home was important to him.

What were their initial deceptions? Sarah knew full well that if you ve an immediate, mouthwatering attraction to a man, you don't announce the depth and urgency of your desire for marriage and kids. She also feigned interest in sports. But so what? If she dismissed all men who were mad about sports, she might remain single forever; so, she rationalized (not a lie at this point) that she might be able to develop a liking for sports.

Here is what John was thinking: I've hit the jackpot here. There is so much I love about Sarah but not enough to even think about marriage yet, let alone having kids. There's too much to do and see in the world. I don't care what anyone says, getting married is a blight on freedom, but I sure won't tell that to her because there's no way I'm going to lose what we have.

John also had a lifelong dream of taking a bicycle tour across the country, and had been saving money so he could take time off to do so. Though this idea had been a driving force in his life, he treated it as inconsequential when talking with Sarah. Intuitively he knew that the idea of him leaving for six weeks would be upsetting to her, and he didn't want to put a damper on the intense passion he was feeling.

Paul and Mary met at a sales conference when he was thirty and she was twenty-eight. The early months of their romance were intense. "We were soul mates," Mary recalls. "It was as though we could read each other's mind." They were similar in temperament and interests. Both were gregarious, but they also liked more contemplative pursuits, like reading and listening to music.

There were initial deceptions. Paul was wary of Mary's ambition. He feared she was high-powered and that he looked like a dud compared to her, but he pretended her accomplishments never gave him pause. He also didn't tell her that he avoided traveling because it made him anxious. He hadn't taken a true vacation in years because of these feelings. On Mary's part, she didn't tell Paul that she had a weight problem (she was at her most slender when they met, thanks to a strenuous aerobics regimen) and that she wanted children. She also didn't emphasize how much she loved to travel. It didn't seem important.

"We Do Everything Together"

Anyone who is even the least bit romantically inclined longs for the feelings aroused by the Honeymoon Stage. This is love's candy. For everyone, the phase that launches your life as a couple is unique and precious. It takes no work to plunge from a great height because gravity does it all; likewise, it requires little or no effort to fall in love. It feels natural, often inevitable. Whether you regard it as chemical, spiritual, or even, as some may say, a kind of temporary insanity, the surrender to new love creates a euphoria like nothing else. Aside from the sheer pleasure of it, the Honeymoon Stage plays an important role in the relationship. It generates a sense of "we-ness," bringing two people together as one.

For some couples, this stage dawns the moment they lay eyes on each other. Other couples meander around a bit before they get there. Perhaps they start out as friends and then—Boom!—it hits that there's more between them than they thought. Both John/Sarah and Paul/Mary were of the love-at-first-sight variety. But whether it begins with a slow-building drumroll or a bang, the Honeymoon Stage is a time when lovers feel that the other person gives them so much that they are meant for one another. They revel in the idea that this sensation of blissful togetherness will last forever. Unfortunately, it won't. In our experience, after about a year, and often much sooner, all couples encounter some trouble in paradise. It's what they do with that trouble—whether they find the courage to confront it or make-believe they're still in Shangri-la—that determines how they will fare as a couple.

How do you know if you're in the Honeymoon Stage? If you are, you may object to the notion that this is a stage. In the throes of the Honeymoon, the idea that this is not an eternal state of being will take you aback: "Sure, relationships grow rusty and people go through difficult times, but that's *other* couples. *Our* marriage will be different, and we will beat the odds."

The Honeymoon Stage is marked by an insatiable appetite for the other person and a seemingly endless store of good will. It engenders a sense of inner completeness that tugs on primitive longings. We all crave a boundless, unconditional love that promises to fulfill us. A couple creates a cocoon, a new miniuniverse, separate from the realm of family and friends. Lovers are likely to marvel at how alike they are and how easy it is to be together. ("You like opera, too? That's *amazing!*") The delight in being "as one" is so intoxicating that both partners are willing to put many of their own interests and opinions on hold in order to sustain that feeling.

In the honeymooner's misty vision, they've happened upon the best of all mates in the best of all possible worlds. Everything about the other person seems marvelous. Someone in this stage can't imagine getting into trouble with lies, so potent is that sense of being able to see into each other's souls. But, of course, couples are lying to each other from the very start. Indeed, the notion that there is a true love waiting for you that does not require heavy lifting, sweating, and exertion is a fiction.

Hints of Imperfection

Throughout this phase, both partners' actions are driven by the desire to keep the romance at the same delirious pitch. If it is a dream, you don't want to wake up. Rather, you want to pull the covers over your head still further, ignoring the alarm clock and the breaking of day. On one hand, the fear of losing the intensity is so strong that whatever doesn't fit the picture is dismissed. On the other hand, you're asking yourself questions and sorting out whether or not you want to be with this person. Even as you're elated by your new love, in some corner of your psyche you're running through the checklist of what you seek in a mate: How does he/she feel about marriage and family? How well do you work together as a team? How compatible are your daily routines?

Just beneath the surface is the awareness that the enchantment can't last forever. In slow or private moments, you may wonder "now what?" Indeed, on the very peripheries of consciousness, you may notice hints of disagreement or shortcomings in your bright fantasy. These are so incongruous, however, that such little blips of discomfort are easy enough to ignore.

Paul, who sometimes felt humbled by Mary's professional success, recalls having some unsettling thoughts about nine months into their relationship:

"We were meeting at a restaurant, and I was a bit early and sat down. The place was empty except for a couple at the table next to me. I couldn't help listening to their conversation. It was clear that the woman had some kind of prestigious job, and the man was more of a lightweight. I noticed that the guy was tall, like me, and the woman was round and kind of sweet-looking, like Mary. I remembered how I felt the day Mary won a huge account a week after I had lost one, and I had this weird flash that this was going to be us in ten years, that Mary would be a star and I'd play backup. The thought of being small fry compared to her gave me a kind of chill. My ego wouldn't allow me to mention this to her and would hardly let me acknowledge it to myself. Then I thought that it could never happen with us. Mary's ambitious, but she helps keep me motivated."

Just as Mary came in, Paul recalls, the place filled up, and he forgot about the couple at the next table. The disturbing thoughts about his relationship with Mary were dissolved by the intimacy of the evening.

Lying—For Better or Worse

We've seen how Paul set aside some of his own misgivings. Although common wisdom tells you to enter into any relationship with your "eyes open," let's face it: With your vision bared to the other person's shortcomings and all the problems the two of you may run into down the line, who would bother to fall in love at all?

The fact is, under scrutiny, people are not as perfect as their partners would like them to be. Or as perfect as they would like their partners to see them. In order to secure the bond crucial to building a relationship, people fudge the truth about themselves and likewise fool themselves about their partners. In other words, we present ourselves as our partners would *like* to see us, and see in our partner what we *want* to see. This results in lying to our partners and lying to ourselves.

This behavior is normal, even necessary, in the Honeymoon Stage. These rosy distortions keep things pure for a while. They preserve the belief that "This is the perfect person for me, and I am the perfect person for him." They keep partners receptive to the good in each other. They save couples from having to confront contradictions, ambiguities, and disillusionment too early in the relationship. They free partners to make a commitment to one another despite their individual imperfections.

Similarly, the capacity to toy with the truth heightens our optimism. The rapture of the Honeymoon tricks us into thinking that this new love will fix all our lingering wounds from childhood and salve the bruises we've acquired over the years. This is, of course, an illusion. But it gets us hooked—and thus committed to the relationship.

On the other hand, Honeymoon distortions can blind you to major flaws in the other person. They can play into your own illusions about yourself ("I haven't been dependable in past relationships, but I'm sure I will be *now*"). They can lead you to make decisions that are unrealistic ("He thinks we'd be great living together, and we'll work out all the details later"). They can beguile you into underplaying matters of importance to you ("I've always thought marriage and children were important to me, but maybe it *is* healthier to be a free spirit"). They can throw your expectations out of whack.

As one woman found out, it's tempting to simply brush off hints of doubts rather than take an unflinching look at what's going on.

Amy met Brian, a restaurateur, on an adventure hiking holiday. Though she lived in the Midwest and he lived on the West Coast, they were able, much to Amy's delight, to see each other frequently because Brian came through town "on business." On a few occasions, he brought her out to the Coast for the weekend, first class. To all appearances, his business was thriving and everything was in synch. She loved the glamour of it all. After a fancy wedding that Brian paid for and then moving into a large new house, it came as a shock to Amy when she learned that Brian—and now by extension, her as well—was up to his nose in debt.

"There were signs," she later admits. "In retrospect, I see that Brian always grew uncomfortable when I raised substantive questions about his assets. And he hadn't had, as far as I could see, any huge successes that would justify his spending. But I really didn't want to know. I didn't look any further than what he dangled in front of me."

Let Me Count the Ways I Deceive You

In our experience, the theme of most Honeymoon lies is "We are just the same" or "We are perfectly compatible." The reason these fictions are so effective is that both parties want them to be true. During the Honeymoon Stage, every liar has a willing audience. Someone ready to question the fantasy, however, may not find such an agreeable listener.

LYING BY OMISSION

To maintain an illusion of compatibility early in the relationship, people may deceive each other by failing to give a prospective partner significant information. Deceptions take this form because people are reluctant to reveal anything that might introduce doubt as to the viability of the relationship.

Gary, a successful attorney, went on a sailing trip with friends and met Janet, a freelance photographer. Galvanized by a shared love of outdoor sports, they dated for an adventure-filled year (skiing, scuba diving, but Janet set the limit at skydiving) and then got married, on the top of a mountain, no less. They were passionate explorers, in their work, in the wilds, and in bed.

Although they had talked about previous relationships (each was divorced), Gary never told Janet that his marriage and a subsequent long-term relationship were entirely celibate after the first year or so. He wasn't necessarily trying to hide anything from her. He simply thought it irrelevant since he sincerely believed that things would be different with Janet. But after about a year, Gary lost interest in sex. When Janet tried to make the first move, Gary complained he was too tired. Things were strained, but neither knew how to talk about it.

Gary's lie to Janet was his failure to tell her about his tendency to withdraw sexually. He hadn't meant to deceive her—at least not consciously.

Yes Lies

Back to John and Sarah.

Early in their relationship, John thought Sarah was interested in sports because she told him so. She even said, "I don't mind going to games or watching them on TV. It's nice to sit close and snuggle." Misleading John about liking sports was a lie, but she certainly was honest about the snuggle part.

So what's the big deal about such a minor fib? After they were married, John could sense Sarah's irritation with him when he watched sports on TV. The hints she dropped ("Do you really need to watch that?") confirmed his suspicion. But John disliked arguments. Had he said, "You don't like me watching sports, do you?" it would have led to a tense discussion. John had little confidence in his ability to resolve disagreements, so he kept his mouth shut. Sports time increasingly meant tuning out Sarah.

Back to Paul and Mary.

Mary, who tried to take a trip abroad at least once a year, subscribed to several travel magazines and loved to read about exotic places. On quiet evenings, she sometimes would look up from her reading and invite Paul into her fantasies: "I'd love to go on a birding safari in the Okavango Delta. Or maybe the Galapagos Islands. How about that?" Paul, who might be scanning the newspaper or reading about his favorite subject, American history, would say, "Sure, sounds great." He assumed Mary was just being playful, but sometimes he quietly wondered how serious she *really* was. Would she indeed stretch their scarce resources by taking such a decadent trip? Even raising the possibility seemed chancy. By giving credibility to her daydreams, might he in fact be encouraging her to pursue them?

A common Honeymoon lie is what we call the "Yes Lie." The Yes Lie is when one person agrees quickly, without recognizing the implications of what they're saying yes to. Most people do this; it is impossible to do a risk-benefit analysis of everything said. A fairly innocuous example would be, "I don't mind eating in dives." Maybe the first few times you don't. But guess what: He knows every hole-in-the-wall in the county. Or the proverbial sports lie, as when a woman says, "Sure, I like football" and the next thing she knows he's bought season tickets, and she thinks, "Oh no. There go my weekends."

A Yes Lie can easily and suddenly grow into something you regret.

Fran, for instance, met Joe when she had left her job in public relations to work on a freelance basis. Joe put her on the payroll, and Fran, already smitten, assured him that she thought it was wonderful to work with him. In some ways it was: They would lose no time in finishing the day's work and heading out to an early movie. When one of them came up with an idea late at night (which Fran tended to do), they could share it with the other. On the professional front, however, Fran grew frustrated. Joe favored traditional campaigns, whereas Fran wanted to take creative risks.

When she questioned his style, Joe, genuinely hurt, said, "I thought you liked working for me." Well, she had said that. For Joe, working together was integral to the romance; for Fran, it was the one down side. She finally set out on her own, as she had originally intended, but Joe was disappointed and felt a great loss.

GRAY LIES

Who hasn't, in the uncertainty of a new, untested relationship, misrepresented or hidden certain aspects of who or what you are? You're not quite lying, but you're not giving your lover the whole story. You give yourself credit for fixing bad habits before you've done the work; you gloss over things that matter to you. All this in the name of putting on a good show for this most important observer. Common areas for such subtle fibs, fronts, and evasions are

- *Habits:* You may hide or deny basic everyday tendencies that, you fear, could put off the other person. Examples would include: You're a spendthrift or you're cheap; you procrastinate or are a stickler for being on time; you leave cracker crumbs around the house or are a clean freak.
- *Psychological Style:* You may say, "Oh, I don't mind disagreement" rather than admit that you crawl into a shell at the slightest hint of discord. Or claim that you're sociable and love meeting new people when the thought of a roomful of strangers makes you break

out in a sweat. Other lies might involve someone's love of adventure and willingness to take risks, or the capacity to be alone and tolerate silence.

- *Differences of Opinion:* One partner may sit quietly while the other spouts off political opinions rather than voice his or her own views and risk an argument. Similarly, someone may let the other go on believing that he or she wants the same things because he or she has never said otherwise. You may be mute about lifestyle choices, religion, politics, culture, taste, or any topic that comes up.

The reason these fall into a gray area is that they feel true at the time. For instance, you honestly believe that your tendency to withdraw from a conflict isn't a problem because you can't imagine it happening with this lover. Or you don't make a point of your desire to live in a city because at the moment it doesn't seem important. Or that you have trouble budgeting money because you sincerely intend to fix that.

Here's an example from our own relationship:

When Ellyn and I were getting to know each other, I did not want her to know the visual wreckage that was my apartment. So, whenever I knew she would be coming over, I had a cleaning service overhaul the place, and it actually looked pretty good. Did I know this was deceptive? Absolutely. Did I think I could keep up this appearance forever? Absolutely not.

How did I rationalize this? "Well," I said to myself, "the longer I'm with Ellyn (this was a very vague time frame) the more opportunities she will have (I hoped) to see my good sides. When the day of reckoning occurs and she knows I live like a pig, I hope to have gained a storehouse of goodwill so she just might overlook this one quirk of mine. And, hey, if I really hit the jackpot, she may even find my messiness endearing.

I suspected Ellyn was neater and more organized than I was (most people are), and I didn't want to risk looking bad in her eyes. What if she had paid a surprise visit and seen my apartment for what it was? Would she have run away? Perhaps to go get a sponge mop, but probably not for good. But it might have been like getting a ding in a new car right after driving it off the lot. Everybody knows cars get dings, but we want to savor the sheen before the scratches appear. And if I could delay the moment when Ellyn detected damage marks, I figured she would feel better about me.

Fooling Yourself

During the Honeymoon Stage, we lie to ourselves for the same reason we lie to our partner: Everything seems great, and we don't want to ruin it. To keep the romance rolling at the same rate, we overestimate the positive and underestimate the negative. We make excuses. We give lovers the benefit of the doubt. We have blinders on to shield us from looking at whatever might blunt our enthusiasm.

To a large extent, self-deceptions are fueled by cultural messages about love and its transformative powers. You want love to work magic, so you believe it will. You kid yourself that if this is "real love," then you and your mate will always agree, that you'll never have bad feelings, and that neither one of you will change. It's common to get seduced by the wish that there can be someone so tuned into your needs and desires that they *share* those needs and desires completely.

In general, we lie to ourselves about the same sorts of things we lie to others about:

- *Habits:* "He seems a bit finicky about his belongings, but I don't think that's a big deal."
- *Psychological Style:* "So he gets moody from time to time. Who doesn't?"
- *Differences of Opinion:* "He doesn't think women with children should work. Well, my mother survived not having a career, didn't she?"

We inflate things that make the other person look good and deflate what could interfere with the "rightness" of the match.

We also delude ourselves about the other's capacity for positive change: "He's not terribly ambitious. But I'm sure once he finds the right job, it will all fall into place." And your *own* capacity for change: "My other relationships have broken up over problems with jealousy. I can't imagine him doing anything to make me jealous."

Mary, for instance, noted Paul's reluctance to travel but said to herself, "Maybe he's had some bad experiences on the road. But I know traveling with me will be different."

Here are some common types of lies we may tell ourselves during the Honeymoon Stage:

- *I Don't Mind:* "I don't mind if we go to his church rather than mine."
- *It's Not His Fault:* "He doesn't get along with anyone in his family, but they just don't understand him."
- *I Think It's Kind of Cute:* "He's not good at expressing himself, but I think it's kind of sweet when he gets all flustered when he's trying to say something."
- *I Can Change Him:* "He used to get in huge fights with his ex-wife, but he'll never get that angry at me."
- *That's Not the Real Him:* "He did act kind of arrogant at the dinner party, but that's definitely the exception."

These lies allow you to perpetuate the idea that there is one reality that you share. It keeps alive the notion of a perfect fusion between you, even if it's just an illusion.

"LOVE CONQUERS ALL"

Another kind of self-deception occurs when we are so in love with the state of being in love that we imagine it can do more for us than it possibly can. For example:

"If this is real love, I won't have those familiar bad feelings."

"If this is real love, he will want exactly the same degree of closeness between us and exactly the same style in achieving it."

"If this is real love, he will never be any different from the way I see him."

There's also the fantasy that this is what you *need* in order to be happy in life. A lot of this comes down to being able to take care of oneself in a relationship. No one can bolster/fix/improve your mood twenty-four hours a day, and it's a huge letdown to accept this as the reality. In the romantic fury of the Honeymoon Stage, fantasy gets confused with fact.

Five-Alarm Lies

An extremely damaging kind of deception that can occur early in a relationship is a fraudulent lie, when a person deliberately misleads a lover about who he is in order to win that person over or hold on to the romance. For example:

Ben had noted that Cara always declined alcohol, even a glass of wine. "It doesn't sit well on my stomach," she once explained. But soon after the wedding Cara told him that she was a recovering alcoholic. Ben was surprised and felt he had been misled, but Cara was quite up front about the reason for her secrecy: She was afraid Ben wouldn't have married her had he known.

Early in their courtship, Dave involved Gloria in his plans for starting a business. She was so swept up in his enthusiasm—and by him—that she agreed to invest in the venture. Dave had failed to take certain import laws into consideration, and the business went belly-up. Gloria felt so betrayed that the relationship failed, too.

George was stunned to realize that Melody, his wife of two years, was eight years older than he was (rather than two years older, as he had been told) and that she had only received an Associates Degree. (She had led him to believe she had a B.A.) As a result, it led him to be wary of much of what she said.

Fraudulent lies are extremely difficult to repair. Once broken, trust is hard to rebuild. Sometimes lies of such magnitude signal that the person is simply dishonest and not to be trusted, that you've got a problem liar on your hands. (We discuss these liars in the next chapter.) That turned out to be the case with Dave, who had a trail of unmentioned failed businesses behind him and the soured romances that had helped to finance them.

But that's not always the case. Both Cara and Melody, for example, consider themselves extremely honest. They lied about specific attributes because they felt that the truth—about a former drinking problem and age, respectively—would have chased their lovers away. The fact, however, that someone lies in a calculated way once suggests they may well lie again.

Deceptions where one person misrepresents himself are impossible to sustain. If a relationship gets built around that lie, the couple is already on shaky ground.

What to Do About Those Lies

We always find it astounding that people in therapy will say all sorts of horrible things about themselves but will almost never admit, "I've been a weasel." This suggests how difficult it is to acknowledge deception. Stay aware of the typical reasons for Honeymoon lies: wanting to please the other person, wanting to bask in the mutual good feeling of a young romance, feeling unready to deal with a partner's complexities and contradictions. This awareness will help you stay open to the possibility that you're being overly free with the truth, without needing to make a harsh judgment on yourself about it.

The deceptions we create in this stage often begin beyond our awareness. The way to contain deception, then, is to learn how your unconscious talks to you: Is it a voice of conscience? Do you feel a twinge in your nervous system, or in your gut? Take notice of those signals and run a reality check over what's being said.

Here are some things to keep in mind:

- *Be alert to major incongruities that may signal trouble.* Are the things your partner is telling you in agreement with what you see?

    Let's say that your new partner claims to have many friends, but you've never been introduced to any of them, and he never speaks of anyone specifically. You may start to wonder if the said friends exist. And that may start you wondering not only about whether he has any friends but also about his credibility.

- *Don't hide significant aspects of yourself.* You don't have to announce, "A large family with lots of children is important to me" on the first or second date, but don't allow your romantic feelings to cloud you into denying those truths or assuming that the other person feels the way you do.

- *If you have make or break questions, raise them.* Are you uncertain about your partner's attitudes concerning fundamental issues?

    Artie wanted to marry someone ambitious and intent on making a lot of money. Because Jessica was working hard as a manager, he concluded that she was ambitious. Five years later, Jessica was home caring for their child and didn't want to return to work. Artie felt that that Jessica had duped him. Her response was, "I worked hard in that job, but I never claimed to be ambitious. He could have asked."

When Pete and I met, we lived in different states. I knew that if Pete hadn't said that he'd be willing to live in California, I probably would have stopped things right there. That gave me solid ground and made me feel I could take the next step. But sometimes people are afraid to ask those questions, or they create fantasies about what the other person wants in order to avoid finding out that reality is more complex.

- *Beware of the too-perfect package.* Do you have a vague feeling that your relationship is just too good to be true?

  John's desire to support his wife and children fit Sarah's ideal, and she concluded that he also felt as strongly about attention to early child development as she did. Had she asked, and had they taken time to explore it, however, she might have learned that when John was a child, his father had been laid off and his mother was forced to work at a tiring and not very rewarding job. His mother had a domineering personality and resented John's father for his failings. She was unhappy, and she tended to blame her only son as well as her husband. John believed that if he could be successful and the sole breadwinner for the family, he could redeem himself and be freed from blame.

LEARN TO COMMUNICATE

Particularly early in a relationship, there is a narrow margin that separates what should be shared and what should be kept to oneself. A good way to ensure that you stay honest is to be alert for times when you're holding something back because you're afraid of your partner's reaction and your dominant concern is what she'll think of *you*.

For example, let's say that a violent movie has been released, and you want to see it. You think, *If I tell my partner that I want to see this film, she'll think I'm sleazy, sadistic, and have a dark streak. So I won't go and will feel a pang of regret. I know I'm being a chicken because I'm afraid my lover will judge me harshly*. Or, perhaps you go to see it on your own and don't tell your partner. Afterwards, you realize that it was easy enough to do so you plan to do it again.

Before you go down that road, say to your partner, "Honey, I have a problem. I want to see the new release of *Die Hard, Part 23*, but I'm afraid you will think I'm one of those people who likes violent movies. You would be right, but I get uncomfortable when you tell me that you hate those movies, and I end up pretending that I agree with you. The reality is that I like them. Maybe we could talk about why you're opposed to me seeing them or discuss why I like them. Even if we don't come to an agreement, at least we would better understand each other's viewpoint."

The "formula" is this: "Honey, I have a problem" plus the dilemma, "I want *X* and am concerned about your reaction. Could we discuss it?"

An example of using this formula follows: "Honey, I like *Playboy*. I'm concerned that if I tell you this, you'll only see me as a pervert, and it will wreck our sex life, plus make you forget that I'm also a supporter of women's rights. Can you accept that I can read *Playboy* without it taking anything away from all that we have together?"

Rather than quietly fuming, Sarah could use this same model to discuss her frustration with John's sports-watching habits. "You know John, we've been together now for several months, and I've discovered that being with you is more positive than watching sports is negative. In fact, I like being with you so much that it takes most of the dullness out of watching sports." The main issue now is one of enjoying time with John instead of her disliking sports. She is true to both parts of herself, and John sees a more complete picture of Sarah.

LISTEN TO THE LITTLE ECHOES

Another way to catch yourself in a lie is to listen for an internal "echo," your own private response to what you've just said. These flash in and out of your mind quite rapidly, but you can train yourself to notice them. Listen for the "parentheses" in your own mind. For instance, you say, "Yeah, I could join you and your friends at the game" but you fleetingly think, *I hope he doesn't think I really mean it.*

Other examples of echoes are

"I think your sister is great, too." *(But don't think I'd welcome her for an extended visit.)*

"No, you're not too old to wear that." *(You're not really thinking of buying those hiphuggers are you?)*

Other common echoes include these, as well as their variations:

(. . . not really.)
(. . . is that true?)
(. . . I actually hope that won't happen.)
(. . . do I now have to follow up on that?)

Also be aware of instances when you find yourself (again, on the mere edges of consciousness) trying to talk yourself out of saying or feeling something.

Take note of these echoes. You don't need to respond to every one. That would get tiresome for each of you, but if they start to pile up and speak to you through a bullhorn, you need to take action. You can say, "Honey, I have a problem. I've been noticing *X* and have been reluctant to bring it up because I don't want to start an argument. Do you want to know about it? Is this a good time to talk?"

STAY OPEN

In the Honeymoon Stage, you're still gathering data about the other person. There's a lot you don't know but might sense. You need to be receptive to the notion that your initial assessment of your partner—no matter how much you've invested in it, emotionally or otherwise— won't be completely accurate. No one is one-dimensional. In the beginning, one side of someone's personality may predominate. Remember that other sides, and everyone has a darker side, will emerge. These undercurrents of character may be the kind of thing you can pick up through your intuitive responses.

CLEAR UP THE SMALL STUFF

Some Honeymoon lies (particularly Yes Lies, those that convey agreement) are small fibs, so small you may even feel silly bringing them up later. Here you can ask yourself if it's worth calling attention to. Generally, if the lie concerned an isolated incident which is unlikely to reoccur, you can let it go. But if you anticipate that the situation is going to crop up another time, you might want to correct the fib even if it means an awkward moment. This will prevent turning it into a larger deception.

If you do decide to amend such a lie, to avoid looking petty, you can bring it up with humor. An absurd exaggeration can make the point gently: "Honey, you know when I agreed to go to that movie *Daffodils in the Spring*, and I said it was okay? Well, the truth is that the only reason I was able to stay awake was that I had fourteen cups of coffee in me. In my opinion, movies like *Daffodils* rank right up there with watching parking meters expire. I was afraid if I told you what I really felt, you might poison my coffee."

Or give it a context. For example, your statement that you liked eating in dives was a Yes Lie. The next time he threatens another cheap meal you can say, "When we first got together, every place we went to was wonderful. I wasn't as interested in dives as I was in being with you." In another kind of situation, you could say something like, "I liked that pink sweater on *you*, but I don't usually like anything in pink."

LISTEN FOR THE TRUTH

You can often tell if your partner is feeding you a Yes Lie if you shift your focus away from wanting her to agree with you ("Oh, I'm so glad you like jazz as much as I do!") and try to emphasize to yourself what your partner is like as a separate person. In that case, you can assess whether their yes is genuine or chiefly an effort to satisfy you.

For instance, let's say your partner grew up on a farm and gets self-conscious around urban "sophisticates." If he echoes your zeal for going to a famously chic restaurant that he's never suggested on his own, you might ask yourself whether he would really be comfortable there. Or you can ask him how comfortable he'd be. Even if he says he'd be uncomfortable, however, that doesn't necessarily mean you shouldn't go. He may be curious, or he may legitimately want to please you. But knowing where he stands, and letting him know it's okay to feel like an outsider there, will help both of you to have a better time.

Moving On

As time goes on, it requires more work to achieve that emotional rush and greater levels of intimate revelation to maintain that incomparable Honeymoon feeling, that sense of knowing and being deeply known. You start to see your partner's failures as well as his successes.

Because the Honeymoon was so lovely, you will have buried in your emotional memory bank an equation: "Falling in love=good. Losing that feeling=bad." This leads to the conclusion: "Uh-oh. Our romance doesn't feel perfect anymore. Something must be wrong with me. Or with my partner. If things were okay, we would still be crooning together in harmony. It must be time to get out, or to try to get my partner to make adjustments, or to scramble desperately to try to recreate what we had." The Honeymoon becomes the template you measure yourself against. If you don't conform, you conclude that you or your partner have failed.

That assumption of failure is wrong, for this is the point where you can start to ground your relationship in truth. Sure, you'll get a wrench in your gut when you discover he's not your Galahad, but now you can get to know him as he really is. You're finding new dimensions to your partner, some a lovely surprise (he comes through in a crisis, or is great with kids) others a downer (he is painfully shy at parties or can hardly fry an egg). These new sides of your partner are news to you either because the Honeymoon didn't present any opportunities for them to surface, or because one of you lied them away.

It's normal to find some kinks in the relationship. It's inevitable that your partner will disappoint you. You observe that he's a dreamer, not a doer, or that religion is a lot more important to him than it is to you. These are growing pains. If you try to evade them, the relationship can't grow, and you won't be able to grow within it.

The challenge lies in how you deal with the disillusionment. You can overlook it, which means lying to yourself and your partner about its significance; you could pressure your partner to change in ways that make you comfortable, which may cause more conflict; you could cover up what you do and how you feel, which may lead to a succession of escalating lies; or you could try to address the situation as it stands. Every choice carries with it psychological distress. But if you can gather the fortitude to confront what's really going on between you, you have the chance to build something resilient.

The first disillusionment acts as a kind of test, gauging your willingness to hear the other person's truths as opposed to clinging to what you want to believe. Here your courage is tested. When you try to freeze the frame at the Honeymoon Stage, you get stuck; unacknowledged truths impede your growth. But when you take the plunge, your relationship may shift in unexpected ways.

In the Honeymoon Stage you're in the "blueprint" phase of your relationship. You're designing a new entity, establishing relational patterns that reflect what you want and who you are. When an uncomfortable truth comes up, you can ask yourself, "How do I want to be as a partner?" You will encounter this question continually throughout your relationship. The choices you make are going to be significant and have consequences down the line. You can begin to define for yourself what's important to you and how truthful you will be. Honesty takes courage, and you will meet many temptations to cut and run. Over and over you will ask yourself, "Is the risk worth it?"

Embedded in the Honeymoon Stage is the opportunity to either create an exceptional foundation or to build a relationship on quicksand. The question is, "Is the Honeymoon the end of the beginning, or the beginning of the end?

5 ✳

The Dark Side
of The Honeymoon:
So Anxious for Happiness

*A*s their first year together wound down, John and Sarah held fast to the storybook image of their relationship, although their story lines—what they wanted from here on in—increasingly diverged. They each began to "try out" their own dreams for the future on the other. Sarah made a point of how happy their settled friends were ("Now that they're married and have a baby, Sue and Mike seem so complete"), but John simply shrugged.

Sarah was in a dilemma: Pursuing the conversation meant confronting the harsh likelihood that John either didn't want kids or was a long way from wanting them. It was infinitely easier to avoid the discussion and hope she was wrong than to bring up the topic and risk having her fears confirmed.

John tried to include Sarah in mapping out his bicycle trips, but she seemed to always want to shorten them. His solution? Stop sharing plans with her. What he didn't do was inquire about her discomfort about his trips. He didn't want to chance finding out that a potential mate wouldn't support his dream.

It wasn't only the dream trip that was important to John. Bicycling was a personal sanctuary for him. It was a time he could be completely himself, open to the elements, as hurried or idle as he wanted to be.

Perhaps most important, he felt free of others' demands. But he didn't know how to reveal himself to Sarah at this heartfelt level.

Unbeknownst to them, the foundation of their future was being poured in concrete. Shortly after the one-year mark of their romance, Sarah became pregnant. She had forgotten to take the pill and "accidents do happen." Sarah told John that she couldn't imagine not having the child. John was not able to tell Sarah that he wasn't ready to be a father. But he did not want to lose Sarah. So he proposed marriage.

Sarah took John's proposal to mean a strong desire to be with her—not as a sign that he was afraid of losing her. She replayed over and over in her mind his statement that he wanted his wife to stay home.

Paul and Mary were "a couple" for a year when they decided to get married. Their families were pleased, but no one was surprised. "It's as though you're already married," more than one friend had said. They started talking about doing some projects together (both were marketing consultants) even though Paul felt intimidated by Mary's confident style. They planned several training seminars together, including one in Europe. Paul didn't want to go; he said he got a headache every time they talked about it. But Mary was so enthusiastic that he went along with it, privately hoping that something would come up that would interfere with the venture.

Mary had kept her weight down to fit into the slinky wedding dress she had her eye on, but after several months of marriage, the pounds began creeping back. She started avoiding sex—complaining that she was tired, pretending she was asleep—because she didn't want Paul to see her body.

"Of Course, Everything's Perfect"

As we know, the Honeymoon Stage does not last forever. But some people never truly let go. This happens through one of two deceptive strategies and often a combination of both: (1) holding on to the fantasy that the relationship is perfect and all-fulfilling, and (2) avoiding any conflict or disagreement.

With the first, each partner hides out, not reckoning with the reality of life together, not willing to give up illusions of the past. This happened with John and Sarah, who each saw the other as their "ideal mate." Many couples expend huge amounts of emotional energy desperately trying to hold on to some ideal moment that has already slipped away. They remain determined to present the perfect front to other people and to each other.

With the second strategy, the couple minimizes or ignores any differences or potential conflicts between them, often resorting to lies and withheld truths to do so. Both Paul and Mary, for example, remained quiet about things that concerned them: their conflicting ideas about working together, Mary's weight problems, and their waning sex life, to name a few. When such deceptions persist, each person's true feelings, opinions, and desires are cast in shadow. This is the Dark Side of the Honeymoon, in which many really important things never get said. The relationship is holding its breath.

The defining feature of the Dark Side of the Honeymoon is that things are no longer fun. In the Honeymoon, the relationship is great, and the partners want it to last forever. In the Dark Side of the Honeymoon, there's an edge of desperation. The relationship *has* to be wonderful for fear the whole thing will fall apart.

You see, the Honeymoon, all ease and brightness, has a flip-side, terror. This is the emotional backdrop for the Dark Side of the Honeymoon: the terror each feels over being found lacking, and the terror of finding out that one's partner may *not* be as wonderful as had been hoped. The roots of this are the universal anxieties about being desirable and being alone.

Not every couple gets trapped in the dark side. Couples who struggle to stay honest will be able to slough off the inevitable Honeymoon lies and allow the relationship to evolve. Others resist and dip in and out of this sticking point before they're able to move beyond it for good.

Couples may get snagged by dark-side patterns as early as six months into a relationship; for others, it might happen after a year or even two. This stage can go on in perpetuity. A pair that begins as passionate lovers can become two people coexisting in silent resignation simply because they don't know how to speak the truth.

Pete recalls, in particular, one couple that could not remember a single fight or heated argument in thirty years of marriage. Perhaps they both raised their voices once or twice. They couldn't talk about what was bothering them. The tension in the room was unbearable. Pete felt claustrophobic, which is no doubt how they had been feeling for years.

It is possible to steer yourself out of the Dark Side of the Honeymoon, especially if deceptive patterns are not entrenched. But the farther you head down this road, the more backtracking you will need to do. The dark-side couple becomes increasingly concerned with perpetuating the fiction of the perfect marriage, and resentment builds up between them because neither feels they're getting their due.

Telltale Signs

How do you know if you've detoured into the Dark Side of the Honeymoon? Often there's an undefinable dissatisfaction, as if the marriage were a set of clothes that doesn't quite fit. You may be aware of significant truths you're stowing away; there may be things you want to know from your partner, but you're not asking and she's not telling. Other clues are

you find yourself obsessing about things you want to say, but it never seems like the right time;

you make love less often and/or enjoy it less;

you allow your partner's seeming lack of interest to dissuade you from raising subjects of importance to you;

you confide to friends about things you want to tell your partner but feel you can't;

you feel more alone than involved with your spouse, despite your conviction that there's "nothing wrong";

you're frequently aware of long, awkward silences or a sense of forced cheer.

Ironically, pairs stuck in the Dark Side of the Honeymoon may be seen as "the perfect couple" by others. True, they may rarely fight. True, they may seem magically to agree. But the real problems, those steady waves of discontentment that build on each other and never quite subside, are invisible.

In our experience, we've found that some people are particularly prone to the kind of illusions and conflict-avoidant behavior that lead to the Dark Side of the Honeymoon. These include those who

would describe themselves as "thin-skinned" or "hypersensitive"

have trouble being assertive and are likely to overaccommodate and overadapt to others

grew up believing that they had to put their best face forward

were abused as children and are afraid they will be punished for speaking the truth

The Dark Side of the Honeymoon is awkward, uneasy, and at times grim. However, a couple who illuminates those dark corners will find their marriage greatly strengthened. They will have overcome fears about mastering the demands of a real relationship and will have handled fears about standing on their own. They will learn that they do have the resilience to hear what their spouse has to say. They will have come through something difficult together and will arrive at a capacity for truthfulness that is hard-won but well earned.

Discontent is what fuels growth—in marriage, in oneself, and in institutions. It's what propels you to come up with creative solutions and to seek novelty and change. Merely accepting this represents a huge step in keeping a marriage alive and frees you to move onward, out of the dark side.

Hear No Evil, Speak No Evil

Many people stave off terror by taking refuge in Honeymoon illusions: You can avoid the dismay of finding out that your new love is trouble as long as you ignore what you don't like. Naturally, this becomes harder as you get to know each other better. Maybe you learn about some messy affairs in his past, or you differ in how you handle money, or you feel uncomfortable with the haughty way she talks to her employees.

Any resulting disillusionment leads to some choices: What do you make of this knowledge in the context of the relationship? Does it change the way you feel about your partner or the way the two of you relate? Can you use this knowledge to reach a point of resolution, or must the truth be driven underground? Are false assumptions from the romantic phase recast in a more realistic light, or will they grow into larger deceptions?

Couples in the Dark Side of the Honeymoon do everything they can to avoid accepting disappointment and relinquishing their cherished illusions. If their partner isn't perfect, if their relationship isn't perfect, if their own behavior isn't perfect, they just *don't want to know*.

The lies in this stage protect couples from the painful reality that no romance will fulfill all their needs. This may seem obvious, but many people refuse to face this fact until they're dragged into it kicking and screaming. Hallie, who has been with Mark for nearly a year, explains it well: "Mark and I had such a powerful connection. Then when he stopped wanting to be with me every minute of the day, I threw myself into my work rather than find out what was going on with him."

In the early years, Sarah accepted John's working long hours without complaint, even when she was lonely. She overlooked his occasional comments that he would like to be free of demands. She configured him in her mind as a sensitive kind of guy who was working hard to build a future for them. Her part was holding down the fort at home. She had this oddly romantic notion that they were like pioneers, working together to forge their destiny. This made her increasing isolation seem tolerable.

My Perfect Partner

One self-delusion that can surface in the Dark Side of the Honeymoon is the Lie of Deification. The revered partner is perfect, the embodiment of all that's wonderful. He or she can do no wrong.

The fantasy of the flawless partner is inevitable to some extent whenever there's a strong attraction. In the Honeymoon Stage, you're giddy with how terrific your partner is. And then you get to know him. Finding out he's not superhuman may be disappointing, but it's also a relief. A couple gets trapped in the dark side when that illusion of perfection is nonnegotiable, when it's so central to the relationship it becomes the glue holding it together.

Or the glue holding *you* together. The person who idealizes often places all the good in the partner and feels horribly deficient herself. The underlying attitude is: "I need my partner to be perfect and competent, or I'll crumble."

Lies of Deification include beliefs like "My partner can do no wrong" and "My partner is better than I am." They create a false portrait which both partners strain to preserve. They lock each person into fixed roles with awkward power imbalances. If the "weaker" party suddenly becomes stronger, what happens? And how can anyone live up to such an image all the time? Once a couple has taken a position of one partner's infallibility, they must continually lie and distort to maintain the appearance.

From the time they first met, John looked up to Sarah. She was in control; she knew what she wanted. John had felt somewhat lost at different points in his life, and he came to believe that Sarah could help to keep him in line, give him a sense of direction and purpose. He would often tell her how wonderful and how smart she was.

After they had their children—Dylan, followed a year later by Nicholas—Sarah bought into the image of the "Supermom." Someone who was always clear about what she wanted, Sarah enjoyed the sense of being in charge and doing things her way at home. She started working part-time, but still did all the drudge work at home. She had repeatedly told John that she wanted to create a harmonious household. John latched on to the phrase "she wants to create" and breathed a sigh of relief; he was happy to let her do the creating. He disagreed with some aspects of how she handled the children, but he didn't say anything. He would just brush aside his own views, telling himself they weren't important.

Sarah wanted John to be more involved but couldn't reconcile this with the part of her that thought she should be able to do everything. Inwardly, she resented John. Playing with the kids and getting them all fired up before bedtime was not her idea of "help." Meanwhile, John kept telling Sarah that she was terrific and a wonderful mother. He was afraid that if he didn't continue the praise, she would stop loving him.

The irony was that they each idolized each other in different ways: John looked to Sarah to be a master of organization, while Sarah saw John as the ideal, if often absent, husband and breadwinner. John was clueless to the fact that he was helping to reconstruct the family dynamic that he had found so painful as a child.

I'd Rather Quit than Fight

In most people's minds, the fewer their differences, the less potential there is for arguments and conflict. The less conflict, the lower the possibility for a cascade of bad feelings and an explosive end to the relationship. The less conflict, the less the vulnerability for self-exposure. The less conflict, the easier it is to hold on to the mirage of a perfect relationship.

Since frankness brings the risk of bruised feelings, it makes sense that partners want to downplay discord, for emotional self-preservation if nothing else. But while avoiding conflict may avert, or at least postpone, some highly flammable encounters, it will put the marriage in another kind of peril, the threat of slow suffocation.

Such was the situation with Fred and Allison.

Allison had been in an abusive marriage before she met Fred. Spontaneous shows of affection set her on edge. "I always felt I was tiptoeing around her," Fred explains. "I had the feeling that if I made one false step, she'd bolt."

Fred was so careful around Allison that he restricted his thoughts, his words, his actions, and he never told her how anxious he was that she might leave him. Every day he had the chance to speak up, and every day he pushed back the truth. The atmosphere in the house became so oppressive that it was no surprise when, after eight years of marriage, Allison moved out.

Avoiding conflict isn't a bad thing in itself. We all pick our battles and may decide that a given argument isn't worth the effort. Sometimes you're simply too tired to protest. If two people tried to work out every disagreement and discrepancy in taste, they probably wouldn't have much energy left.

Avoiding conflict certainly makes things easier in the short term. It maintains the status quo and keeps things predictable, so no one has to worry about the unknown. It can dictate behavior so that no one has to take personal risks. It may give one partner a gratifying role in the relationship (such as the "strong" one or the one who gets pampered) that's hard to give up. It may allow people to postpone having to take themselves or their goals seriously.

But any immediate benefits are soon outweighed by the sense of marital paralysis that sets in. Conflict avoidance is problematic when it's used to shield a relationship from necessary growing pains. When every potential conflict seems like a major threat, and married partners lie to evade any disagreement, that marriage is setting itself up for trouble.

The longer an uncomfortable truth or point of contention is denied, the longer it festers. The secret that no one dares talk about—the drinking, the bad temper, the overzealous flirting—becomes the invisible core of the relationship, an undetonated grenade that both partners tiptoe around.

Once established, a pattern of conflict avoidance only intensifies. When people avoid speaking their own truths, they fail to develop any ability to elicit truthfulness from their partners. As a result, the fear of conflict increases with time. Partners become suspicious, assuming the worst rather than finding out for sure. They get caught in a cycle: The less they know the more they suspect, and the more they suspect the less they actually ask.

Fears about telling the truth tend to become self-fulfilling. You may think, *If I lie, I don't have to face this ugly scenario.* As time goes on, you begin to realize, *If I speak up now, I'll have to open an even bigger can of worms.* So you put it off and continue lying as the stakes grow even larger.

Whatever You Say, Dear

The lies partners tell each other at this stage generally fall into the category of Lies of Accommodation. The lies serve to keep the "we" paramount and minimize the two individual "I's." The overt sentiment is, "Anything you want, dear."

Sarah remained invested in the idea that their marriage be wonderful and harmonious. Thus, she would always find a way to accommodate herself to whatever John asked. She agreed he could accept a new position that required extensive travel, and she told herself the trade-off would be worth it because if he gets ahead, they will have a sense of working together. Her increased responsibilities at home would be her price to pay and her contribution to family progress.

John was rather relieved when he was offered the new job; he didn't mind traveling because he got to be alone. Plus, he could sense that Sarah was discontented but wasn't sure how to bring it up. Travel meant a double bonus: time to be alone and an escape from Sarah's disgruntlement.

Paul kept his feelings of inadequacy secret from Mary. At one point he exaggerated how much money he had coming in because he didn't want Mary to think he was a slouch. Once Mary nominated Paul to chair a local committee, a role that required a lot of public speaking. Paul backed out at the last minute. He had wanted to look good so he went along with it, but he really didn't feel confident enough to go through with it. Had he spoken up at the start, he would have avoided a lot of embarrassment.

We saw one couple that decorated their entire house in a way that *neither* was happy with because they were constantly lying about their preferences in an effort to accommodate the other: "The wallpaper you chose is just fine"; "No, I don't mind that particular rug at all."

Another couple went on a weekend jaunt that neither one really wanted to take. They traveled a few hours north, far enough that there was snow but not far enough to ski. As they sat around, bored after breakfast, they wondered, "How did we end up here?" The wife said, "I was going where you wanted to go." The husband replied, "I thought you didn't want to go too far." They were so concerned with not upsetting each other that neither got what he or she wanted.

Dark-side lies may start out as seemingly benign, only to spiral out of control. When people don't speak up, they each make small concessions. They continue to lop off the part of themselves that feels discontent. In time, they feel they're giving up more than they're getting. Soon, each harbors spite toward the other. Either that, or they start feeling trapped by lies intended to purchase good will.

People who habitually slight their own interests in order to sustain the "we" may become completely out of touch with themselves; they can go on acquiescing to the other's whims in order to preserve the peace indefinitely. After repeatedly acceding to the other and denying oneself, someone may literally wake up one morning and say, "Hey, I never wanted to be here. What am I doing?"

This is exactly what happened to Angela.

For several years, Angela and Bruce had lived in eight different university towns, following Bruce's academic fellowships. Angela, also a student, continually shifted her focus of study depending on where Bruce wanted to be.

By the time Bruce finished his studies, Angela was feeling rooted in the last locale. She loved the safe but cosmopolitan atmosphere of the large university town and had a part-time research position with the promise of growth. The last thing she wanted was to start over again. Bruce, however, wanted to move back to New England and launch his own research company. He also wanted Angela to work for *him*.

She said no to both counts. This was the first time she had put her foot down and spoken up for herself. Bruce was taken aback by this unexpected turn and said he wanted a separation. A few months later, he introduced Angela to "the woman he would marry next." Later, during divorce mediation, he said to her, "The day I heard you say no, that was the day I decided to find someone who would say yes."

Angela had gone along with Bruce's wishes so often that he had taken it for granted that she would agree. On some level, she probably knew that Bruce wouldn't compromise, that it was his way or nothing. On the other hand, she never tested it out. If Angela had spoken her truth earlier, maybe they would have negotiated solutions that fit both of them. At the very least, she would have learned much sooner that they were ultimately incompatible.

One fallacy in operation here is that it's admirable to be selfless. There is the perpetual martyr who thinks, "I'm so good because I always let the other have his way." The martyr may feel she's doing her partner a favor, but all she's doing is effacing herself into invisibility and storing up animosity in the process.

Excuses, Excuses

People find a variety of reasons to avoid speaking the truth when they simply don't want to deal with reality. If there's something uncomfortable to be said, certain people automatically revert to finding an excuse *not* to be truthful. Rationalizations that spouses use to dodge the truth and avert conflict include

"I'm protecting my partner."

"I don't want to upset my partner."

"I'm a good guy and don't want to have to be the bad guy."

"I'm protecting the kids."

"It's not worth making a fuss about."

"What I think doesn't matter that much."

Mary knew that Paul was concerned about her weight. She started resorting to tricks she never dreamed she would turn to: She would sneak food or hide snacks in different spots in the house so Paul wouldn't catch her going into the kitchen. She told herself Paul wouldn't be able to handle her "dirty little secret," but the truth was that she didn't want to reveal this confused, shameful side of herself.

She was deceiving herself that her behavior wasn't a problem if she concealed it.

Under the guise of protecting a partner, lies to the self often lead to avoiding difficult but important self-confrontations. Self-fooling excuses can immobilize a marriage when one partner stops being conscious of the truth altogether and allows the rationalization—"He/she can't handle the truth"—to govern the entire relationship. Things grow dull quickly because so much that's important gets edited out.

This is what happened, for instance, with Larry and Gail when they were married for five years.

Larry was a steady, even-keeled sort; Gail was always struggling. She complained of feeling helpless and insecure, and leaned on Larry for support. Larry loved Gail, and often withheld information—illnesses in his family, potentially important changes at work—for fear of upsetting her. His fears about her stability were so constant that by the time they came to us, he shared very little with her at all.

In treatment, Larry revealed his weariness with Gail's vulnerability and his loneliness in the marriage. I pointed out that if he gave up catering to Gail's sensitivities, he'd have to relinquish his role as her rescuer. His rationalization for protecting Gail, "She can't handle it," had given Larry his role in the marriage, that of Gail's protector. For a time, this worked for him. But ultimately he felt stifled.

Once Larry started deceiving Gail "for her sake," Gail's emotional fragility became the strongest force in their marriage. Each small deception built upon larger lies: the lie of Gail's overriding helplessness and the lie of Larry's omnipotence. These, in turn, generated the delusion that came to frame the relationship, that Larry knew better than Gail what Gail needed.

Problem Liars

One woman logged on to the computer she and her boyfriend often shared and found that he had downloaded pornography. She asked him to explain. He waffled. Then he told her he wanted to have dinner with an "old female friend" who turned out to be an ex-girlfriend. His response: "If you had specifically asked if she was an ex-girlfriend, of course I would have told you. And if you had directly asked if we slept together, I wouldn't have thought of hiding it from you. But I don't really consider her an ex-girlfriend because we only got together a few times."

Soon afterward, she reminded him that he promised they'd move in together after a year. Then he said, "Well, I didn't *really* say that. What I said was, I never live with anyone until I've known them for a year."

Truth is frightfully compromised when a partner has to ask harder and harder questions to get to the bottom of things. It's extremely frustrating and leads to layers of cynicism that are hard to remove.

There are people who would lie to their partner no matter who they're with. These are often people who are constantly changing their story and parsing terms in a manner you might call "Clintonesque." His words: "I have never broken the laws of my country." Okay, so he tried pot in *England*. His claim: He didn't have a "long affair" with Jennifer Flowers. Well, he had sex with her, he admitted under oath, but still contended that the affair wasn't of long duration.

Typically when the couple cruises through the Honeymoon without specifically addressing habitual deceptiveness, each partner either ruefully accepts it or makes weak attempts to confront it, with no effect. This establishes the couple in a Dark Side of the Honeymoon pattern.

This scenario may creep up on a couple quietly. At first there may not be a compelling reason to push the truth. Ted says, "I think having kids is a fine idea" because that's what Joan wants to hear. She may suspect, but she won't know that this is a lie until the child issue is actually confronted. Or, Ted might say, "Just bear with me until my business gets off the ground." It could take a long time for Joan to realize that his company isn't going anywhere.

As with many dark-side predicaments, the longer it continues, the harder it is to extricate yourself. The longer you delude yourself, the more likely it is that you will either need to get out or to accept that you're with someone who will be less than forthright about many things. Each time you intend to bring it up and then collapse, your uphill battle grows steeper.

Dark Spots

Some couples are honest with one another, for the most part, yet have a "dark spot" in their relationship—a sensitive topic they cannot touch. In such instances, deception is used strategically to put a boundary around specific issues.

Martha, who is married to Ken, a highly paid lawyer, has taken to stashing money in her stocking drawer. She's already the veteran of one marriage and subsequent messy divorce. She has told Ken of her reluctance to be financially dependent on him. Ken's response was dismissive. "Don't worry," he said. "You know I have plenty of money. You will always be taken care of."

Essentially, Martha tested Ken: "It may not be completely logical in terms of dollars and cents, but I want the security of feeling that I have my own funds. Can you hear me on this?" The answer was no. Ken was inadvertently telling Martha to lie by letting it be known that he wasn't interested in hearing her monetary worries. The message was: "If you have money concerns, don't tell me." She was reluctant to push so she put those feelings elsewhere—along with the money she wanted to feel safe.

Many couples have dark spots. Here are some common ones:

A rough time earlier in the relationship: "We've gone over that as much as we can. I won't bring it up anymore if you won't."

A friendship the other person disapproves of: "See Terry if you feel you must. Just don't tell me about it."

One partner's liking for erotica: "I don't want to catch you reading porn in our house."

While not necessarily problematic, dark spots can spread into a kind of dark sprawl. For this reason it's important to test the subject from time to time and to make sure that it isn't exerting a stronger pull on the relationship than it warrants. Is the dark spot an isolated area, or does it represent pervasive hiding? Can you two confront conflict in other areas? Do you know why this particular subject is off-limits? Does it thwart the relationship in any way?

It's important to recognize that if you choose to have a zone of deception, you may be prone to imagining your partner engaged in the same kind of lies. This is what happened to Martha. She started worrying that Ken was being secretive about his finances, too. This caused her a great deal of anxiety—more, in fact, than the original stash was intended to resolve.

What to Do About Those Lies

When people get stuck here, they can become completely disconnected from their own vibrancy and spontaneity. The reason to take the risk and speak the truth is simple: to reclaim your vitality, even your personhood. Sometimes an inner sense of being cut off from what's alive in yourself is sufficiently painful to motivate change. But mostly, it requires blind faith. Ultimately, the best reason to speak your truth is that it is the only way that you can live with integrity. Encouraging your partner's truth encourages him to live a life of integrity with you.

CHANGE YOUR ATTITUDE

The way to come out from the dark side's shadows is this: Face what it is that you fear about the relationship. There simply isn't any other way.

That's the bad news. The good news is that it's rarely as bad as you think. Most of the discomfort comes *before* you make the decision to move forward; once you do, your internal tension lessens. The more you feel compelled to hide—the complaints you never mention, the mistakes you won't admit to—the larger these secrets loom. Bringing matters into the open also pulls them down to scale. It often turns out that your partner is not as shocked/distressed/disappointed as you thought she'd be. You may even wonder why you stressed yourself so much.

If, however, you try it and it turns out messier, more intense, or more painful than you want to deal with on your own, do yourself and your partner a favor and call an experienced therapist.

For people who habitually suppress their discontent, expressing what they feel seems a drastic measure. They may compare it to jumping off a cliff. We try to help them see it as closer to jumping off a diving board: a bit of a free fall but there's water below.

We see our job in therapy as helping couples speak truths despite their fears and to do it again and again. Typically, once someone has finally reached the point where he can air a long-smoldering grudge or ask something he's wanted to ask for years, the reaction is, "Phew, I'm glad that's over. I don't want to have to go through that again."

Well, guess what? These challenges will surface continually. People who have trouble saying one important thing to their partners generally have trouble saying *lots* of things to their partners. Once they move towards truthfulness, they have many lies to undo. It does, however, become easier. As you persist and grow stronger it will seem less scary.

In our experience, there is generally a palpable moment when someone makes the conscious choice to speak the truth. The breakthrough usually occurs when (1) you say to yourself, "I can't sit on this any longer," or (2) you test out being truthful and find you can manage it. At this point, your attitude shifts. You decide that your mate really does want to know more about you and that the benefits of closeness are worth the price of initial discomfort. Once you have that resolve, it clearly comes across.

Mary decided that concealing her eating habits was becoming too painful. She didn't want to struggle with her weight in private anymore. She wondered if this was something she could discuss with Paul, and how supportive he would be if she sought help. She wavered back and forth: She dreaded the thought of putting into words something she wasn't sure Paul could ever understand, but she also hated the idea of keeping secrets from him.

She realized she didn't want to continue hiding, not if she and Paul were to have the honest marriage she wanted. After rehearsing different dialogues in her head, she finally approached Paul and said she had something extremely important to say to him. She said, "What I'm going to tell you touches some very raw emotional spots for me, and I hope you can withhold judgment of me until after we talk. All my life, my weight has gone up and down like a yo-yo, and the way I feel about myself along with it. I was teased about my weight as a kid, which only made me more sensitive about it. I beat myself up for eating too much by calling myself a pig for days on end. I hide some of my eating from you so that I don't get those dirty looks, and then I feel like a naughty child because I'm hiding."

Paul was stunned by this revelation. He had no idea his supremely self-confident Mary had been living two lives. There was no way he could be critical of her after she had opened up to him this way. He felt compassion. He also felt strangely closer to her. His own self-doubts made it easier to identify with her struggle. The problem remained, but now that the issue had been laid out, they could get some traction on it for future discussions.

How do you decide to break that barrier of silence? Sometimes I ask people to look at role models around them. If a client, for example, comes from a family that was made fearful and secretive by alcohol, they'll have a visceral understanding of the cost of pretending everything's fine. A movie or novel—*Ordinary People* is one chilling example—can also bring that home.

Another exploratory method is to pay attention to how your family resolved conflict when you were growing up and how this has affected the way you handle your anger and frustrations. People often adopt patterns of resolving conflict and dealing with anger from their own families without even thinking about it. We all tend to do what we see as routine and may think that what our family did was the "normal" and only way. Conflict avoidance in particular may be passed down from generation to generation. Learning to manage conflict is a learned ability that requires practice. If no one teaches you, you're likely to struggle with it.

Decide how you want to handle things. This needn't be in defiance of your family. Maybe, in retrospect, you see that your parents were shy of conflict, but you appreciate that they were respectful of others' feelings. Select a role model who demonstrates the qualities of directness, forthrightness, and conflict management that you respect. It's likely that this person didn't happen on this facility by simple good fortune. Observe this person and ask them how they're able to handle disagreement.

Hearing the Truth

The way to steel yourself for what your partner has to say is this: Remind yourself that it's not about you; it is about him or her. Try to take a step back and interpret his words that way, rather than taking it personally. Even when your partner is furious about something you've done, remember: There's a reason that this particular thing is upsetting to him that does not pertain to you.

For example, let's say you're late for dinner for the third day in a row and your mate is ticked off. Since it's your behavior at issue, the natural response is to get defensive: "Quit bugging me. I'm someone who tends to be late, so get used to it." But you'll get nowhere if you continue to regard the problem as "about you." Even a promise, "I'll try to do better," will only make you feel more stifled. You're still in the dark as to why this is so upsetting to him.

By shifting the focus from yourself to your partner, you may ask questions and learn that your being late reminds him of being left alone for long stretches of time. Understanding this gives you a stronger and more heartfelt incentive to be on time.

Renee and Matt disagreed about how to handle their demanding two-year-old twin sons. Even though she was doing everything she could think of to slow them down, Matt complained that she let them get too wild. Rather than arguing with him, Renee would choke off her response and say, "I'm doing the best I can" and then be a nervous wreck when Matt came home, hoping the kids wouldn't act up. This was a lie. What she really wanted to say was, "Get off your high horse. I desperately want your help. I'm stretched thin already." Instead, she continually felt criticized and hurt.

In treatment, Ellyn encouraged Renee to ask Matt more about himself.

RENEE: "What else—besides frustration with me—do you feel when our kids seem undisciplined to you?"

MATT: "Sad."

RENEE: "What are you sad about?"

MATT: "Sad that I don't see them more."

RENEE: "What would you feel if you disciplined them when you are around?"

MATT: "I would feel guilty that in the short time I see them I'd have to be tough with them."

They had a situation where Matt was home at the roughest time of day—dinner and bedtime—and didn't want to do any of the disciplining. The children were losing out on the limit-setting guidance their father could offer, and the marriage was suffering. But now Renee came to understand that Matt's anger *wasn't* about her. Rather, whenever the twins were "undisciplined," he was confronted with contradictions in himself. This was something she couldn't grasp while trying to avoid conflict. After she explored what disciplining the children meant to him, the entire matter looked much different.

Moving On

The reality is that you and your partner will bump up against each other from time to time. You will have differences of opinion, values, interests, and goals. You will frustrate each other. The next stage, Emerging Differences, is about learning to use disagreement to recharge your romance and help you grow as individuals. If you're both hiding out in the dark side, you'll never get there. Unless you begin to reckon with some truths, you will slowly strangle life out of yourself and your relationship. Sometimes the charade becomes so untenable that a couple is forced to call it quits.

Keep in mind a picture of how you want to relate to your partner. Do you always want to be guessing what the other is thinking? Do you want to live in an emotional vacuum? Can you find productive ways of expressing disagreement? Give yourself a chance to live up to how you want to be. The time is now.

6 ✹

Emerging
Differences:
Getting to Know
(and Like) You

*B*y now, Paul and Mary were settling into marriage, but certain points of contention proved harder and harder to ignore. Finally, Paul said plainly that he didn't want to pursue any joint business projects with Mary. She was crushed. She really did value his contributions, viewpoints, and energy. She believed so strongly that they could work as a team. What was this if not a rejection of her?

Ready or not, they now had to face the next hurdle. When Mary said, "When are we going to have children?" Paul mumbled half to himself, "In another life." He could see the vast repercussions of his words, so he quickly backtracked and said, "Well, maybe soon." Mary did not pursue the precise definition of "soon." She was still reeling from his response.

Sometimes problems seem relentless in their ability to appear at bad times. Paul and Mary both knew their sex life had deteriorated, but Paul was the first to raise the subject. Mary thought she would feel sexier if she lost some weight but when Paul suggested as much, she snapped, "This is my body. Take it or leave it." At each flash point, one partner pushed and the other resisted.

Reality and Its Discontents

The first nudge towards differentiation comes unbidden. You feel an internal twinge, a vague awareness that something is happening between the two of you that challenges your vision of the relationship. Maybe you acknowledge that your partner has assumptions about you that don't quite square with what you feel. Maybe you thought you shared the same views on important moral issues but now see that you're miles apart.

Discovering differences between the two of you can be exhilarating and exciting. Your partner can introduce you to something novel, anything from a new ethnic cuisine, to a sport you'd never thought to try, to a fresh way of thinking about things. But sometimes new aspects of your partner contradict your own value system. And that will give you a jolt.

Here's what happens: You're riding in your boyfriend's car, and you notice a half a dozen unpaid speeding tickets lying on the dashboard. You think, *Oh gee . . . what are the implications of this?* Or, you're out for coffee with friends, and your husband makes a blatant antifeminist remark. You think, *I can't just sit back and listen to this stuff.*

You know you're in the Emerging Differences stage when something about your partner sets off an alarm, and you're not quite sure what to do. You find yourself wrestling with the question: *Should I speak up or not?* If you do voice your concerns, you risk validating your fears (*He really is irresponsible—or a chauvinist*). There's the hope that if you *don't* bring it up, the issue will simply disappear (*Maybe he's learned his lesson and will be a careful driver from now on,* or *His bigoted remark was just careless chatter*). But now, as opposed to the Honeymoon and its dark side, ignoring inconvenient knowledge doesn't work. You're listening to your intuition, or that intuition keeps resurfaces despite your best efforts to repress it.

We Are Not the Same

At some point in a marriage, differences erupt. It was pleasant to dwell in the fiction that nothing could blight the serenity you shared.

You could smirk at couples who argued, certain that you would never find yourselves at loggerheads. But no more. Troublesome topics that had been relegated to the background now clamor for attention. Once one or both of you begin to divulge what's important to you, you'll land yourselves smack in the midst of some pretty rough strife.

Why go there? Because it's necessary. Because after the intense togetherness of the Honeymoon Stage, there's a need to assert separate desires. Because, if you don't, you'll get drawn back into the dark side and feel smothered. Because the realities of who your partner is and how you function together are hitting you in the face. Because the old deceptions that you had relied on for equilibrium don't work anymore.

And also because you're intrigued by what you're finding out about your partner. You intuitively feel that your partner has something to teach you. When you struggle through serious disagreement, you may understand and appreciate each other more deeply.

We find with most couples that significant differences begin to emerge about six to nine months into the relationship. When you can deal with differences that arise, you will bring both tolerance and dynamism into the marriage. If you suppress them, however, you're setting yourself up for trouble. We can say this: If, after a year, you haven't expressed any meaningful opposition to your partner in terms of attitudes, beliefs, or desires, you're on the trajectory to a conflict-avoidant relationship. The longer you wait to speak the truth, the harder it is. Conversely, the earlier you address differences in smaller disputes, like differences in personal tastes, the more practice you will have in tackling the big ones.

Here's a small example from early in our own relationship. I remember that Ellyn would buy bananas, and I would eat them. I was eating them because she bought them. She was buying them because I was eating them. I didn't even like bananas that much. One day I said, "You don't have to buy bananas." She said, "Oh, I thought you liked them, that's why I bought them." This was, admittedly, not a make or break issue, but there was a kind of epiphany: "Oh, I don't have to keep doing this thing to please you. I can tell you what I want."

The process of reckoning with differences is essential to the vitality of a relationship. Couples need to know that they can work through conflict; otherwise, they'll always live in fear of it. Partners need to know that they can speak their minds; otherwise, they'll bottle up everything, and wind up angry and estranged. You must be able to own up to the lies that you've told yourself and each other. If not, those lies will dominate the relationship.

The differences that arise at this time run the gamut. They can involve leisure (he likes to get on the road the minute he can; she prefers to lounge), friends or family (he contends that "for better or worse" includes all his relatives; she wants to keep a comfortable distance), sex, money, work, or any number of areas. They can start with simple habits (he can't get anywhere on time; she's always prompt and thinks being late is the height of rudeness), or deeply held beliefs (she's a fatalist; he believes we create our own fortunes and regards her view as a cop-out). They could stem from the fact that one partner has a greater investment in certain goals, such as keeping a tidy home, getting the kids to bed on time, or building a nest egg. They can be sparked by an outside event, or by one person's determination to change.

One task of the Emerging Differences Stage is to reckon with the realities of your relationship. Who is this person you've promised yourself to, aside from what you've wanted to see? What do you want in your marriage in order to develop yourself more fully? What priorities do you share, and where might you have to carry the ball? An important aspect of this phase involves confronting the lies that distort how you appear to each other and how you act. If someone tends toward being a Lie Invitee, this means asking for information straight, without a 'slant to the question. Getting past lying and lie-inviting behavior will allow you to be true to yourselves and will give the marriage a renewed sense of openness and possibility.

Breaking Silences

The process of bringing truthfulness into your relationship triggers many emotions: curiosity (*Oh, is that what he's really like?*), surprise (*Oh, is that what he's* really *like?*), and disenchantment (*Oh, so* that's *what he's really like.*) The dominant feeling is apprehension. There's an awareness that the marriage is changing; there's no turning back. You're nervous about discovering things about your partner. You're scared because you are arguing more often.

This apprehension differs from the anxiety that forms the backdrop to the Dark Side of the Honeymoon. In the dark side, the anxiety is more global and diffuse. The fear of losing the relationship overshadows everything. The specific conflicts are not acknowledged, certainly not between you and possibly not even to yourself. In Emerging Differences, the issues have risen up to the surface. Yes, you're rocking the boat, but it's more complex than that. You're thinking: *What does it all mean? What's most important to me? How can we talk about it? Can the relationship survive this?*

Another prevailing element in this stage is frustration. As you're learning more about your partner, you have to accept that you can't change him. In the Honeymoon, you might have thought, *Since he really loves me he'll change—and do so willingly.* In the Dark Side, you'd work desperately to pretend everything is wonderful as it is. In Emerging Differences a spade is called a spade.

Here, you have a head-on collision of values. Information comes out that arouses strong feelings. You hit upon touchy issues, things that are hard to talk about. The partner who breaks open the truth may find his own integrity put to trial.

Let's say you're involved with a man who is divorced and sees his two school-age children every other weekend. It's Friday, and you're having supper with him and his kids. You see the way he relates to them, and you don't like it: He has a bullying style that gets them stirred up and belligerent.

You're reaction is *This isn't good. These kids aren't learning how to behave. Do I need to speak up? How much of this is my business? But I thought he was so easygoing.*

You're faced not only with the question of how to approach this with your boyfriend, but also what you can live with. You think kids should learn how to solve problems without fighting. Do you follow your own convictions and speak up? Do you take the risk? Powerful feelings— surprise, disappointment, apprehension, indignation, frustration—boil up as you hash this out on your own and with your partner.

Advance, Retreat

What couples do in the Emerging Differences Stage is take a step forward and then they step back. People generally alternate between putting their foot down (*I'm not going to let someone talk to a child like that*) and pulling it away (*I'll wait and see how he is in a calmer moment*). There's a lot of back and forth, testing to see what will fly with the other partner, pushing a bit further and then withdrawing. You put a strong opinion out there and try to hold on to it ("This isn't okay with me") and back off again ("Maybe it's not such a big deal"). You decide to share some of your long-considered opinions about raising kids, and then you retreat. With your partner and within yourself, you go around and around: engage, discuss, resolve, retreat, *re*engage, and again.

Worth the Risk

The Emerging Differences Stage is pivotal. When both partners can take responsibility for how they feel and who they are, the marriage is fortified. If you can begin to grapple with difficult issues and continue talking, you will build a stronger bond. You will find new reasons to respect each other. You will understand in a more visceral way where the other individual is coming from. You will establish ways of handling conflicts and differences of opinion so that you needn't let your fear of them force you into deception.

Confronting differences challenges both of you to grow. It also encourages you to accept your relationship as an ever-changing union rather than as a static coexistence so fragile that the slightest discord threatens to tear it apart. The capacity to reckon with differences, especially in ticklish areas, teaches you about your own reserves, and your partner's as well. If you're able to speak up about what's important to you, maybe your partner can take it. If you show you can handle the truth rather than encourage lies, you'll receive more honest answers.

A huge benefit for those who chance the truth is that little squabbles—those nitpicking quarrels that bog down many couples—start to disappear. An attitude of accepting differences makes it possible to work out effective solutions. For the longest time, Pete kept telling me that he would make the effort to pick up after himself. He kept promising, and I kept waiting for him to do it. It drove me crazy. It was a very good moment for us when he said to me, "You know, I'm never going to be somebody who cleans the house the way you would like." That freed me up. I could then say, "That creates a big problem for me. So how about you hire someone to take care of your messes?"

Pete's lie was the empty promise he used to avoid disappointing me. It only layered on more frustration. Once we labeled the situation as it was, we could apply more creativity to finding other options.

Some shifts that take place are internal; each person is working towards being able to say, "This is who I am. This is what's important to me. These are my desires." When you can be truthful about who you are, it releases energy that had been shackled by lies, secrets, and the fear of acknowledging truths. It can lead each of you toward further self-definition, a deeper sense of knowing what you want. And the better each of you knows yourself, the greater your tolerance and understanding of the other will be.

As you learn more about your partner, she may seem increasingly complex and even contradictory. You may think, *Is this the person I thought she was? Is this what I bargained for?* You may also think, *I never really appreciated the strength she has. I'm impressed and proud.* The question is: What do you do with any contradictions you discover? Do you shy away, seeking comfort in illusion? Do you feel wronged? Do you use any disenchantment as ammunition against her or as a rationale for retreating? Or do you regard this as a launch point for your own growth and the growth of your relationship? It takes guts to view her complexities as a challenge to your own ability to love. More commonly, partners pout and feel wounded when they discover contradictions in one another.

Wrenching Choices

After a year of promises, the will-we-have-a-baby question came to a head. Paul had hedged about it for a while, and Mary finally gave him an ultimatum: "Neither of us is getting any younger. I want a baby. Are you with me or not?"

This didn't come out exactly as she wanted it to, but after wrestling with her own values, it clearly represented how strongly she felt. Paul's answer, "I'm not quite ready" made him feel like a cowering fool, but he wasn't about to make another commitment he might have to renounce.

This was their exchange:

PAUL: I don't want to lead you on. I don't think I want to have a child.

Mary: I don't get it. You'd be a great father. You like kids.

Paul: It's a huge responsibility. I just can't see it.

Mary: Why are you so afraid of responsibility?

Paul: I know it seems like I'm being nonchalant about this, but that's not the case. I'm really torn up about it. I love kids, but I have no model for being a father. All I have is a lot of ugly memories about being a miserable kid. I don't want to revisit that stuff.

Mary: Paul, you are not your father!

Six weeks later they had this conversation in therapy:

Mary: I've been thinking about your decision. At first I was furious and thought you were just being stubborn, but I'm beginning to see that maybe you are never going to feel ready to have kids. Recognizing that has pushed me hard to figure out what I want. At times I haven't been sure, but I'm increasingly clear that I want a child very badly. I can't see my life *without* children. I'm not sure I can back down on this. We may have to separate. Please don't take this as a threat. I'm just starting to see how much this means to me. Now I'd like to hear more about your reluctance and why you think you wouldn't be a good father.

Paul: Part of it is that my father wasn't around much, but it's also that I feel I can't give enough. I want to throw myself into my career. I want to make something of myself, and I don't know that I'd have enough energy left over to be the parent I'd want to be. I know you don't want to wait another five or six years for me to feel more settled.

Mary: You're right. It's painful for me to say this, but I think I've come to recognize that I am prepared to leave you. If I don't stay true to myself on this one, I'll resent you. I don't want to do that to you. This is very scary because I might never get married again, and I might have to do it myself. However, on something I value so deeply, I need to be honest with you and myself. I don't want to corrupt our marriage. I know that if I were dishonest about how central this is, our marriage would be destroyed and so would my spirit.

After two months of intense discussion, Paul decided to say yes to having a child. Through these conversations, he recognized that Mary's longing was not a power play and that the loss he would feel if she left was more than he wanted to bear. Mary's desire pushed him to do some hard self-reflection that he wouldn't have chosen to do on his own.

"Why Didn't You Tell Me That Before?"

One sticking point in situations like this is accusations of deception. It is only when one partner starts being honest that the other partner gets the sense that he hasn't always been offered the full picture. There's often a feeling of betrayal, or even being tricked.

Accusations prompted by disentangling old lies or retracting false promises include

"You should have told me before";

"You were hiding the truth so we would get married";

"You didn't show me who you are";

"You were pretending to accept the real me";

"You led me to believe that you wanted the same things."

The question of whether or not to have kids lurked in the background a long time for Paul and Mary. Mary would test the waters by saying, "When we have kids . . ." as though it was simply assumed that they would. Paul wouldn't protest these statements, and he still felt like a wimp. Was he lying? Well, he wasn't quite lying, and he wasn't quite telling the truth, either. Paul was wary about kids, but the prospect felt so far away that he couldn't imagine what he would feel when kids actually became a reality. In the moment, it felt okay to just go along with Mary.

When you get the query, "Why now?" some possible answers might be

"I was deluding myself";

"I was hoping to talk myself out of it";

"I didn't want to risk you being so disenchanted with me that you would leave";

"I hate to admit it to myself, let alone someone else";

"I don't like it when I feel that way."

These are answers to give your partner so that she can understand the struggles you've had with speaking the truth and then can better understand you.

Growing Pains

Can confronting the truth lead you to a place of greater understanding, even though the road there will be bumpy?

One week before Sandra and Mac's wedding, Mac was picked up for drunk driving. It turned out that he had received several prior warnings. Sandra knew that Mac liked his Scotch, but she had no idea how much he consumed on a regular basis nor how careless he was. When they were out together, he had always made a point of not drinking whenever they took his car. Sandra realized that Mac was hiding his drinking problem from her.

The next day Sandra said to Mac, "I'm not going through with the wedding." Mac protested and promised it would never happen again. Sandra objected. "I'm not going to say don't drink anymore," she said. "The point for me is that I don't like the way I would react if I married you. I would be nagging and suspicious; I would be wondering what you were doing; I would be sniffing your breath. I'm breaking the engagement because of me, not you."

Sandra didn't say, "How dare you do this to me just before our wedding? How could you deceive me like this?" She didn't back Mac into a corner, making him beholden to her, coercing him into refashioning himself to suit her. She called off the wedding because she was unwilling to compromise herself. On his own, Mac went to Alcoholics Anonymous and worked hard to wean himself from alcohol. A year later, when it was clear things had changed, they decided to get married.

Sandra looked the situation square in the eye and chose what was right for her: She couldn't marry Mac because she didn't want to be a suspicious wife. She didn't minimize her discovery or deny it to herself. Instead, she did some introspection and gained a deeper understanding of what she wanted—and didn't want—in a marriage. She expressed her convictions and let Mac know that she intended to stand by them. Mac learned that he would have to take responsibility for his own behavior; this would not be a marriage in which he was constantly testing what he could get away with. And when Sandra and Mac did marry, they knew they could regain balance after a serious upset.

Honesty: An Uneven Process

One reason the revelation of truth is so tense is that the process is inherently asymmetrical; the quest for deeper truthfulness in a marriage starts with one person. One of the delights of the Honeymoon Stage is that sense of perfect congruity, of inhabiting the same emotional space. But any significant shift, change, or evolution in a relationship originates with only one person. It's rare that two people will begin to get restless or feel the need to come clean on something at precisely the same time. The trouble is that the partner on the receiving end is taken completely by surprise. And that can shake things up.

When your partner reveals an unsettling truth to you, it will feel as though the ground is trembling beneath your feet. Nothing seems quite certain anymore, nor are you prepared for this! We're taught to regard tension in a relationship as a sign that something's wrong, rather than being something necessary. Sometimes it will feel that if you pull a single thread, you'll unravel the whole fabric of your marriage. But by reclaiming personal truths and strengthening your integrity, you're stitching with a stronger yarn. The alternative is to take cover in outworn deceptions and live with your mate on perpetual hold.

My Turn, Your Turn

You may take turns being honest. You disclose something and your partner, thrown off guard, accuses you of lying. You hash this out for a while and begin to digest the new information. This sparks your partner to admit something. And she gets blamed for lying. And so on. That's the story of this stage: back and forth, advance, retreat.

When Paul and Mary started being more open about their career plans, they bounced on an emotional seesaw for a while. The more they explored their differences, the more tense it became—and the more they ended up contesting deeply held beliefs about what they wanted from their relationship.

Mary's initial response to Paul's wanting to work separately from her was, "Why did you have to pull the plug on this? I think you're great the way you are." As she received more revealing responses, her reaction became, "Why couldn't you have told me sooner?" Paul persisted in describing his efforts to become stronger, which would mean doing some things without her. Although that would be much harder, he had to do this for his own self-respect. Finally, Mary was able to say to him, "I guess it really was hard for me to acknowledge that other side of you."

At first she couldn't see beyond her own sense of rejection. There were so many advantages to pooling resources, she thought. She couldn't understand what was getting in the way.

However, when Mary was able to set aside her own hurt feelings enough to ask Paul why he couldn't go along with her, she discovered that he was struggling with feelings of professional inadequacy. Paul felt he lacked Mary's animated style and worried that he would always be number two if they teamed up. She saw that wanting to strike out on his own wasn't a personal rebuff to her but part of his desire to build his own confidence. Once Mary grasped this, she was no less disappointed about the lost opportunity, but she was able to support Paul's separate work efforts.

The subtext to Paul's solo venture proved more disconcerting, however. When Mary saw that Paul was so unsure of himself, she realized that he wasn't as cool and self-sufficient as she had thought. For all the time they had been together, it had never occurred to her that they were anything other than equals. In fact, one of the reasons she was attracted to Paul was that she thought he was smarter than she was. That was important to her in a man. With Paul's impressive height (6'2") and easy wit, she saw him as poised and self-assured. But here he was, telling her that he felt like a second fiddle *to her*.

Mary had to deal with her dismay and disillusionment that Paul was not the suave, unflappable hero she took him for. She didn't like that. In fact, she felt cheated, but she made an effort to understand where his insecurity came from. She learned more about his background and how paralyzing it was to grow up with a critical father whom he could never satisfy. She also adopted the attitude that Paul may not *always* be so self-deprecating, and that he might grow more confident as he tested himself. She believed he had lots of untapped strengths.

Ironically, learning of his sensitivities helped her discover that she didn't have to protect his ego as much. Before, she had wanted to keep the illusion of his swagger and, often unconsciously, kept building him up. Now she could accept, and empathize with, his frailties.

Lies: Denying Differences

The lies that crop up during Emerging Differences are attempts to avoid dealing with difficulties in the relationship. In the step-up/step-back routine that characterizes this stage, truthfulness is the step forward, the move towards facing differences; deception is the step back, the sign that you're scurrying away.

The two main lies in this stage are

1. telling your partner the differences between you aren't important, and
2. telling *yourself* the differences between you aren't important.

Let's return to the example of the boyfriend bullying his kids. You say to yourself, "I'm sure this is an aberration. I know we really do agree about how to handle children." This is a lie. You *know* it's a lie. You think: *Ugh. I don't like having to look at this*. In the Honeymoon Stage, we talked about the little echoes that let you know when you're lying. In the Emerging Differences Stage, the reverberations become positively *thunderous*: Your better senses scream out "LIAR!" when you're trying to avoid looking at the truth.

With Paul and Mary, Paul originally told himself that it didn't matter to him that he felt professionally inferior to Mary. He was lying to himself. The sense of being inadequate gnawed away at his pride to the point where he dreaded any joint efforts. Paul also lied to Mary when he'd say, "Sure let's work together" because he felt his opposition seemed irrational. Ultimately, however, he realized that working together was not an option for him.

Truth versus deception is an active dilemma in the Emerging Differences Stage. You're continually being faced with: Do I reveal more truths? Do I lie or not lie? Am I going to start a scene if I say what I want to say? But if I don't say something, am I going to perpetuate a bad pattern?

Not So Fast!

There are also lies that put reins on the uneasy passage towards honesty, slowing things down and sending the message, "I don't think I'm ready to deal with this." For example, one couple had a sexual conflict. She liked lovemaking to be spontaneous, but he felt he needed to "plan" sex. They both felt they were making progress in therapy, through talking but at one point the man was edging too close to some raw feelings. If he didn't know they were going to have sex, how would he know she would ever want him? At the end of the session he stood up abruptly and said to the therapist, "Everything's okay now. We don't need to come back."

His lie allowed him to take his time and regain his balance. As he began to feel secure that his wife wasn't judging him for his fears, he was able to reopen the dialogue. He returned to therapy after he had a chance to collect himself and felt more ready. Danger arises, however, when deception is used as a ticket out of facing an uncomfortable reality.

I Can Look Away

Another hazard is the gloss-over lie. Again, you see your date browbeat his kids. You say, "Please don't act like that when I'm around." He says, "Okay," and you drop it. This is a 100-yard dash through the problem. You both breathe a sigh of relief and congratulate yourselves on resolving the matter. But you haven't.

This is typical of the Lie Invitee. A tense issue breaks the consciousness barrier and the Lie Invitee reacts by thinking, *Give me a lie that will allow me to avoid facing this reality.*

What to Do About Those Lies

In the Emerging Differences Stage, lies serve as beacons: They call out to you, "Here's something you need to look at!" The lies are useful when you pay attention to them. They can help you pinpoint problem areas in your relationship. You can then initiate a conversation or, at least, explore your own feelings about it. You have to fight the temptation to retreat into the lie, using it as a safe harbor to evade uncomfortable truths.

HEED YOUR BODY SIGNALS

In the Emerging Differences Stage you allow yourself to register those transitory thoughts that tell you you're a bit uneasy. We generally train ourselves to override the faint whispers of suspicion, but the more truthful we are about our own core values, the more attuned we will be; likewise, the more attuned we are to these glimmers of candor, the more we respect our own longings and limits.

It's helpful to learn to recognize body signals that betray strong feelings, especially desires that your partner doesn't share with you. These include signs of discomfort, like a queasy stomach, a cramped feeling, or shortness of breath, and also hints of excitement, like a quickened heartbeat or a surge of energy. Excitement often gets squelched for fear that the partner will somehow deflate it or be jealous.

What's essential is not to allow yourself to be talked out of your own feelings. Let's say you want to spend time alone with a close friend. Your spouse says, "Hey, let's all get together." You really want a night out with your friend. You get a slight pit-in-the-stomach feeling: *Oh, darn.*

Your typical inclination would be to drop it. We're saying *don't* drop it. You might say something like, "Maybe we'll all be together this time because it seems it would really suit you. But next time I'd really like to be alone with my friend."

When you express excitement or a desire to do something, a partner often makes light of it or tries to neutralize it. It ends up going on the "feelings I'll ignore" shelf. We're urging you to give voice to what you want. This will allow you to pursue what you want without having to be misleading about it. It will also help clarify—for both your partner and yourself—what's important to you.

HOLD ON TO CORE TRUTHS

The deceptions that most need to be addressed in the Emerging Differences Stage are those that compromise core parts of yourself. These are the ones that will come back to haunt you if you fail to bring them to light.

The way to dismantle those lies is to *stick with it.* Stick with your convictions—despite how awkward you may feel. Stick with the truth—despite your partner's accusations. Stick with your partner through the disillusionment—despite your dismay. Stick with what your partner is telling you—despite the fact you wish things were different. Stick with all of this *despite* the anxiety it will cause.

The same applies to the person whose partner calls them on a lie. Rather than dismiss the accusation, *stick with it.* This is the time to start admitting what's really going on with you. If you don't, the gulf between what you say and what your partner sees is going to grow dangerously wide.

This is what Paul and Mary were able to do with their disagreements. Each had their turn to hear things they would rather not hear; each had a turn to be disheartened. They took risks with their honesty and had to tolerate not knowing what would happen—whether they would get what they wanted and even whether the marriage could survive their differences. They each had to admit difficult truths. They relied on inner resilience to help them through it and built additional resilience as they did.

With the accumulated momentum of truth telling and truth seeking, they found they each did a better job of expressing themselves and of hearing difficult things from the other. They also saw that the more they learned about the other, the more there was to discover. This was daunting but also exciting.

START SMALL FOR A TEST RUN

Sometimes a couple may begin by using a small matter as a testing ground.

Brad and Lily made household thrift a priority. They had a pact to buy only generic products. After several years of marriage, Lily, now in her early thirties, felt confined by their austerity plan. She wanted to enjoy things and live a little. She wrote up a shopping list and, along with the usual cheese, milk, and peanut butter, wrote down "Godiva Chocolate Ice Cream." Brad came home with Price Chopper chocolate ice milk. A week later, she did the same thing, and underlined the words *Godiva Chocolate Ice Cream*. Again, Brad brought home Price Chopper chocolate ice milk.

This time Lily called him on it. "I have to say something," she said. "I asked you to get Godiva Chocolate Ice Cream, and you got the Price Chopper brand. You know, I really wanted the Godiva." Brad said, "We had this agreement. . . ." Lily then said, "I don't want to stick to subsistence anymore."

Brad had intuited that this was about more than just ice cream. The change had made him anxious. *What else is Lily going to want?* Well, she didn't know. But she did know that a no-frills lifestyle wasn't working for her anymore.

FIND YOUR MOTIVATIONS

With most couples we see, the toughest aspect of the Emerging Differences Stage is sitting on the powder keg—living with the tension of not knowing how things will work out. Tolerating the tension is not simply a matter of endurance. It involves understanding yourself and your motivations. Ask yourself the following questions:

1. How important is this issue for me?
2. *Why* is this so important to me?

It also involves trying to understand your *partner's* motivations and desires. This means giving up any anger you may feel because your partner isn't a mirror image of you.

The clients we see generally fall into two categories. Some say, "I will do what I can" to change or save the marriage. This translates to, "I will do what isn't going to require too much effort on my part." Others will say, "I will do what it *takes*." Often the stances differ within the same couple.

If your motivation is strong, you have more choices. You don't have to wait for a *quid pro quo*. You can take charge. You may have to carry both backpacks for a while because your partner is too depleted or unsure to put in much effort, but if you're hoping for a resolution, you do need to move.

MAKE SURE IT SINKS IN

When you're initiating a change, it might take a while for your partner to "get it." In general, it will suit her to ignore what you say and deny the differences that are beginning to bubble up. You may need to bring it up more than once if it doesn't click the first time. It's up to you to make sure that your message comes through rather than blaming the other for not picking up your cues.

Remember Lily, of the Godiva ice cream? She literally underlined her craving for a tiny taste of luxury in her notes to Brad. And Brad still disregarded it. It can be frustrating. The temptation is to go back and lie, minimizing to yourself the importance of what you want. Emphasize your request; don't delete it. Help your partner get used to your reality rather than trying to protect him from it.

CONCENTRATE ON TONE

Speak in a way that diminishes defensive reactions. Initiate discussions in a nonjudgmental way. Answer your partner's questions. Take for granted that you're not going to be in the same place, and recognize that what you've been musing about for a long time may come as a surprise. Try not to be impatient. Know that if you make a dismissive comment, you're going to push your partner to lie or suppress how she feels. What you want is to have her slowly understand where you're coming from.

Anticipate a defensive response and be prepared to hold your own. Your challenge is to stand your ground and not use the other person's anxiety as an excuse to cave in and lie.

Try to present feelings in a way that helps your partner to empathize with you. When you can arrive at an emotional understanding—not necessarily an agreement—the need to lie will diminish.

DON'T FORCE AGREEMENT

Be clear that your goal is not to convince him that you're right, but rather allows him to understand your position. It's uncomfortable to disagree. But forcing a partner to agree with you means that you're misrepresenting the case or you're asking him to lie.

Identify what you would like to have happen rather than focusing on what your partner should do about it. If you stress what you want from your partner, you're going to encounter some resistance, or you're going to push her to fib or make false promises to get you off her back.

HOLD YOUR GROUND

Regardless of your partner, you need to stick to what's important to you and understand why it is important. You then will help your partner gain a clear perspective of things by reaching a clear perspective *yourself*—such is the interdependence of marriage.

If your partner says he really wants to raise the kids to be religious, it forces you to explore your own beliefs. If you don't want to make religion a priority, you'd better figure out what you *do* want. Sometimes people simply react instead of reckoning with themselves.

Don't toss in the towel too soon. A quick capitulation suggests you're acquiescing rather than agreeing, and you'll both pay later. Tensions might ease temporarily, but whatever problem is resolved is usually the wrong problem, and you'll have to deal with the real one sooner or later.

HEAR ONE PERSON AT A TIME

Only address one partner's side at a time. The person who is sharing her views wants to be heard fully before the other interrupts with his concerns. Often people try to be honest, but nothing gets resolved because they haven't openly exposed their own conflicts.

One couple, for example, was battling over spending habits. He was conflicted about money; he didn't want to buy for the sake of buying. He preferred a subsistence lifestyle and grew upset when his wife purchased things he thought were unnecessary. While growing up, he idealized his grandmother, who was exceptionally frugal. Whenever he or his wife spent a lot of money, he felt like he was betraying the lessons he'd learned from his beloved grandmother. His wife, meanwhile, felt controlled by him. She grew angry because he complained whenever she bought fresh flowers for the house. Underneath her anger was tremendous fear that he was trying to take away everything feminine from her.

They wanted me (Ellyn) to help them figure out how often it was "reasonable" to buy flowers. I told them that flowers and what they cost weren't the problem. Exposing each person's concerns would set them on the path to a more permanent solution.

Avoid relying on deal making. This couple wanted to negotiate the flowers as a shortcut through the problem. Making a deal is easy compared to the real task, which is for each person to articulate the feelings beneath the dispute. If you put in enough energy up front, the solutions will more easily fall into place.

HEAR THE TRUTH: ASK FIRST, SPEAK LATER

The key here is going slowly and staying curious. Again and again, we have seen couples turn things around simply by asking a lot of questions in the spirit of inquiry, rather than by jumping in to explain themselves.

The rule to remember is this: Understanding comes before explaining. Most people reverse this and try their hardest to get their partner to see things their way. It's truly uncanny how it shifts when you can really hear your partner, when you can say "tell me more" and mean it. This, of course, is difficult when what your mate is telling you is hard to hear. But when you can hold on to it, this approach creates absolutely the right atmosphere for intimate disclosure.

In one of our workshops, Ned and Janine, married fifteen years, were quibbling about Ned's addiction to TV sports. Janine quipped that he'd only pay attention to her if she turned into a box and sprouted antennae. She asked him, "Do you really like watching ESPN better than you like talking to me?"

Ned took a deep breath and said, "Frankly, I do."

Rather than breaking down in tears ("See I told you he was a terrible guy!"), Janine held tight. She looked straight at him and asked, "Why?"

Here Ned mustered the courage to tell his wife how uncomfortable he felt with too much togetherness. He was using television not to shut her out, but rather to escape his own awkward feelings.

PAY ATTENTION

If you make the effort to be observant, you can often help your partner be more truthful. You may notice an incongruence between his words and actions. For example, you can say, "I notice it's difficult for you to give the kids the meals I suggest. Do you have different ideas about what they should eat?" rather than, "Hey, what's with the macaroni and cheese again?"

Watch for behavioral changes. Sometimes people start to alter their behavior before telling their partner. This could be a sign that your partner is going to open up to you at some point soon. You then can make an effort to be receptive to her.

Paul and Mary went through a challenging line of questioning when they tackled the twin issues of Paul's desire for more sex and Mary's difficulty with losing weight. In therapy, Mary was encouraged to shift her approach and to try to learn why her weight was so important to Paul. We reminded her that what he said would be more about *him* than *her*.

MARY: Why is my weight so upsetting to you?

Paul: Do you think you can listen without getting mad at me? This is very sensitive.

Mary: I'll do my best.

Paul: I know it shouldn't be a big deal, but it is. My mother was heavy. I never wanted to marry someone who looked like my mother. I picked you because you were so petite. But now that you have put on weight and your shoulders look broader and your thighs are bigger, I start feeling queasy. I'm afraid I'm getting into bed with my mother. I don't know if you can even appreciate how creepy I feel. It almost makes my skin crawl. I do love you, but I can't get that image of my mother out of my head. I am also concerned about your health. You know I've been into health foods and vitamins for years. I worry about your cholesterol level and your heart. Sometimes I feel mad when you eat high-fat foods right in front of me . . . almost like you're trying to get even with me.

Mary: What do you think about when you see me eating desserts?

Paul: If I can deprive myself, why can't you? If you really love me, why won't you make some effort?

Mary: You make it sound like we're in a power struggle.

Paul: Well, aren't we? Are you?

Mary: I never thought about it before, but maybe I am. My feeling about losing weight is that I want you to love me no matter what my weight is.

Paul: I do love you, but sometimes I feel angry and think, *Couldn't you give this to me because you do love me?*

Mary: It's starting to sound like we're both testing out how much we're loved. Maybe I'm being rebellious until you prove it to me.

Paul: Could you ever want to lose weight or be healthier just for you?

Mary: I sometimes forget that appearance isn't the only issue. *(She laughs)*. It is kind of liberating to think I might do it just for me instead of for you. I have an idea. Let's not talk about this for a few weeks and let me see how this new awareness sits with me. I'd rather not talk about it or even have you comment if I'm eating less. Is that okay with you?

Paul: Yes. I'd love to be in a different place about this.

Mary: Thanks for talking about your feelings without blaming me.

SPEAK UP ABOUT YOUR CONCERNS

Allow yourself to voice vulnerability. You might be afraid that your partner may, for example, make more money than you. When, without trying to scare or stop your partner, you can expose the vulnerability underneath, you can deal with things in a direct way without the need to cover up your true feelings. For example: "Sometimes I think if you earn more than me, I'll always feel inferior to you. I can't feel inferior and be equal at the same time."

When your partner is making changes that you don't know how to handle, don't fall into the lie of "It's okay. It doesn't bother me." Quick dismissals push the other person away and leave her guessing what your true feelings are. It's better to express the truth: "I'm feeling threatened" or "I'm confused." Being truthful maintains the connection.

LISTEN, DON'T SURRENDER

Recognize that listening to your partner is not the same as surrendering to his opinion. Giving in to your partner may get you through a rocky moment, but it is not necessarily what your partner wants. Acknowledging his heartfelt feelings doesn't mean you have to agree with them. The challenge is to reveal without capitulating or rebelling.

We saw one couple where the woman wanted to live a simple life organized around her growing sense of spirituality, but the man was attached to their large home in the suburbs. When she told him what she wanted, he said, "Fine, we'll sell the house." She reported that, rather than pleasing her, this made her both sad and angry. "I knew he didn't really mean it and that he would regret it."

The fate of their house—and their marriage—was in abeyance for a while. They kept chipping away at the reasons behind each partner's wishes, and it emerged that, for him, the house was more than a ticket to the upper middle class. He had designed and built it, and it represented years of work as an expression of his creativity. Understanding how much the house meant to him was very poignant for her. It did not change her desire to live more in line with her beliefs, but she was open to exploring ways to keep the house as well.

Moving On

The need to assert differences brings many couples to the brink, but once a couple can discuss what's underneath those differences—what fuels different aspects of themselves—they learn profound truths about their partner. They discover the extent of the other person's convictions, the strengths of their commitments, and the impact their own behavior has on them. Not only is it then possible to get through the immediate challenge, but they are able to understand each other in a deeper, more intimate way, which leaves them poised for still greater depths of understanding.

The central question is, do you accept the differences you discover and relate to your partner in a more genuine way? If so, you're building something special. Being able to manage difficult issues creates a sound bond. Being true to yourself generates real self-esteem; being true to your partner makes you indispensable to each other. Your marriage then is planted in rich soil, ready to flourish and grow.

Or, do you fight against the reality of your differences, continually sparring with your partner to get what you want? If so, you're choosing the Stalemate route, which means exchanging one kind of lie (the lie of denying differences) for another (lies that polarize you).

7

Seething
Stalemate:
Starting to Know
(and Dislike) You

*W*hen we last left John and Sarah, they had become a family of four. John was a rising star at work. With steady pay raises, he didn't have the financial troubles he feared, and he was able to do what he had planned, provide for his family.

In spite of demands at home, Sarah remained active in the professional world and often took on business projects. Although she liked running things her way at home, she still resented John for not helping with the kids and around the house.

She became overwhelmed and exhausted, but she didn't know how to talk to John about it. She found it hard to let on that she felt inept and out of control. She also recalled that when she did try to bring these feelings up, nothing happened, so there was little incentive to risk another rebuff.

Instead of describing those contradictory sides of herself and the bind she felt she was in, she took to criticizing John: "You're lazy, inconsiderate, and selfish. You don't care about anything besides sports, bikes, and work." When the harangues didn't change his behavior, she gave him the silent treatment, and then back to another tirade.

This had the predictable effect on John. Once again he was battling the forces of evil in his own home. Once again everything that went wrong was his fault. He tried to provide the best he could and still it was not enough. What happened to Sarah's desire to stay home with the kids? It wasn't his fault she continued working. Didn't they have an "understanding" that this was the way things were supposed to be? Wasn't their home supposed to be a place of refuge from the trials of the world? What happened?

John felt helpless about Sarah's unhappiness and fell into the habit of apologizing the minute she seemed upset. This appeared to have no effect, and John couldn't figure out why. Even shared activities that used to bring them together were now causes for argument. On summer weekends, Sarah would want to go swimming with the family while John wanted to cycle. Rather than humoring each other's taste, as they used to do, they would fight over who would control the day. Often, Sarah won and John seethed quietly.

No Exit

Imagine two male deer vying for territory. They lunge and push and then their antlers lock together. Neither can escape. Neither can get what they want. Night comes, then day, then night again. They both starve.

This is the dynamic of the Seething Stalemate, the deep pit couples fall into when they can't reckon with their differences. If the "ideal" marriage could be described as a "win-win" situation, the Seething Stalemate would be labeled "lose-lose." Deceptions have so obscured the realities of what's between you—the conflicts and the love—that no one knows what he's dealing with anymore. The arguments and the lies have taken on a life of their own.

You can be pretty sure you're in the Seething Stalemate when the two of you are always growling at each other, when you hardly have a conversation that isn't peppered with zaps and zingers, screaming fits, or the occasional slamming door. You and your partner get ensnared in quarrels that never reach a satisfying conclusion. You can't seem to find a way of dealing with disagreement that works. You feel you're playing the same tape over again and again.

By this point, the lofty adoration of the Honeymoon is but a distant memory. From time to time you may experience a flash of good feeling that reminds you of what you once had with each other. But it's fleeting. If in the Dark Side of the Honeymoon you might have said, "Who us, argue?" now the response would be, "Who us, get along?"

A stalemate pattern can get launched as early as one to two years into a relationship and then persist for years afterward. Sometimes couples proceed into it directly from the Honeymoon. One or both start to feel disillusioned with the relationship or encounter conflicts that they aren't able to manage. They may venture towards Emerging Differences, only to collapse because they don't have the skills to prevail. At this point, the mood deteriorates quite rapidly from blissful togetherness to being at each other's throats.

A couple may also arrive at Seething Stalemate via the Dark Side of the Honeymoon. For many conflict-avoidant couples, the pressure of suppressed feeling grows too intense. With time, often a number of years, dissatisfaction turns into outright hostility. This, for example, is what happened with John and Sarah. Typically, one person realizes that avoiding conflict isn't getting him anywhere in the relationship, and he starts to think, *What do I have to lose if I come out fighting?* And fight he does. But because anger has been stored up or unexpressed for so long, there's a tremendous backlog. And neither partner has mastered the skills necessary to deal with conflict.

At least half of all couples who come to us are in the Seething Stalemate. This is a stage at which many couples raise the question of divorce. It is possible to haul yourselves out of this marital quicksand, but you need to take active steps to do so. First, instead of getting sidetracked by each other's defensive tactics and misconceptions, you need to zero in on the problem you're dealing with. Second, you need to develop the ability to tolerate and resolve conflict.

Sleeping with the Enemy

The emotional climate of the Seething Stalemate is often nasty. Both partners are likely to experience anger, loneliness, disillusionment, loss, and, above all, incredible frustration. What they generally feel toward each other is hostility. The distinction between anger and hostility is important here: Anger usually implies displeasure stemming from some kind of insult or injury, and it is often mobilizing towards a constructive solution. Hostility, which derives from the Latin word for "enemy," suggests ill will, and may imply intent toward retaliation. Hostility now dominates a couple's interactions, leading to everything from frequent barbs and competitive insults to outright vengeful behaviors.

Partners typically have built up an arsenal of grudges and complaints against one another, to be deployed when needed. They've become invested in a negative view of the other person. When angry, all they see in their spouse is a barrier to their own wishes. The assumption is that the other person is guilty unless proven innocent. In the Dark Side of the Honeymoon, both partners desperately cling to the Honeymoon. In the Seething Stalemate they annihilate it.

The tip-off that a couple is in Seething Stalemate is constant defensiveness. The pair is either fighting or on the brink of a fight. They prefer combat to compromise. This approach describes their relationship to each other as well as to the truth: They rail against whatever slice of reality doesn't suit them.

The five major defenses that keep a couple in a locked-horns mode are as follows: blame, withdrawal, resentful compliance, whining, and confusion. These, we find, are at the root of most faulty communication patterns in marriage. In our workshops, we invite couples to brainstorm and list the things that they and their partners do to destroy communication, and they invariably come down to some variation on these five defenses.

We've found that couples are well aware that these behaviors don't solve anything, but they feel helpless to stop them. These defenses are intended to bring relief from psychological pain or the threat of it. Behind these defenses is an avoidance of truth and self-revelation. Someone withdraws rather than saying to a partner, "I feel hurt or scared." Someone acts confused rather than saying, "I don't want to say no to what you are asking of me." Instead of being addressed, the pain gets volleyed back and forth like a Ping-Pong ball. Your relief is your partner's distress, and vice versa.

People become defensive in many situations, but what stands out in the Seething Stalemate is how pervasive the defensiveness is and how rapid the ensuing reaction. The antennae are always up. The defenses become so central to how a couple relates to one another that the two end up fighting *about* the defenses. When a marriage gets caught in cycles of blame and withdrawal, the defenses do become offensive to the partner.

Matt and Hilary are deciding whether to buy a new car. Hilary feels they already spend enough money and starts to pout.

> MATT: "I can't talk to you about anything without you putting on that face."
>
> HILARY: "Oh, like *you* never pout. How about the time . . ."
>
> MATT: "You're always judging me for what I want. I feel like I always have to argue with an expert on who I am, especially my faults."
>
> HILARY: "I can tell you're going to be stubborn about the car. I can't deal with you when you're stuck on something. There you go, ripping off my energy again."
>
> MATT: "You've certainly got enough energy to nag at me."

The many layers of defense and disagreement make it hard for a couple to be honest with each other, or to cope effectively with the problem at hand. Like most family feuds, nobody really knows what the original fight was about.

In Attack Mode

Another feature of the Seething Stalemate is passive-aggressive behavior. This is the irritating kind of behavior that is very difficult to effectively confront. For example, the person who continues to say he or she will be on time and then is late or agrees to do important things and then forgets. Or he or she continues to refuse sex.

At other times the hostility is more open and unmistakable, like yelling, slamming doors, and breaking household articles.

Stalemate couples fight constantly. They'll repeat the same script again and again without resolution. Sex, money, child rearing, in-laws, chores, errands—all become forums in which to express displeasure. It escalates until people are afraid to bring up certain issues because they know it will catapult them into another round of battle.

The longer the war continues, the tougher the fighting, the more depleted the troops. Until you take the risk of making the hidden parts of yourself alive, your marriage is going to be a never-ending battle. You're fighting about many things but are withholding key vulnerable aspects of yourself.

Stubborn Beliefs

In Seething Stalemate, people often operate from faulty presumptions about their partner, themselves, and the relationship. These are based on entrenched ways of seeing oneself in the world. Such beliefs create a kind of tunnel vision that constricts the way you relate to others and leads you to see your partner through the pinhole perspective of your own assumptions. This tendency interferes with you recognizing when a partner is being genuine. It stops you from pursuing conversations that may bring you closer together. It blinds you to your partner's truths and, because you become invested in confirming your own beliefs, prevents you from expressing your own truths.

Stubborn beliefs can be about:

yourself (e.g., "I'm unlovable.")

your partner ("He's selfish and never interested in what I feel.")

your interaction ("I give and give and never get anything in return.")

The entire relationship then gets filtered through those fixed beliefs. For example, say your creed is, "I give and give and never get anything in return." If your partner does something generous, you may automatically think, *I'm sure I'll have to pay sometime.* Such attitudes lock a couple in Seething Stalemate because the other person can never be whole, and the relationship can never be seen in its complexity.

Jared and Lindy, who just moved in together, came to therapy. They both greatly want things to work out, but their intractable belief systems keep them in a Stalemate tug-of-war. Jared can't stop thinking, *Nothing good ever happens to me.* Lindy's stuck on the idea, *I get blamed for everything.*

JARED: "I've wanted this for so long, but I don't know if we can make this work."

LINDY: "What do you mean, 'make this work'?"

JARED: "I mean, can we really afford such a nice home?"

LINDY: "It feels like you're taking the dream away from me."

JARED: "No, it's just that it's almost too good to be true."

LINDY: "That makes me think you don't believe I'll hold up my end of the bargain; like you don't see I've been supporting myself for the last ten years."

It's as if they each have an audio device that only detects the tones it was made to pick up. Jared keeps hearing: "If it seems good, it can't really be happening to me"; Lindy only hears: "All he does is find fault with me."

Instead of really listening and getting to know each other, Seething Stalemate couples try to read each other's minds, and they operate as if their assumptions about the other's beliefs are actually true.

Lies: An Escape Valve

The most common function of lies in Seething Stalemate is to diffuse the bad feeling. They're like the whistle in a sporting event, calling "time out" and sending contenders back to their respective corners. Let's say one partner says to the other, "I promise not to complain anymore." This is a lie, but it can relieve momentary tension in the aftermath of an argument. It keeps a nominal truce. In Seething Stalemate, a lie provides peace in the immediate moment, but in the long run it merely exacerbates the couple's sense of desperation. The next time that person *does* complain, that particular lie gets added to an already long list of unforgivable offenses.

For couples prone to Stalemate, lies often cover up feelings of weakness or vulnerability. Part of being truthful is showing vulnerable feelings; part of the intimacy between two people is accepting those feelings in each other. But revealing vulnerability or shame is hard for many people. The more partners keep the human, essential self hidden, the more they believe they can't be themselves with their partner.

It's a self-perpetuating process. Rather than testing truths out on their partner (Can I show contradictory aspects of myself to this person? Can I express love in new ways?), people wary of sharing uneasy feelings seek the safe haven of lies. This, in turn, keeps a couple in Seething Stalemate.

John found it hard to tell Sarah how lonely he felt and how much he missed their sexual closeness. When he tried to give her cues that he wanted to make love, it was invariably the wrong time. Even though Sarah also missed her physical bond with John, she believed if she "gave in" it would just reinforce his selfishness, so she put him off.

Types of Lies

It's crucial to address deceptions that arise in Seething Stalemate; you've got to stop them before they stop you. The lies grow more habitual and more treacherous as time goes on. Lies designed to disguise vulnerability become lies to shut the partner out; passive-aggressive lies can turn into aggressive ones, lies that leave scars. But if you can work through the obstacles posed by this stage, you'll strengthen your marriage and develop new skills and capacities through the process.

LIES TO KEEP A HOLDING PATTERN

Lies allow some couples to remain a couple. The idea is, "We may be miserable, but at least we're together." Some people do—consciously or unconsciously—make that decision.

Amazingly, John and Sarah still held on to the fiction that they were "a team working to get ahead," but because being home was less and less appealing to him, John started lying about working late. He knew full well that he was now deliberately lying but saw no reprieve from those unpleasant contretemps with Sarah. A part of John knew he wasn't carrying his weight, but he also felt men shouldn't do housework—it was emasculating. Other than playing with the kids, he didn't feel confident about parenting. Rather than discuss his painful feelings and reservations, he simply absented himself. But, hey! Didn't Sarah say she wanted to be home with the kids? What was this anyway, a bait and switch on him? As for Sarah, she continued fighting instead of describing how helpless and hopeless she was beginning to feel. Had any of these secrets been laid bare, John and Sarah would have been forced to deal with some very real and very difficult truths about their conflicting desires and fears.

PASSIVE-AGGRESSIVE LIES

With the constant fighting that marks Seething Stalemate, lies are often used as little jabs to "get" the other. Passive-Aggressive Lies can be anything from throwaway lines ("I just forgot your birthday," or "It's hard to find a color that flatters you") to those that get back at or get even ("I've always been turned on by your best friend," or "I went out with you because I felt sorry for you").

Another passive-aggressive ruse is to go behind the other's back. For example, one man started a secret banking account because he was angry at his wife for spending money frivolously. Another man stopped having sex with his wife and spent long hours chatting on the Internet about sex.

"GET OFF MY BACK" LIES

One common type of passive-aggressive deception is the "Get Off My Back" Lie. One person agrees to something that they have very little intention of following through on. Everybody does this to some extent: "Yeah, yeah, I'll clean the boxes out of the basement (*We've been talking about this for years, and neither of us has done anything about it, but I'll say I'll do it just to get off the topic*)."

When they're chronic and involve more than just minor concerns, these lies betray a Seething Stalemate pattern. One example is someone saying he'll be someplace and then failing to show up: "Sure I'll get there (*No, I won't, but get off my back about it*)."

HOSTILE LIES

In Seething Stalemate, people will say things they don't even believe themselves just to spite the other. Often, the lying begins in a less harmful way, but with constant fighting it grows malicious. The use of deception becomes a weapon. After a point, someone may feel, *I don't care if I hurt you, I just want to get my way or have some peace and quiet.* In time, the partner can seem insignificant, or someone may feel she's been hurt so much that she doesn't care if she hurts the other in return.

This is the case with Jake and Erin, who are separating after twelve years of marriage. Erin believes Jake is a terrible father. She'll say, "You never pay attention to Nora," or "All you ever think about is yourself."

Erin's assertions are untrue. She knows Jake tried at times to be a good father and that their daughter is quite attached to him, but she denies that truth just to hurt him and pile on guilt. She knows that fatherhood is a matter of deep pride for him, so she's sure he'll feel the blow.

Another spiteful lie is inaccurately reporting what others have said about your partner. Erin, for example, said to Jake, "You think Joe is a good friend of yours, but he says he can't even talk to you." Erin and Joe did speak about Jake, but in this instance, Erin made sure that something got lost in the translation. Joe might in fact have said something like, "Jake is hard to talk to sometimes" but Erin recontextualized the comment so that it became a slam.

"MY FAULT, YOUR FAULT" LIES

No one in a Seething Stalemate will take responsibility for nastiness, either felt or vented. Couples avoid accountability, however, in different ways. Those who come directly from the Honeymoon will leave all blame in the other's court: "Maybe you don't like it when I snap at you, but look at what I have to put up with," or "You asked for that." No apologies there.

Those who stumble in from the Dark Side of the Honeymoon, on the other hand, may passively apologize without meaning it. They can't seem to *stop* apologizing even though their behavior never changes.

Excessive apologies are lies in that the speaker continually backs away from what he wants and is pretending to feel badly about what he does.

Here are some snippets of dialogue from John and Sarah.

> JOHN: "If you're going to go ballistic on me for coming home late, I'm going to think twice before coming home at all."
>
> Sarah: "I can't believe you're so mean and nasty. Pull another rug out from under me, why don't you?"
>
> John: *(sees that she's hurt and about to attack):* "I'm sorry. I didn't really mean it. I'll get myself home earlier tomorrow, I promise."
>
> He still comes home late—just not *as* late.
>
> Sarah: "I have a splitting headache today."
>
> John: "It's my fault. I've been an awful husband. I should take you out more."
>
> Sarah: "What makes you think I want to go out with you?"

As soon as John would say something, he'd retract it. If Sarah grew the slightest bit angry, he'd leap forward and accept the blame, as though she might read his mind and see the animosity he was beginning to harbor, and he needed to quickly dispel that. Rather than assuage Sarah, however, this merely frustrated her even more. Because John kept revoking what he said or did, her anger never led to any constructive discussion.

Often, the apology becomes an inextricable part of the fight cycle. The couple begins to argue about something important in the relationship, then, just as they're rolling up their sleeves, one partner pulls back and says, "I'm sorry. Let's just forget it." But of course it isn't really forgotten. And one partner is angry because the other has just belittled his concerns. So it surfaces again and again.

This is what happens with Bert and Suzy. Suzy is home full time. She wants Bert to be involved with their three kids, and every night when he comes home from work, they fight about what he isn't doing. "You brushed his teeth, but you didn't read him a story; you played ball, but you didn't put away the toys." Later, Suzy will feel guilty and disturbed by so much fighting and think, *I shouldn't be asking this of him. He's*

the breadwinner. It shouldn't matter to me whether he does much with the kids.
She talks herself out of how she feels and apologizes to Bert for making
a fuss. And again the problem isn't solved.

However, it does matter to her. Suzy was the oldest of seven siblings
and took care of her brothers and sisters without feeling cared for herself. Regardless of how she tries to convince herself that Bert's partici-
pation isn't a big deal, it *is* to her. And so they will fight about it again.

The trouble is that they never talk about parenting when they're not
actively fighting. Bert doesn't know why his help is important to Suzy,
and her constantly changing demands—it's important, it's not important—create a shifting target that's impossible for him to hit. Suzy
avoids taking the risk of being honest with Bert about what she really
wants. Her deceptive apologies rescue her from the tension such honesty might create, but they also leave the couple in a deadlock.

"IT'S NOT SO BAD" LIES

Another type of self-deception that takes hold in Seething Stalemate is
telling oneself, "It's not really that bad" when it *is*. Even when dissension sneaks into every aspect of the relationship, someone may maintain
the illusion, "We'll work this out." Or someone reflects upon a bitter
fight the previous night and thinks, *We got through that. It could be worse.*

This frequently happens when alcohol is an issue. No one wants to
acknowledge the situation, so its severity and destructiveness to the
relationship is minimized. This keeps the marriage in a holding pattern,
but there's tension, frustration, fighting, and denial, and it won't
improve until the underlying cause is addressed.

John and Sarah often fell back on "It's Not So Bad" Lies to cover up
the sorry state of their marriage. After a fight, the tension between them
would soften, and they would again believe, "We're working as a team
to get ahead." In truth, they were getting ahead financially but emotionally they *were* in a steep decline.

LIES THAT BIND

In Seething Stalemate, it's common for one or both partners to be reluctant to accept solutions that acknowledge their differing interests. Each

person competes to get what he or she wants, trying to force his or her own perspective on the other. The attitude is, "I'll push harder to try to get you to be more like me" rather than, "Let's be who we are and make room for that."

If you're trying to maintain the illusion "We're alike" or "We want and need the same things," you're going to miss possible solutions. In Seething Stalemate, this can lead to a lot of stress as both partners try to push each other into agreement.

If you lie and say things like, "I'm your best and only friend, and you can't go alone because you'll be lost without me," or "You need me to do your packing for you," you may be pushing for a degree of togetherness that isn't possible and could be destructive. At the extreme, this kind of lie can lead to threats and domestic violence. In many other instances, it creates huge dependency problems.

"IT'S ABOUT ME" LIES

A good way to get a rise out of your partner is to personalize everything he or she says. This tendency, typical of the Lie Invitee, is endemic in Seething Stalemate. One partner siezes the role of victim and thinks things like:

"You're doing this to *spite me*";

"You say yes because *I say no*";

"You want to pursue new interests *because you don't love me*";

"You've been so cold to me that *there must be someone else*";

"You say the trip is inconvenient *just because you don't want to be with my family.*"

Wes and Pauline have moved several times to accommodate Wes's work. When Wes announced that he was planning another relocation, Pauline said, "Underneath it all, you're just doing this because you really don't want me to be happy. Every time I start feeling happy, you wrench me away."

No, Wes is not choosing to move to keep Pauline perpetually

unhappy. In fact, he's so focused on his work that he only cares about his advancement and his self-esteem. He's indifferent as to whether or not she's happy. Perhaps Pauline has created an alternate narrative so she doesn't have to confront his lack of concern for her or to accept how self-focused he is.

The partner who overpersonalizes has trouble seeing beyond her small field of self-awareness and misses what may be true for her mate. The failure to acknowledge that there are two sides to every story can also result in the lies discussed below.

"It's About You" Lies

Many of the deceptions of Seething Stalemate involve some type of projection, attributing all the problems to the *other* person: "If only my partner would change, I could reexperience the Honeymoon bliss again." The stalemated individual will fault his partner rather than admit his own hostility, immaturity, lack of inner resources, or refusal to compromise. Here are some common self-deceptions:

1. *You tell yourself: My partner doesn't understand me.*
   What you meant: If he understood my pain, he would give me what I want. And I won't stop screaming until I get what I want.
2. *You tell yourself: He won't let me express my feelings.*
   What you meant: I want to get even and have complete license to dump on him.
3. *You tell yourself: He has problems communicating.*
   What you meant: I don't like what I'm hearing, and I want him to stop saying it.
4. *You tell yourself: He let me down.*
   What you meant: If he loved me enough and gave me enough, everything would be fine.

Self-deceptions like those in the examples above evolve into distortions about your partner and what the relationship should be. You attribute too much responsibility to your mate. These distortions also reinforce your own immaturity, and that keeps you in Seething Stalemate.

SLIPPERY LIES

In the Dark Side of the Honeymoon chapter (see page 77), we discussed problem liars, classically untrustworthy sorts who manipulate the truth. In time—and it can be a long time—the partner grows tired of being lied to and starts expressing frustration.

Often, the partner must continue to ask questions, turning the marriage into an ongoing interrogation. The problem liar may say, "If you wanted to know if I had sex with her, I would have told you." This puts the onus on the partner to ask more and more skilled questions, leaving her chronically suspicious.

When you notice that it's hard to grasp your partner's slippery responses, and realize that, to get anywhere, you have to ask just the right question in just the right way, remember that you're dealing with a rigid personality trait that is unlikely to change. Problem liars can catch honest people by surprise. During the Dark Side of the Honeymoon someone may have ignored or denied the pattern, but now the realization, and the anger that accompanies it, erupts.

The liar may say something like, "You have a problem with trust," or "I don't see why it's a lie." These are danger signs. When the lies have accumulated and your partner says, "What's the matter, don't you trust me?" the only good answer is this: "Frankly, in this area I don't."

What to Do About Those Lies?

Many couples trapped in Seething Stalemate relationships are reacting to some very old hurts. For these people, defensive responses are automatic because, in part, they want to avoid being hurt by an intimate partner as they may have been in the past. A couple may find that their relationship in fact, offers a chance to move beyond old pain—*if* they can ask for honesty, stay present to hear the partner's reality, and relinquish some of the deceptions and self-deceptions that keep them adversaries.

GET A MORE REALISTIC PERSPECTIVE

An important part of the attitudinal shift needed to break the Seething Stalemate depends on forming more reasonable ideas of what you *can* expect from your partner. Many stalemate scuffles arise when partners ask for more than the other can possibly provide. There's often a fantasy that the partner is the one and only person who can make up for losses experienced in early life. When the partner isn't able to erase every bad feeling or memory, the other person feels disappointed. Then angry. And the fights begin.

I (Ellyn) remember one stalemate couple who claimed they'd been married for ten years and had been fighting for nine. The wife wanted constant attention, support, and reassurance from her husband. She also wanted him to provide this support without her having to ask for it. I asked her if she thought her husband was intentionally withholding all the things she expected. Her response was, "Actually, that's what I prefer to believe."

Her response was illuminating. She would rather argue with her husband each time he disappointed her than admit that he really couldn't do all that she wanted. She clung to the belief that if she yelled often enough and loudly enough, he would fulfill her wishes. She kept pushing, and so they continued fighting.

GET A BROADER PERSPECTIVE

To overcome the stalemate-style deception that can paralyze a marriage, each person needs to step back from the quarrel of the moment and see the larger picture. Think again of the two deer, antlers entwined, and imagine prying them apart. This is essentially what you want to do. Put aside the immediate argument. Trying to simply hammer things out has been getting you nowhere.

To get that needed distance from your fights, do the following:

- *Give up the notion that an argument can be won.* People desperately want to win because prevailing and "winning" seem the only way out. When you try to win each battle, nobody ever wins.
- *Make the assumption that neither of you is blameless.* Ironically, this reduces the pressure to twist the truth in order to be "right."

- *Go on the presumption that your partner has a bigger picture.* You may not see it now, and it may not be logical, but it will make emotional sense if you can allow yourself to hear her story. You have a better chance of learning that story if you can continue asking questions like, "In addition to anger, what else do you feel? . . . And what else?"

- *Don't get stuck on getting your point heard.* In Seething Stalemate, you tend to put the bulk of your energy into coercing your partner to hear your side. Once you give that up, you're likely to obtain clearer focus of what the argument is really about.

- *Stop fighting so hard to avoid saying who you really are.* Lies that lock couples in Seething Stalemate mostly stem from the inability to be truthful about one's sense of vulnerability or fear of inadequacy. Accept that this is part of being human. The more you try to present a mask of invulnerability, the more you'll have to lie. Dropping the mask is uncomfortable and takes tremendous effort, but then your partner has a chance to know you better, and you won't have to devote so much effort to hiding yourself.

- *Recognize that what your partner does is a problem, but it's not* the *problem. The* problem is how *you* react to what your partner does. If you make your partner *the* problem, all you can do is hope that he changes or try to get him to change. That's a disempowered position. As you increase your ability to respond to the negative things your partner does, you are going to empower yourself and increase your own self-esteem. This single concept is the driving principle behind almost all books on improving relationships.

  When things get difficult, it is normal for most people to think they have done all they can do, want to do, or should have to do. Then they resort to finger pointing saying that it is the partner who has to change. If their partner has little motivation to change, the result is Seething Stalemate gridlock. It may seem counterintuitive, but you will regain some of your lost power by expanding your thinking and by developing new behavioral reactions.

- *Know that if you don't get what you want immediately, things often can be worked out later.* In Seething Stalemate, you can't see your way out of a fight; it becomes your entire world. Remind yourself that this isn't your only chance.

HAVE A FAREWELL TO ARMS

In Seething Stalemate, both partners' defenses shift into overdrive. To break the impasse, each person must learn how to manage his defenses in a more mature way. How do you react when you become uncomfortable? What do you do when your partner brings up something you don't want to hear? Do you withdraw? Blame the other person? Lash out? Know that everyone has defensive patterns and hot buttons that trigger their anger. Approach the question like an archeologist on a dig, with a disinterested, even intellectual curiosity about what you will find.

Once you label your habitual defenses, you can learn to remind yourself that if you give in to them, they'll send you down the same old path. Counteract them when you talk to your partner.

Replace your defensiveness with more productive responses such as support, concern, curiosity, and encourage these responses in each other.

Here is an exercise that can give you insight into your own and each other's defensive patterns:

Draw three concentric circles. In the middle circle (2), list the defensive tactics and immature behaviors that you'd like to change. In the innermost circle (1), write out the vulnerable feelings or truths that these behaviors cover up. In the outside circle (3), describe how you want to be.

Doing this exercise will reward you for years to come and may actually require less effort than most change attempts you have tried in the past. First, select an ineffective behavior that you tend to fall back on during stressful communication with your partner. For example you

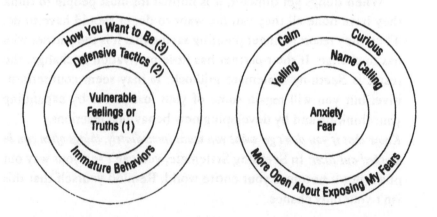

might yell, cry, pout, get sarcastic, withhold affection, make various threats, or get hostile.

We will walk you through this exercise using the example of you becoming angry when your partner spends more than you both budgeted on a household project. For example, when you are angry, you tend to yell and call names. So in the middle ring (2) you would write in yelling and name calling.

Because anger is rarely a single emotion reflect on other emotions that you might feel in addition to anger. Perhaps a part of you feels anxiety and another part of you feels scared. Now list anxious and scared in the innermost ring (1).

Next think about how you would like to respond in a better and different way than yelling. Perhaps you would like to be calmer in these discussions. Maybe you would like to be more *genuinely* curious about why your partner continually goes over budget. Possibly you would even like to take a risk and let your partner know what scares you when you exceed the budget. So in the outer ring (3) you would put calm, curious, and more open about exposing my fears.

How do you put this all together and express it to your partner? Think of the credo of the Mexican cliff divers—timing is everything. So when the time is right, you can approach your partner and say something like the following: "Honey, I would like to talk about the disagreements we have had over the budget. I know that too often I have become nasty. I want to discuss it again without getting angry. Here's my internal reaction: When you overspend the budget, I get scared. I get scared that we aren't saving sufficiently for the future. Then I start lecturing, criticizing, and ranting. I really don't like that I do that because I don't like how I feel about myself and I don't like the wedge that it drives between us. I would much rather discuss money calmly and understand more of how you think about spending money and what a budget really means to you. I know it is hard to learn more about you when I'm preaching, so I want to curtail that very unproductive approach. Can we start again and have a discussion about our values regarding money, what it represents to us, and why I react differently than you and why you react differently than me?"

The above expression could be one way of approaching the discussion. The "formula" is, first, here's what I do that is unproductive on this topic, second, here are my vulnerabilities that have been hard for me to express, and third, here's how I would like to be instead. This is very different than blaming your partner for your ineffective, defensive behavior.

Now here is how you can make those changes permanent. First, picture in your mind's eye how you want to be. That is represented by the outer ring (3). In this case you would picture yourself being calm, curious, and more openly expressive in different dialogues with your partner. Second, you will say affirmations to yourself that support the picture of yourself in the outer circle. For example, you might say to yourself, "I am a calm person when I discuss difficult topics like money. I can be really curious about my partner's thinking about money. I can listen calmly to my partner's thoughts about money. With patience I can work this out with my partner."

These affirmations will basically tap into the left or more logical side of your brain. The picture of yourself doing it will tap into the right or more intuitive side of your brain. Combining the left and right sides of your brain will create a self-image that is consistent with how you want to be. When you act in ways that are consistent with your self-image, the change is more natural and fluid. Change doesn't become a teeth clenching, will power approach that won't last longer than a New Year's resolution.

How to Keep Arguments from Escalating

Stalemate pairs get into serious trouble when their fights spiral out of control. A common ploy, then, is to lie to get out of the situation. Try this exercise on setting limits, which will help you diffuse tension without resorting to deception.

Complete the following four statements:

1. The following behaviors are acceptable for me to use during an argument or disagreement: _____

   _____

2. The following behaviors are acceptable for my partner to use during an argument or disagreement:_____

   _____

3. The following behaviors are unacceptable for me to use during an argument or disagreement:_____
_____

4. The following behaviors are unacceptable for my partner to use during an argument or disagreement:_____
_____

These suggestions provide a safer and more predictable structure for arguments. Make only agreements both of you will be able to keep. If you can't agree to a point raised by your spouse, try to find an alternative that's acceptable to both of you. As a backup, use "time-outs" if the discussion grows too intense.

Agree not to end arguments with a power play. Some people, when under the gun, call time-out as a way of staying one up on the other, but this tactic will only put you back at square one. If you take a time-out, specify when you will be ready to continue the discussion.

Even when not relying upon written limits, you can set your *own*. You can say to yourself, "I don't have to be nasty just because she is. I don't have to stoop that low."

APOLOGIZE TRUTHFULLY

As we explained on page 134, apologies are often lies, used in the Seething Stalemate Stage to diffuse tension or retreat from a strong stance. Apologize effectively by using the following techniques:

- *Don't apologize grudgingly.* If you're not sorry, don't pretend that you are.
- *Be specific as to what you're sorry about.* Many people apologize in a pitifully exaggerated way, saying something like, "I'm so awful." This type of response puts the person being apologized *to* in the position of comforting the one who did wrong. In addition, it prevents the apologizee from venting his own disappointment and may force him to lie ("Oh, it's okay. The outfit you ruined wasn't one of my favorites").
- *Make sure that your apology signals that you are taking responsibility for*

your own behavior in a mature way. It is not a token of "giving in" or a means of extricating yourself from an uncomfortable situation.

- *Don't overdo it.* Excessive apologies are condescending to the other person, suggesting that they are too fragile to handle a minor setback or a slight.
- *Empathize with how your wrongdoing affected the other person.* This will give closure to the entire episode. If you're able to say, "I'm sorry because I put you in a bad position" the deed can be acknowledged and put behind you.

CONFRONT YOUR SELF-DECEPTIONS

Couples stay immobilized in Seething Stalemate when neither partner will sacrifice his illusions. If you can be open to revising your own views, some of that tense animosity may ease.

- *Don't be afraid to recognize that you're angry.* People often deny their anger even as they hold on to it. This reaction merely fuels hostility, grudges, and the feeling of being a victim.
- *Seek alternatives to easy blaming.* Ask yourself, "What has blaming and attacking produced so far?" Know that blaming your partner isn't going to get you anywhere. Can you stop yourself from blaming and find another way of looking at a situation? For example, if your usual complaint is, "My partner doesn't communicate," you can say to yourself, "Maybe what I'm hearing is difficult, and I could be more receptive. I wish my partner didn't feel this way, but I do need to understand him better."
- *Avoid immaturity.* Even if immature behavior (demanding you get your way, blaming someone else, etc.) has worked for you in the past, know that it's not going to help you achieve a more enjoyable, stable, or resilient relationship.

BREAK THE TUNNEL VISION

When someone holds on to a limited view of a partner to justify her own combative behavior, she's not going to admit any evidence to the contrary. One useful exercise that can break this pattern is to write a list of everything your partner does that *doesn't fit* your assumptions. Just one exception can help you see another side of your partner.

For example, let's say your complaint is that your mate never helps around the house. If you sit down and think about it, you may recall that he cleaned up after a dinner party when you went to bed. And that he put up bookshelves. And that, when you come down to it, maybe he's not as selfish as you've been thinking. Can you tell him these pluses?

COME CLEAN ON LIES IN A PRODUCTIVE WAY

- *Be clear:* Vagueness leads to more tension, and more tension leads to more lies. Tell your partner what's important to you, how important it is to you, and why. Then she'll have a better idea of how to respond.
- *When you talk to your partner, limit your points to one topic at a time.* Otherwise the conversation can turn into a muddle.
- *Give up the labels you impose on your partner:* People in Seething Stalemate often have a complaint about their partner which acts as a kind of default response, something that gets dragged out as an excuse for all sorts of behavior.

Hearing Truths

When your partner is telling you something, remember that it's not about you; it's about him. People tend to personalize everything in Seething Stalemate. However, personalizing what your partner says leaves you little option. You'll feel you have to complain back, deflect, or withdraw. You won't be able to ask your partner what's going on with him.

Be particularly wary of personalizing everything when either of you is angry or under stress. Such times are when people are most prone to attack.

When an angry partner walks in the door and launches into a verbal assault, it feels very personal to the other partner. If you can try not to get entangled in the contagion of that anger and say, "Wait a minute.

Why are you angry?" you'll realize that those angry feelings relate to her and not to you—even though it's you she's ostensibly angry with.

Seething Stalemate is like a wide-open invitation for the Lie Invitee. Be aware of that and try to resist being one.

Moving On

In Seething Stalemate you have a choice: You can stay in the misery you know, or you can take the risk of being more honest with each other. Rather than railing against each other's imperfections and the differences between you, you can commit to the hard work of laying down your weapons and divesting your armor.

Relinquish the notion that you can solve all your relationship problems by turning your partner into your double. Being clones does not create marital happiness. Know that your partner will be true to himself before he will be true to you—and that it has to be that way.

An intimate relationship provides an opportunity for enormous personal development. It can help release you from false beliefs that have interfered with your happiness and growth. That happens best when there's empathy and when the two of you can support each other through emotional stress. It can't occur when a couple views marriage as a zero-sum game: "I win; you lose." By replacing contention with caring, you can find that you're each other's best allies, and move into a more rewarding—and more liberating—phase.

8 ❀

Freedom to
Explore:
The Surprising
Gift of Space

*P*aul and Mary did have a child, a little girl named Anna. And indeed, Paul was smitten. Between working and parenting, the next few years were a blur, but by the time Anna started kindergarten, things grew more relaxed. For years, all their free time had revolved around Anna's activities, but now they each began devoting time to their own pursuits. Mary was steadily advancing professionally and became active in the local PTA. Paul, meanwhile, spent much of his free time volunteering with an environmental group.

Working for a cause bigger than his own immediate interests gave Paul a boost of confidence and self-respect. He was able to breathe life into the cause with his heartfelt passion and would organize breakfast meetings as early as 6:00 A.M. He was amazed at the energy this work unleashed in him. One morning he got up quite early and left without telling Mary when he'd be back. This prompted a huge argument because she thought he was gone from home too early and too often.

Before they had a chance to resolve this issue, Mary was offered an extremely lucrative project in Japan. Paul was irritated by this possibility. With Mary gone for a full month, he would have to do more work at home. He also was unnerved by the huge fee she would receive. It reawakened some of his old qualms about his own self-worth.

About Face

At some point in marriage, the energy shifts. Early in an exclusive relationship, lovers turn to each other for sustenance and satisfaction. They each go about their lives—jobs, family, friends—but the focal point, the vivid core of pleasure and interest, is the marriage itself.

Suddenly, however, attention is drawn outward. The outer world, once only the background setting for romance, now dazzles and beckons. Challenges outside of the relationship—new interests, new friendships, newly awakened dreams—become compelling. The marriage remains a central part in each partner's life, but it's not the main focus anymore. The partnership is a constant; excitement and risk are now elsewhere.

This directional shift, from focusing on the relationship to other aspects of one's life, fuels the Freedom to Explore Stage. It's almost like coming up for fresh air.

You know you're in the Freedom to Explore Stage when you start channeling more energy into your own self-development than into your marriage. You may revive friendships that you had let slide when you were completely consumed by love. Long-dormant interests reclaim your attention. Children or other family members may become more central. Early in the relationship, you could feel high on your partner's very presence. Now, your high points often have nothing to do with him or her.

Paul, spurred to action by a development deal that threatened an historic site, ran a local political campaign. He gave speeches and became known for his views. Mary went to Vermont for a ski weekend with her college roommates and mastered a black-diamond slope for the first time.

It's not that you're pursuing outside interests to spite your partner; you're genuinely excited about what you're discovering.

We Can Do Different Things

The boundaries that guard the borders of any relationship can only remain fixed for so long. In the Freedom to Explore Stage, the external world, previously held at bay by the intensity of romantic love and the struggle to accept one another's differences, breaks down the barricade and exerts its influence upon the marriage. The couple repositions itself into the ever-larger contexts of family, profession, friends, community, and the limits of togetherness begin to stretch.

After traveling for Thanksgiving to be with her in-laws for more than a decade, one woman decided that what she really wanted to do was spend the day at home with her own mother and sister and eat a gourmet meal rather than the standard overcooked bird. So that's what she did, while her husband traveled to be with his family.

Ever since college, when he switched his major from English to Economics, another client of ours yearned to try his hand at a novel. For two years, he chose to devote all his vacation time—and many evenings—to a Master of Fine Arts in writing. This placed a strain on his wife as he pursued his degree and threw himself into writing.

The Togetherness Myth

Freedom to Explore Stage couples are often forced to confront a cultural lie—the belief that the more activities and opinions a couple shares, the happier and stronger the marriage will be. Many people buy into this belief and find it hard to give up. Couples who happen upon the Freedom to Explore Stage often encounter powerful or subtle external pressures to conform.

Dina called her mother with her exciting news: She had been accepted to a prestigious artist's retreat. Her mother, however, didn't appear to share her enthusiasm. "You can't just go off for a month," she said. "What about meals?"

Dina answered, "That's the beauty of the whole thing. They take care of everything. I don't have to cook for a whole month!"

"I'm not worried about you," her mother said. "I'm talking about Brian. What's he going to do while you're gone?"

The notion that togetherness is always better isn't true, certainly not for the couple who gets a taste of freedom. The yearning for self-development is powerful; the prospect of giving it up, painful. Freedom to Explore partners want to create space to accommodate their independent strivings. Though apprehensive about the implications, they believe it's possible. And it is, once the pair has established a base of truthfulness and understanding from which to work.

The Path to Independence

It usually isn't until a few years into a relationship that the Freedom to Explore Stage materializes. Ideally, the couple would have relinquished Honeymoon lies and developed the ability to accept differences between them before beginning the branching-out process that marks this stage. When two people know how to talk honestly about what's important to them, they will be able to take some liberty without going AWOL or feeling pressed to lie about their intentions.

The duration of this stage could take a long time or be relatively brief. It depends on how much exploration each person had done before they met. Frequently, partners who link up later in life have challenged themselves and developed more of an individual identity. For them, the Freedom to Explore Stage might be a brief interlude before they again crave more solidarity. But for those who pair off at a relatively young age, or before each person had a chance to test his own mettle, it will take a longer time, even many years, to get through.

We don't see many Freedom couples, perhaps ten to fifteen percent of our clients. When they do come in, it's usually because the issues under consideration are potentially divisive and therefore merit skillful negotiation. An example would be when one partner's quest makes such demands on the other that they know it will strain the marriage. Either that or they haven't successfully worked through the Emerging Differences Stage and need to go back and master those skills first. This pattern occurs more frequently now because many couples start out their marriages living independent lives.

For the fifteen years she's been married to Will, Francine has basically fit herself into Will's life. She moved into his well-decorated house, traveled with him on business, and spent time with his three grown children from a previous marriage. Despite her happiness in their marriage, urban life began losing its charm. She began reflecting on her love of horses and yearning for wide-open country spaces similar to those she had enjoyed as a child.

In therapy, Francine explored these equestrian dreams and realized that she had neglected that part of herself during her years with Will. It wasn't Will's fault that she had gotten swept up in their cosmopolitan lifestyle and downplayed the importance of her country heritage, but this no longer felt good to her.

She decided to take dressage lessons, working with trainers whose style she admired. This meant traveling out to horse country and spending time developing new skills and new friendships with both men and women. At first Will objected, "Don't we have enough to do in the city on the weekends?" But, as Francine was able to convey to Will what working with horses meant to her, his reluctance gave way to support.

The Freedom to Explore Stage is not an exercise in "finding yourself" as during the "Me Generation." Back in the '60s and '70s the main concern was individual freedom. Here, the questions are "How do I respond to my own desires and maintain a collaborative, loving relationship? How can we loosen the reins without becoming completely disengaged?" In our experience, once a couple has arrived at Freedom to Explore and has begun to earn each other's trust by giving the other room to grow, they feel much more solid as a couple.

Opportunity Knocks

The Freedom to Explore Stage is a contemporary phenomenon. In past eras, the chance to follow your own aspirations was something most people could only dream about. Even a generation ago, gender roles were rigid enough that marriages in which each person had the chance to pursue his own endeavors were rare. For this reason, there are scant models for how to operate independently in the context of an intimate relationship. In particular, there are few precedents for how to speak truthfully about your dreams and desires. This is important because attaining those desires often requires effort and involvement from your partner.

About ten years into our marriage, I started playing on a local women's tennis team. This was a totally new direction for me. I had never considered myself particularly coordinated and had avoided competitive sports my entire life. With some good fortune and an enormous amount of hard work, my team qualified for the United States Tennis Association Nationals. The experience was fantastic. It was a women's bonding experience, a confidence booster, and a chance to discover a new part of myself. I learned that I could actually enjoy competition.

For me, the tennis team kept one part of the Freedom engine running. It was something I joined for myself. It had nothing to do with Pete, although I know it would have been more convenient for him if I hadn't been running to practice Thursday and Sunday nights. If Pete had been threatened by me traveling to Texas to play in the Nationals, I would have missed out on a tremendous experience. Fortunately (and this wasn't the case with some of my teammates) he understood what it meant to me.

The path to Freedom can be laden with hazards, with plenty of bumps and sharp turns along the way. First, there's the blind-curve factor: You have no idea where it's going to take you. Second, one of you will have to sacrifice something—time, security, companionship—in order for the other to pursue his interests.

And here's where it becomes messy: The advent of Freedom for one partner can be threatening to the other. You'll probably hit the Freedom trail at different times. If one partner is still wholly oriented towards the marriage as the other partner starts to spread her wings, huge anxiety will result. The extent to which each of you can be open about your aims, fears, and jealousies will determine whether you become more intimate and collaborative or whether lies create more barriers between you.

Feeling Your Oats

One defining feeling of the Freedom to Explore Stage is the emotional rush of doing something positive for yourself. You feel a trust in yourself, a knowledge of what is right for you.

You will feel trepidation. Moving towards Freedom is scary because you know there will be repercussions in the marriage. If you're authentic in your desire for more independence, it's bound to stir things up. The larger the dream you hope to fulfill, the more nervous you'll be. You hope you're not going to crumble and give up. You will flounder a bit and then regroup—more than once.

As you work through the Freedom to Explore Stage, you also learn to trust each other. When it's your partner who's taking more latitude, you find you can listen to dreams and desires even when feeling a huge knot in your gut. You learn to find ways to help each other excel. You're not afraid that you'll be forced to compromise what's important to you; you begin to believe your partner wants the best for you. You can rely on your mate to be honest with you, and speak up when something is important. You know he's not going to inflate the importance of anything merely to get what he wants.

But you may also be nervous. You'll wonder, *Is this a first step on the way out?* If, however, you've been flirting with ideas of what *you'd* like to pursue, you may be relieved. Either way, your mate is working to relax the restraints, and this presents you with an opportunity to try new things.

Several discomforts accompany this stage: the fear that you won't hold on to your desires; the fear of clashing with your partner over conflicting goals; the fear of being left out or left behind. It is the expression of these fears, as well as other significant concerns, that moves you through this stage. The issue here is regulating togetherness and independence, determining how elastic or constricting your bond is going to be. You're trying to answer this question: *On the grand continuum of togetherness and separateness, where do I want us to be?* The means of achieving the answer is through negotiation based on the current circumstance, not holding on for dear life against some unnamed terror.

In the Freedom to Explore Stage, couples give each other more leeway. You probably do more things independently, staking out your own turf. At the same time, you remain connected with your partner in important ways. You tell the truth about what you want; you engage in negotiation, rather than simply demanding that your partner let you do as you choose; you tell each other what your relationship means to you, and you hold on to that knowledge when you're apart.

Strong Partners, Strong Marriage

A successful Freedom to Explore Stage advances your relationship in several ways. You discover that you can be a couple *and* be an individual without having to sacrifice one for the other. You learn that you can stay connected despite physical and even emotional distance. When you find that you can vacation alone without your mate throwing tantrums, he becomes even more desirable.

Far from being an impediment to personal growth, the marriage offers a platform from which each person can venture out—tentatively at first, perhaps, but then more surely. There's an added sense of security in knowing that your goals aren't a threat to the marriage. You learn that you can pursue what you want without diminishing the other person; you find that you can stay committed to the marriage without forgoing your dreams. Your relationship has real ballast, born of honesty and trust.

This stage is where people solidify their own identities. Each partner learns important skills like negotiation, flexibility, and self-sufficiency. These, plus the strength that comes with taking the opportunity to be authentic, make both partners less prone to lie. When you find that you can be truthful—truly yourself—with each other, the marriage becomes even more precious. Trust increases, is tested, and increases again. Some couples say that the liberation and excitement they feel sparks a renewed sense of romance.

Deception: A High Stakes Game

Telling the truth at this stage is a matter of sink or swim. If you say you want to go to a Greek island by yourself and part of the reason is that you've got an old flame waiting at the port, you will undermine the entire stage. Being duplicitous while experimenting with freedom is disastrous. The stakes are high. You and your partner will push the margins of trust. The potential gains are great; the potential for destructiveness is huge. If you essentially say, "Let's be more authentic while I lie to you," you've toppled over the edge of the Freedom to Explore Stage and into its warped counterpart—Freedom Unhinged.

Not all the lies that occur at this stage are so devastating. Some are process lies, little glitches or slight detours along the way to truth.

THE "JUST A LITTLE INDEPENDENCE, PLEASE" LIES

The truths that arise in the Freedom to Explore Stage revolve around autonomy and independence; thus, the lies that are stumbling blocks to mastering this stage are about those same issues. Typically, the partner who's seeking independence will lie to veil the degree of independence she wants.

Rick decides he wants to run in a high-profile marathon. He has turned fifty, the age when his own father fell into ill health, but Rick feels fit and wants to celebrate that fact. The marathon is important to him, but he doesn't want to make a lot of noise about it until he knows he really has the makings of a runner. He's still unsure. He tells his wife, "Oh, I don't think it should be a big deal. I might take long runs once or twice on a weekend." Even as he says this, he doubts that's the only change ahead (he's already vowed to improve his diet and cut out most alcohol), but he chooses to play it down. He's thinking about upcoming races he'd like to enter, but is wary about telling his wife just how much training it will take.

Lies can be useful when you zero in and decode them. They alert you to tension between you and the issues that make you anxious. For example, a lie at this stage may suggest that you want a lot more independence than you are saying and perhaps more than you have acknowledged to yourself.

Negotiating space is not easy. In a marriage, it can be nerve-wracking to carve out more liberty, just as it will be unsettling to be asked for it by your partner. Because people seeking freedom often feel guilty, they will start out with a little testing, suggesting that they want something without spelling out exactly what that is. Instead of stating outright, "I want to get an M.B.A." someone may say, "I'm thinking of going back to school."

That's okay. You want to test a new idea on your partner, and you want to try it on for size yourself. The key is to be aware of any discrepancy between what you want and what you admit. There's a steep price to be paid for sidestepping the truth about your desire for independence. If taken sneakily, you may believe you *have* to be sneaky to realize your dreams. When you journey without the collaboration of your mate, you risk veering off in completely different directions.

The main danger is that any lie about autonomy that isn't corrected is likely to evolve into a bigger lie. Let's say that you'd like to spend some time with a friend of the opposite sex. You may balk at telling your mate so as to avert any jealousy. In order to see this friend, you fabricate so many excuses and do so much sneaking around that it looks like you have something to hide. That behavior becomes uncomfortable, and you begin to feel more relaxed with your friend and more distant from your spouse. Where are you now? You've skipped right past Freedom to Explore into Freedom Unhinged.

LIES TO AVOID STATING YOUR DESIRES

You plan a day skiing. Your partner wants to know why you didn't mention it. You say, "I didn't think you wanted to go." Well, maybe. But you didn't ask. The truth was, "This is something that I really want to do by myself."

You buy a computer and tell your partner, "I decided to buy a computer to better manage our finances." You're not telling the whole story, which is that you're thinking about changing your career.

When someone starts to feel the Freedom itch, they're often concerned that making a foray into new terrain will threaten or alienate their partner. It's common, then, to lie about it.

Ellis, an amateur guitarist, started lying when he joined a local rock band. He wouldn't tell his wife, Sylvie, because he was afraid that if he told her how late he'd be out at night, she might say, "Don't go." He wanted to avoid conflict and to stay out without worrying about obtaining Sylvie's approval; so, he'd say, "I'm not going to be out very late," knowing full well he wouldn't return much before 3:00 A.M.

Therapy revealed that Ellis's mother had been quite strict, and he feared Sylvie would keep him on a tight string, too. Sylvie assured him that she didn't mind his late nights but just wanted an honest answer from him. When he tested her, she stuck to her word and let him know she wanted honesty.

LIES THAT CAMOUFLAGE AUTONOMY

We've often found that when women, in particular, reach the Freedom to Explore Stage, they want control over their own money; yet, they may be afraid to state this desire because they're worried that their partner will think it's a prelude to leaving him. So they hedge in a way that masks their desire for more autonomy. Rather than say how badly they want to manage their own money, for example, they might come up with a half-hearted excuse for doing it or try to keep it a secret by, perhaps, setting up an independent account through a business address.

Many people begin the Freedom to Explore Stage with half-truths. The question, however, is: Do you start telling more and more half-truths, or do you become more honest with yourself and your partner? Do you hold on to your integrity, or let it crumble?

Paul told some half-truths regarding his morning environmental meetings. He didn't want to risk Mary's stubborn refusal to cooperate with his desire to *add* another meeting. Instead, he said he was changing his meeting schedule. That was true enough. The deception was that he wanted to add more meetings to his schedule. Half the truth was easier than the whole truth.

By now, Mary wasn't going to back down. She pushed him to define "changing" his schedule. This time Paul admitted the truth and said what he wanted and why it was important to him.

"HERE'S WHY YOU SHOULDN'T DO IT" LIES

When one partner is on the ascendant, the other person might feel that offering encouragement is like giving a pyromaniac more matches; so, he lies, extinguishing the fire—and often coming close to squelching the spark that started it.

Let's return to our would-be marathoner. His wife senses this race means more to him than he's letting on. She becomes nervous, and thinks, *He's getting into shape and looks great. If this continues I'm going to feel like an old lady. I don't know what to do to get out of my own rut.* Her first reflex is to dissuade him, "I'm not sure you're healthy enough to do this." This is a lie but an effective one: It zooms right in on his anxieties about his age and condition.

In general, one partner will try to dissuade the other from doing something because of (1) physical danger or (2) emotional danger. If your mate informs you that he's planning to start rock climbing, take up sky diving, or buy a motorcycle, you may be anxious and try to discourage him because there's actual physical risk.

It's much less clear-cut when the threat is emotional. It's difficult to say, "I'm really scared about your excitement about activities that don't include me. I'm also afraid I won't find anything as exciting for myself, and you'll find me boring." The inability to express concerns about what Freedom taking means leads to lies.

Let's say that a woman learns that her husband has been given an assignment abroad and thinks, *I know what it's like there, and I'm afraid he might experiment with drugs and sex.* Instead of saying this, she says, "Why can't so and so do it instead of you?" She's being deceptive by reframing the issue, creating a smoke screen for her real concerns.

Or an anthropology professor decides to take two months of the summer to do fieldwork in Kenya. Her husband thinks, *It's summer. The kids and I want to be with you and here you are trotting around.* But instead he says, "Isn't summer a horrible time of year over there?" Or, in an attempt to stir up anxiety, "I think I read that they have terrible storms, not to mention rattlesnakes, poisonous spiders, and possible political unrest." Or, laying on guilt, "The phones are erratic. What if I really need to reach you?"

In these cases, the other person has a hard time coming up with responses. Generally, individuals leaning toward Freedom are conflicted about taking clear steps in that direction. They may fear losing their nerve if they explore possible reasons *not* to do something, so they don't mention their own misgivings and refuse to acknowledge their partner's concerns. This creates a scenario in which the two are polarized on either side of the debate and often lie to maintain their positions.

Paul and Mary found themselves in a situation similar to the one described above, but they were able to move beyond the tug-of-war. When Mary received her travel contract to Japan, she wanted the whole family to go. She wanted to share her bounty with Paul and thought it would be a good experience for Anna.

Paul felt otherwise. First, he used Anna as a cover: "What if Anna doesn't like it? She's too young to travel so far. Also, Japan is so expensive. We won't be able to see very much."

MARY: "I'd love to have you with me."

PAUL: "There is work here that I want to do. This month looks so busy for me. I'll be overwhelemed. Even if you go alone, I don't know how I can be really reliable with Anna. It takes me twice as long to do the things you do. Why don't you stay home this time, and we'll go together another time."

MARY: "I really, really want to go. There must be a way to work this out."

PAUL: "I don't see how. I really, really don't want to go. And I'll be swamped if we are gone that long."

MARY: "What else is bothering you? [A very effective question] You don't usually get demoralized so easily."

PAUL: "Well, I want to be able to throw myself into my work here . . . and not have to worry constantly about picking up Anna after school and fixing meals."

MARY: "Anything else?"

PAUL: "I'm also afraid I won't look very good to you after you spend a month with all those successful businessmen. [A rare admission of vulnerability for him.]"

What emerged was Paul's fear about Mary making more money and it reinforced his feeling of inferiority. When Mary was able to understand this fear and to listen empathically, he was capable of being more supportive of her trip. They made an agreement to talk frequently, and Mary helped arrange some carpooling and playmates for Anna so that Paul didn't feel so burdened after her departure.

Paul lied in order to stall until he felt he could be more honest. He thought that if he could prevent Mary from leaving, he wouldn't have to face the fears prompted by her success. He was afraid that her success would take her away from him, but in fact, his support of her success strengthened their relationship and her commitment to him. Also, he found his own version of Freedom because he was able to express his real preference, to stay home and expand his career rather than to travel.

THE LIE OF DEFIANCE

People often confuse the idea of Freedom with rebellion. Freedom occurs when someone reaches out in a positive way toward something appealing and rewarding. With rebellion, the person stepping out is taking a defiant stance, something like "I'll show you!" When this happens, the gesture of autonomy is a lie.

Let's say a man joins his company's softball team though he's not terribly interested in softball, but he does it because his wife has been involving herself in a local choir. He wants to prove to her that he, too, can be independent. This is not an illustration of the Freedom to Explore Stage. He is reacting to his wife rather than strengthening his own identity.

Lies of Defiance give people a false sense of freedom. The danger is that a couple can get caught up in competition. Rather than helping their partner, they start to keep score. This plunges the couple back into Seething Stalemate, competing to be one up on each other, and it stymies potential growth. With real Freedom, someone is truly able to describe the pleasure of growth in something they're pursuing. They wish for the other person to enjoy and understand their excitement, even if they don't feel that same excitement.

Some examples of rebellious statements that may masquerade as Freedom are

"I've got to be me."
"I've got to do it my own way."
"It's my turn."
"I'm not going to let you stop me."
"I've got this coming to me."

Genuine expressions of Freedom would sound more like:

"I want to tell you how excited I feel."
"I feel like I'm learning every day."
"This means a lot to me because . . ."
"I appreciate you helping me do this by holding down the home front."
"When I see that I can do this alone, I feel more confident and competent."

"They're Leaving Me" Lies

It is fairly common to believe that your Freedom-seeking partner is being evasive and making a statement about you and the relationship. Many people observe Freedom desires and construe them personally. Typical erroneous conclusions include

"You don't love me anymore."
"You just don't care about me."
"All you care about is yourself."
"I don't need that kind of independence. Why should you?"

Deceiving yourself this way is counterproductive. These fallacies raise your level of anxiety and leave your partner feeling hamstrung. Either that or, as with the Lie Invitee, he or she will think twice before sharing his or her dreams or ambitions.

"But I Don't Need Freedom" Lies

The anthropology professor has initial stirrings: "Taking the summer in Kenya is what I really want to do." One internal voice exclaims, *Yes! Go for it!* Another voice scolds, *You're just being selfish and inconsiderate, and there must be something wrong with your marriage if you're so anxious to leave.* She wavers back and forth, alternately feeling excited about the project and trying to talk herself out of it.

People often stifle their interest in Freedom before it even registers psychologically. Rather than undergo the cumbersome process of breaking the news to your partner that you want change, you tell yourself that things are just fine as they are. Here are some common self-deceptions about the desire for Freedom:

Why bother my partner about this? There's not much chance of it happening.

I probably don't deserve to get what I want anyway.

I'm sure this is just a phase. If I just stick things out, I'll find something else to be excited about that won't require me asking for support from my partner.

We've worked so hard to get where we are. My partner won't want to hear about my frustrations.

To some extent, such self-deceptions are coping mechanisms intended to minimize stress, but if you risk being honest with your mate, you may find unforeseen possibilities for change. Rather than feeling put upon, as he or she might have been in earlier stages, your partner may welcome the chance for expansion.

The "Sure, Go Ahead" Lie

Rick, our marathoner, gathers the courage to tell his wife the extent of his passion for running, and that he plans to devote a good bit of his free time to training and racing. She says, "Sure, go ahead."

This response is a lie because it conceals how she really feels. She's saying, "If you have to do it, do it" with an edge. The implication is, "Go on, see if I care."

The "Sure, Go Ahead" lie can cover up the fear that besets someone when his or her partner seeks Freedom. Usually the person's facial expression and tone of voice betray his or her true feelings. As with the Lie Invitee, the partner hears a double message: He's free to do what he wants, but not really.

What to Do About Those Lies

For Freedom to flourish, the overriding attitude needs to be an openness to change, to each other, and to new possibilities. In part, you're looking for solutions to whatever dilemma your burgeoning desires provoke, but the process of discussion is itself part of the solution. After you discuss what you want, you can brainstorm about your choices and opportunities. You'll inevitably experience some trial and error. You want to clarify hindrances to your dreams and think about ways to surmount them.

Freedom has to be continually earned and renewed by talking things out and revisiting the questions. You take the core issue and rotate it like a disco ball, viewing it from all angles. You then arrive at Freedom in a manner that's supportive and responsive to each other. This sets the stage for you to handle future dilemmas.

The deceptions that need to be addressed in this stage are those that inhibit one or both partners' growth. These lies either keep the bond between you so tight that you feel claustrophobic or let the bond go slack so that you feel insecure. You can prevail over those deceptions when you (1) learn to tolerate more distance between the two of you and recognize the gift that comes with that, and (2) learn to negotiate.

The primary characteristic of this stage is your hunger for what the the world outside of your marriage can give you. In our culture we don't find this acceptable, but our experience has shown that, once a couple has achieved a certain level of separateness as individuals, it's more than okay. The more you can allow yourself and your partner to experiment—the more fresh air is allowed into the marriage to circulate through it—the more each person can grow. And that growth comes back to enrich the relationship.

When people break through a tough, seemingly insurmountable deadlock, what they've done is

1. talk about the situation,
2. share their emotional reactions to those facts,
3. explain what they do when they have that emotional reaction,
4. talk about what their dilemma means to them,
5. share their vision of what they'd like to have happen.

Here's an example of how this works in practice:

Laura says to her husband: (1) "All of our money has always been shared. When I have to check with you before I spend more than fifty dollars" (2) "I start feeling like a child. I get mad at you and tell myself I'm stupid. I'm a grown woman. Why am I subjecting myself to this?" (3) "The more I think these things, the more depressed I get and the more I start to distance myself from you." (4) "My dilemma is this: I want more freedom to spend without going to you on bent knee, but I also like that you ask me before spending large sums and that we do collaborate about money." (5) "One option I'd propose is that I have my own checking account of $800 a month, and that I can use that money without having to answer to you. Do you have any other ideas?"

CONTINUE DISCUSSIONS

Because of the complexities inherent in any long shared history, it's very rare to work through all the snags in one discussion. You need to return to the issue and connect the dots, allowing one conversation to carry over to the next. This will help you obtain a clearer picture of what's going on. As you are progressively vulnerable with each other, discussions will feel more relieving over time. You'll each feel more confident in yourself, more trusting in the strengths of your partnership, and more of a sense that you're in this together—even if on the surface it looks like you're doing more things separately.

Let's say Eric has a high-level managerial job that requires a long commute, and he finds the situation intolerable. He wants to return to school and change his career. He's afraid to tell Lisa, who is comfortable with the way things are. He will go through these steps:

Facts: "I want to do something different. I bought a computer."

Feelings: "I am afraid of your reaction. That fear makes me (1) want to give up my dream or (2) pursue my dream and hide it from you."

Meaning: "Pursuing a new field would release me from the trap I feel I'm in and enable me to see what I'm truly capable of. Your support would give me the strength to give this new venture all I've got."

Vision: "I want to build something together with you. Right now we have jobs but not a life. Now it's important to me to have a life."

The keys to becoming more honest in the Freedom Stage are (1) don't censor your desire to grow and (2) don't ask your partner to deny his desire to grow.

This is harder than it may seem. When you talk about your own growth, you may have a sense of direction, but you can't know the ultimate destination. This uncertainty raises the temptation to lie. Likewise, you may want to talk your partner out of heading into uncharted terrain.

DETERMINE WHY YOU WANT MORE FREEDOM

In order to relinquish your own lies, you need to be honest with yourself about your motivations: Is this an honest desire for personal growth, or are you seeking defiance or revenge? Are you being realistic about the possible risks to the relationship? Can you keep in touch with your partner and be up front about any perceived risks to your relationship?

It's crucial to stay open with your partner about your steps towards independence. It can be tempting *not* to talk about your plans or to regard your partner as an inhibiting factor; however, if you don't maintain contact, you risk being unnecessarily provocative. You also risk feeling guilty and resenting your partner for that.

How do you remain honest and open through this sometimes awkward process? The simple fact about honesty in marriage is this: You will become more forthcoming and will elicit a more forthcoming response from your partner when you see that (1) the consequences of shading the truth are high, and (2) the rewards of honesty are worth it.

Would you like to continue your journey into the Freedom to Explore Stage? If you do and you're like most people, you would prefer a solution that doesn't require much discomfort or sustained effort. Pete would also like to win the lottery without having to waste money on worthless tickets. Well, as you can guess, making it through the Freedom to Explore Stage takes more effort than buying a lottery ticket. A lot more.

In working with your partner, here are some tips.

- *Have a plan to maintain your connection.* Your partner is going to be a lot less concerned about you going off to pursue a project if it's clear that you've given thought to remaining in touch. As Paul and Mary did, you can set up times to talk. Demonstrate that you'd like to share your excitement with him or her.
- *Be accountable for what you request.* One client of ours demanded that his wife promise never to knock on his door when he was working. This seemed reasonable, until they took into consideration that they had a two-year-old child in the house. Simply disappearing into solitude for hours was not realistic. There are many negotiated ways for him to have focused time on his work without inflicting rigid demands on his family (*if* he weren't afraid to negotiate).
- *Articulate your desire in a way that isn't threatening.* The emphasis should be on *what you want to do*, not the fact that you want to break away.
- *Express your own ambivalence.* Let your partner know that it's hard to pull away from her, even temporarily. This will help her better understand what you're experiencing.
- *Accept that you and your partner don't always have to be in the same place or be excited by the same things.* Your task is to let your partner know

what's important to you, not to try to convince her to make the same things important to her.

- *Don't let your partner's anxieties deter you.* If you believe your interests are legitimate and worth pursuing, try to determine the cause of those anxieties and find a way to alleviate them without giving up your goals.

UNDERSTAND WHEN YOUR PARTNER WANTS FREEDOM

When your partner wants to stretch his limbs, you may feel you're in a tense position, but you needn't feel helpless. Approach the situation as it is—not according to what you fear.

- *Determine your best response.* If being apart from your partner is difficult, ask yourself, "Assuming that I am committed to the growth of our marriage, what will I do to make this work?" Make a list of answers. Once you make the decision to commit to growth, the answers will flow more easily. You might come up with things like, "Find fulfilling things to do apart from my partner," "Do things, like running or drawing, that I enjoyed before we were together," etc.
- *Recognize that freedom for your partner does not mean a rejection of you.* You don't need to "compete." Paul found this hard to come to terms with. He felt that a stimulating experience for Mary would somehow reflect badly on him, as though he needed to prove himself as worthy as everyone she met.
- *Be creative in ways to stay connected.* Some couples we've worked with have taken unexpected pleasure in writing to each other, and even report discovering another side to their romance.

TRY ON EACH OTHER'S SHOES

We often help couples through Freedom impasses by working with both partner's dreams. Not only does this work ease them through the crisis, but it helps them understand each other's truths in a more visceral way. We encourage people to explore: "What are your hopes?

What would you like the future to look like?" This approach helps remove the situation from the immediate context of their lives and encourages them to use their imagination.

Try to brainstorm. Start out by assuming there is no disagreement. What would things be like for each of you? Create a Freedom wish list together. What are the things that you want to do as an individual and/or couple? How can you make those possible within your relationship? Take the attitude that everything is possible until proven impossible, instead of the other way around.

One exercise we suggest when independent desires differ markedly is "Unified Thinking," both partners considering the same side of the issue at the same time; therefore, the energy that would normally be invested in trying to win your partner over to your side can be harnessed for coming up with a solution. The classic example is: "If we both live in the city, how can we make it work? If we both live in the country, how can we make it work?"

A variant on this is the "Switching Exercise." We did this with Stan and Maya. Maya wanted to get married and have a baby (she was thirty-nine and didn't want to wait), and Stan said he wasn't ready. There is no compromise regarding this issue. "Okay, let's have a baby but you have to take care of it" is not a resolution. Generally when couples hit grid-lock, they soon start repeating their own arguments, with little emotional or intellectual illumination for either one. Sometimes the picture can be enlarged when we ask each person to spend some time, perhaps a week or two, "being the other one" in the disagreement. In other words, you trade roles and act as if you want what the other person desires and discuss the situation as though you were your partner.

When they tried this, Stan began to feel what it was like to describe a powerful dream and have it refused—again and again. We encouraged him to continue the exercise through the whole week, even though it was frustrating.

Later they described their experience. Stan said it was actually quite painful to be rebuffed so often and began, for the first time, to feel what it was like for his wife. Maya discussed the ambivalence this provoked. On the one hand, she first felt that she held most of the power, but she soon felt guilty about denying something so important to someone she loved.

Paul and Mary tried this. Paul imagined what Mary might have felt about the opportunity in Japan and how frustrated she must have been by him attempting to dissuade her from going. Mary then put herself in Paul's shoes and imagined the twinge of jealousy he was bound to feel.

When you truly try to experience your partner's quandary this can be a very powerful exercise, if handled with integrity. While this won't immediately create the perfect answer, you will find new ways to approach and discuss the situation.

TAKE TIME AWAY FROM THE CONFLICT

When couples get into a logjam, we suggest taking time away from the conflict. You want to make sure that the conflict doesn't spoil all your time together. If you know there will be times to talk about it, you can suspend the discussion the rest of the time. If not, the conflict will fill every available moment.

On good days, we can apply these approaches to our own relationship. Recently, I told Pete about my very strong desire to have a year or more with a reduced work schedule before our daughter reached high school. It wasn't just a simple suggestion. It would mean increasing my financial dependence on Pete. This dependence ran contrary to my conscious early-life decision to stay solidly on my own two feet financially. Since the notion of being somewhat "taken care of" didn't sit well with another part of me, I had to work this out for myself as well as with Pete.

I also remembered that in previous years Pete would get nervous about financial matters, so I wasn't sure how he would respond. When I raised the issue, a part of me was pleasantly surprised with his answer. "Dynamite. I would welcome the opportunity to take care of you more than I do. As a matter of fact, doing this would give my ego a significant boost. My mother had to work to help support our family, and I would gladly create a situation that was different from my own family."

As I said, this was good news to only a part of me. I still had to deal with the effects of my earlier decision about being independent. As this book was being written, we were still trying to make this work financially and emotionally.

Freedom discussions and decisions take time, energy, patience, and persistence—and still the outcome may be less than perfect. One couple we worked with faced a difficult decision when he was offered admission to a prestigious graduate-school program. She didn't want to go with him. The stakes were high. After many conversations about their reasons, the couple decided that he would go to school, and that they would travel back and forth for the two years. The solution required significant accommodations from both. What made it work was not the logistics but an understanding attitude about their solution.

Freedom in the Electronic Age

The advent of the Internet has created new, electronic opportunities for people to seek Freedom—and new risks for finding themselves cut adrift from their mates. People are establishing relationships via computer. These can be innocent and romantic, or they can be sexual. They can be open or secretive. For those who like to chat online, keeping the following questions in mind will help ensure that some idle tinkering doesn't turn into dangerous duplicity:

Do you share what you do on the Internet with your partner?

Are there any correspondences that you consciously hide?

Why do you hide them?

What truths about the correspondence are you not revealing?

How might your online chatting lead you to shut out your partner?

Moving On

The Freedom to Explore Stage is about building confidence, self-esteem and developing your own unique talents. Your honesty with each other is the core of the relationship, one which strengthens with time. When you learn that your bond is flexible enough to support your explorations, you'll know that the two of you will stay together without stifling each other. But when you betray confidences and flout that bond, you'll find yourself in trouble. Let the next chapter be a cautionary tale.

9

Freedom Unhinged: The Shocking Price of "Anything Goes"

John and Sarah's sons had now reached adolescence. Like many estranged couples, they endured a grinding, joyless relationship. There were pockets of relief, but it was neither profound nor long enough to offer sustained hope for a better future. Sarah occasionally cared enough to get angry at John, but the results were dreadfully predictable: He would clam up, snap back, or apologize without changing his behavior. Ironically, John regarded Sarah's bursts of anger as signs of her dwindling feelings. He didn't realize that apathy—not hate or anger—is the opposite of love.

John had long felt like a dead man in his own house, not fully recognizing that he had brought the rope to his own hanging. He mourned the passing of the highly charged sexual relationship he had had with his wife and felt lonely and lost. He believed that the last hope for any spark of life would be through reawakening his sexual experience. When he decided to go to a prostitute he knew that he crossed the line and that there would be no turning back.

The idea of discussing his distress with Sarah was not even on John's radar screen because they had simply avoided too many earlier opportunities to tackle unpleasant topics. Their marital problem-solving muscles had atrophied. They could not even begin to respond to the complex set of self-deceptions, hidden truths, and disillusionments that had accumulated over the years.

To allay his guilt, John told himself that there was no emotional involvement. He needed sex and Sarah would not respond, so once or twice a month John had a "business meeting" in another city. John had these "meetings" for two years and, just as he thought, they were only for physical release.

But life rarely remains simple. John met another woman at a professional conference and developed a romantic attachment, one that was emotional as well as physical. He felt alive for the first time in years. He hadn't been looking actively for a new relationship because he had resigned himself to staying with and providing for Sarah and the boys. But he was relieved to put an end to one-night stands. They were feeling increasingly empty, and he was beginning to be haunted by the thought of AIDS.

As the months passed, he became more enchanted with the other woman, but leaving the marriage was not an option for him, so he lavished gifts on her. He constantly lied to Sarah to cover up the affair, but he no longer felt as guilty about it. He told himself the marriage was over. He just never told Sarah.

Marital Chaos

Up until now, your marriage has maintained at least a semblance of order. In the detours you stumbled into, you at least lived according to the norms of marital propriety, in fact if not in spirit.

No more. Welcome to Freedom Unhinged. What we have now is marital anarchy. Marriage by mob rule. Marriage as a war zone. Look around and you'll see the scattered debris of all the falsehoods you have told each other, the wreckage of long-held lies. You've annihilated your few remaining connections. There's nothing solid left to stand on.

You can assume you're in Freedom Unhinged when you really don't care much about the other person at all. You're concerned with your own interests and your partner represents little more than obligation or inconvenience because you two haven't worked to understand, resolve or accept your differences. It may be hard to recall what you ever saw in each other. Lying has become so habitual that it's automatic. You don't think twice about it.

Descending into the realm of Freedom Unhinged does absolutely nothing positive for a relationship, and its disintegration serves as a giant SOS. When you suspect that lies have grown completely out of control, you'd better listen to those wailing sirens. This is serious. Unless you take direct action to prevent it, things will explode.

The prognosis for Freedom Unhinged depends on how much damage the lies have caused. With effort and commitment, some couples can and do work through the deception. They do the tough emotional work that had been left undone from earlier stages. They learn that they can reconstruct their union out of stronger material. During the betrayal's denouement, however, it can be hard for anyone to envision a way out.

How Marriages Unhinge

A romance can begin detaching from its base at the outset. From the very beginning in all relationships, there are junctures where a person has to choose between sharing or withholding truths. Many of these moments of decision can set you on the path to deception. When that happens, there may be a vast accumulation of lies, big and small. One person may act as the Lie Invitee, growing more desperate—and thus more likely to encourage lies—as the deceptions increase in size. The accretion of betrayals can continue for a long time before the entire relationship disintegrates.

A marriage gets unhinged by deception in one of two ways: either one partner becomes deceitful or both partners do. When one partner is chronically deceptive, the lies often build until they become large, felony lies—and then the marriage snaps. Infidelity tops the list, though there are different types and degrees of adultery; a one-time, one-night stand will have different implications for a marriage than a long-term, clandestine affair with, say, the wronged partner's best friend. Affairs may involve other secrets that affect the marriage. For instance, family funds may be diverted to keep the adulterer under cover or to maintain a paramour in grand style.

Dangerous lies rarely arise full-blown without warning. Couples often pretend that "the big one" came out of nowhere, that they just happened to be standing in the way when the bomb exploded. But if they focus on the cataclysm without looking at what occurred prior to that point, it's like trying to reconstruct a primitive civilization based on a few shards of pottery. You need to continue excavating in order to slowly piece together the complete picture.

Often, the innocent partners see or sense shady behavior and get frightened, or they take the Lie Invitee position to such a degree that they hide from the impending crisis. If there's a problem liar involved, the lies may have grown so massive that even the most conflict-avoidant mate can't ignore them anymore.

Some felony lies concern money, secret accounts, unrevealed debt, or failure to pay taxes. Other extreme deceptions include hiding significant parts of your life, like a second family, children from a previous relationship, or a criminal record. There may be multiple lies. One woman, for example, lied to an insurance company to get a settlement and then used the money to finance trips to visit a man she was seeing behind her husband's back.

Parallel Lives

In other instances of Freedom Unhinged, both partners take liberties and become so disconnected that they hardly care what happens. When you take a door off its hinges, it's no longer part of the house. When the couple is in Freedom Unhinged, they lose their point of attachment. They go on, leading separate lives and lying to each other, and grow farther and farther apart.

Couples in the Freedom to Explore Stage, too, may conduct significant aspects of their lives independently of one another. For example Jan was quite involved in her meditation practice. She not only meditated on a daily basis, but also went on weekend and even month-long meditation retreats. Mark, meanwhile, had as much interest in meditation as he did in watching reruns of telethons. But Jan was not running off to meet a lover or start a black-market business; she was genuine in her interest in the meditation program. She was being *proactive* in searching out these opportunities. It was actually inconvenient for both of them to adjust their schedules to accommodate her retreats. But they worked it out by discussing their importance to her, the additional responsibilities for Mark, and how she could compensate for her time away. They maintained their connection despite their strong differences.

By contrast, in Freedom Unhinged, one person's move away from the other is often *reactive*.

John, for instance, made lots of outside commitments strictly to avoid having to face Sarah. In her turn, Sarah was angry about John's chronic absence so *she* found reason to be out of the house. Neither was motivated to find additional work for the sheer love of it. They both were simply escaping.

In an Unhinged state, partners don't make the effort to reach out across the divide. Their lies keep them cut off from each other and are also used to steer away from a dangerous collision of truths—a crash that, despite their efforts, will unavoidably occur.

Let's say one Saturday night finds both of you at home without plans. You each think *Why bother having a nice time together? Why should I be the one to extend myself in a meaningful way?* The big lie is that you're a couple at all, when there's nothing keeping you together save inertia. Beneath that, all the other lies maintain the pretense of a functioning relationship.

What's a Nice Couple Like You Doing in a Place Like This?

You may note the squalid goings-on of Freedom Unhinged and conclude that this stage harbors crooks, cheats, philanderers, and other riffraff, but that's not the case. The people that show up here are not necessarily bad people. The deceivers are often those who tested out truthfulness and, either because they weren't effective or were rebuffed, felt compelled to find an alternate route. They chose deception as the less arduous of two options, or backed down when confronted with the shenanigans of the Lie Invitee.

Freedom Unhinged couples are those who have failed to develop mechanisms to deal with differences. They've struggled over supporting each other and have finally given up. They have trouble articulating and negotiating for what they want, so rather than making the effort, they just do what they want. They act as if they're still single, or that certain commitments have become null and void because they've become inconvenient. Regard for the partner is nonexistent.

Lowell, an attorney, was ensnared in a felony lie. Fifteen years into his marriage, he withdrew funds from a joint account and secretly bought a large boat. Rather than being a reflection of the marriage per se, the fraud was an outgrowth of the ingrained ways he related to others.

Lowell was an extremely bright child raised in a nonintellectual family. He loved books and read whenever he had the chance, but his father and older brother teased him. The pain of ridicule led him, at the age of five or six, to start reading under the bedcovers. He wouldn't let anyone see what he was reading and also kept quiet about what he was thinking and feeling. This formed the basis for an ongoing pattern of secrecy.

That pattern was firmly in place when he met his wife, Gwen. The way Lowell put it, he "went from being invisible to being deceptive." As a child, Lowell would think, *I hope Dad will leave me alone.* As a husband his attitude was, *I'm going to say one thing when I mean another in order to prevent my wife from knowing me.* He would lie to Gwen about what he did, what he wanted, and what was important to him. Gwen was not a Lie Invitee; she often complained, sincerely, "I wish I knew you better." Lowell would have lied no matter who he married because the habit of holding back was so entrenched.

Situations like Lowell's make Freedom Unhinged inevitable. The couple never reckons with differences because one person always keeps what's important to him a secret. They don't learn to negotiate because that one person doesn't speak genuinely about his wishes. Every time the person gets attacked for a small fib, it reinforces his decision to be deceptive. And the deceptions grow bigger.

In the case of Lowell and Gwen, Gwen would sometimes get annoyed and aggressively try to coerce Lowell into talking. "It's like hitting a brick wall," she'd yell, and retreat to the bedroom to call her sister or a friend. Lowell's response would be to deceive or shut down altogether. Ultimately, his predilection for concealment led to his secret boat.

We've found that with a significant number of couples, this following process creates and perpetuates Freedom Unhinged:

1. There is a very painful early-life experience or an accumulation of such experiences, including early trauma, leaving home prematurely (running away or being thrown out), and negative family examples (such as having a parent who has multiple affairs or is an alcoholic).
2. Out of that situation, the child makes a decision: "If I'm going to survive emotionally, I have to do X." This is usually some variation on, "I won't express core aspects of myself in a way that reveals my tender areas of desire or fear."
3. This behavior gets repeated in the marriage in a way that frustrates the partner. But this reaction only pushes the person deeper into his or her conviction.

Deception is invariably involved because the person continually tries to make the world fit her model. And it doesn't. Gwen, for example, was not looking to humiliate Lowell as his father did, but Lowell acted as though this was the case. He had organized his whole life around self-protection. He didn't know how to behave otherwise.

Couples drift into Freedom Unhinged in various ways. For a while it can be like wearing a camouflage suit in the jungle; you're not really lying, just blending into the setting so you can't be seen. At some point, however, your partner will put you to the test or catch you in the crosshairs, and then you fool yourself into believing that lying is your only choice.

A Slow Burn

When you're in the thick of Freedom Unhinged, you may feel complete indifference toward your partner or you may feel weary, worn out by the work of pretending that there's anything left in your marriage.

When you finally reach the endgame and all deceptions have been blown into tiny little pieces, you may feel shell shock or confusion.

Some statements we've heard from clients at this stage include, "I don't really care what happens to him," "I don't recognize her as the person I married," "I'm just not attracted to him as a person anymore," "I don't like who I am when I'm with her."

Rebellious anger tends to fuel this stage. People express this in different ways, but the underlying feeling is, "I'll show you. I'll get what I need even if I have to trample you to do it." This attitude stems from feeling wronged, controlled, or stifled by the other person. When Freedom Unhinged is in full throttle, so-called loving partners may feel venomous, vindictive, malicious, and malevolent towards each other.

At this stage, partners are actively or passively aggressive with each other. Hostility pervades. Couples often communicate their frustration indirectly, lacking the desire to engage. One person may antagonize the other while denying being contrary, such as by leaving without saying where she's going or when she'll be back. Frankly, if you're angry with your partner, you're still actively dealing with each other; that's not Freedom Unhinged. In the bitter stage of Freedom Unhinged, it's more of hit and run than an open challenge.

As we've seen, at every phase of a marriage people struggle with being able to do what they want. Let's say you want to play soccer. In the Dark Side of the Honeymoon, you'd be reluctant to say anything about it. In Emerging Differences, you'd begin to understand and express that desire. In Seething Stalemate you'd fight about it ("You never let me play!" "You play all the time!"). In Freedom to Explore, you'd work out a way between you that allowed you to play soccer. In Freedom Unhinged, you'd think (or say), "Screw you! I'm going to play soccer whether you like it or not!"

When you're on the receiving end of major lies, you always feel on edge. You may even feel *crazy* because your partner's ever-shifting stories leave you unsure about what you can believe. For example, some people who have affairs leave clues—telltale lipstick stains, unexplained receipts, suspicious messages on the answering machine—and then vehemently deny that anything's going on. This leaves the partner doubting even her own perceptions.

Another frequent feeling in this stage is jealousy. This can signal that you're not getting the complete picture. The nonlying partner intuits a threat to the relationship but can't pinpoint the source of it. As a result, every sideways glance or lapse in attention causes alarm. This is especially true if your partner is someone who treats the truth like spandex, a problem liar who stretches "truth" to fit any situation.

"Who Needs You?"

Freedom Unhinged is marked by sneaky, vindictive behavior. Examples are spending a lot of money on something extravagant while the other person is scrimping, or telling nasty stories to friends or family members that highlight the other's faults. These actions flaunt your indifference to your partner; you're trying to "get" them. Usually one partner does the overt acting out; the other may retreat emotionally or cling excessively as she feels her marriage slipping away.

Sometimes one partner feigns being nice, out of guilt or the hope that he can avoid being caught.

John tried to hide his affair from Sarah until he felt sure he was ready to end the marriage; he wanted to decide when he would leave. He periodically bought her flowers to allay her suspicions. When things were heating up with his mistress, he took Sarah to the Caribbean. It had been years since they had taken a real vacation. He did this in part to see if he could reawaken some feeling between them, but also to distract her.

Sometimes Freedom can detach from its moorings when one person in a marriage feels controlled by the other and becomes torn between needing to assert her independence and the difficulty of standing up to her partner. She avoids the hard work of truth telling under the guise of "being independent." This self-deception can hold until it leads to a divorce. Rebellious behavior gets defined as autonomy, and the attitude becomes: "You can't stop me from doing what I want." When this happens, the person may become rebellious about all kinds of matters, parental obligations among them.

A Web of Lies

By the time a couple reaches Freedom Unhinged, an entire substructure of lies has developed. Once one partner has decided to tell a big lie, all the smaller lies are instinctive; he does anything he needs to in order to protect that cardinal lie.

John certainly felt the pressure of lying. While he had mastered the art of the rapid-fire excuse, he had to keep the stories about his absences, his expenditures, and his distraction straight. He also knew that he was hurting Sarah, and all his rationalizations couldn't keep the guilt hounds at bay. But the guilt was still not sufficient to provoke any change in his actions.

With another couple, the big lie was $50,000 that the husband lost in the stock market and didn't want his wife to know about. She asked about the status of their accounts. He said, "I need to run some more numbers before I have the real figures." She asked again. He said, "The statement didn't arrive on time. I'd better give them a call." And on it goes. The smaller lies are needed to maintain the big lie.

LIES DRESSED UP IN TRUTH'S CLOTHING

After Erin—who gave her husband some nasty digs on page 134 in the Seething Stalemate chapter—learned of Jake's affair, and the bitterness between them came out into the open, she had a whole litany of things she'd say to him: "You and your relatives are nothing but bitter, nasty money-grubbers. Our vacations were always just for your pleasure. I never had any fun. You've always been a lousy lover. I always faked orgasm." These are brutal lies designed to be hostile. The person saying them goes straight for the partner's sore spots.

These lies are treated like truths but are really only truths in that moment. The reality is probably closer to "I can't imagine ever enjoying a vacation with you." Or, "Knowing everything I know about you now, the best sex I can envision with you is lying back and thinking of shopping at Nordstrom's."

Lies can turn extremely ugly here. They resemble snipes from behind enemy lines. We've heard some wives tell their husbands that his penis is too small, and husbands tell wives that her thighs are too heavy and their breasts are too small. By the time a marriage starts to unhinge, nobody's careful about what they say anymore. They fling insults to get back at the other, to get even, or simply because they feel helpless and don't know what else to do.

This behavior is typical during a separation or divorce. People wound each other in repayment for feeling wounded: "You hurt me and now it's your turn." They keep their vulnerable truths to themselves. The last thing they want to do is expose any sensitivity to the other person. Everything is fodder for deceit: why phone calls aren't returned; why childcare payments are late; what's wrong with the other person.

Most tragic is the big lie: "I only want what's best for the kids." This is a fabrication because what is generally best for the kids is highly inconvenient for each parent, but both may hold on to this fiction at the children's expense. This notion may be calming, but you may be fooling yourself. Try to stay honest with yourself, as emotionally difficult as this is. It is possible to hold on to integrity despite the battlefield of a breaking marriage. Even if you're getting divorced, you can use the techniques we've discussed to stay truthful. For example, Yolanda, a woman from our practice, found her husband guilty of numerous deceptions; however, she decided that her children were her number one priority. This became the driving truth of her life throughout her separation and divorce. She endured the awkwardness of dealing directly with her husband because she felt that it would serve the kids best.

If you find the tough truths of a marital disaster closing in on you, you're not alone. Many couples that reach this stage do split up, but your honesty needn't become another casualty. By remaining honest, you will build your own integrity, maintain important relationships through the divorce, and, undoubtedly, improve your chance for successful relationships in the future.

Extracted Lies

One particularly seductive deception is the Extracted Lie. Your part-ner says, "Tell me you'll never lie again. Promise me you'll always tell the truth." The person demanding "truth" doesn't want to feel the full force of the deception, nor can she express the vulnerability that it sparked. She desperately needs reassurance from her partner and would rather get it—sincere or not—than do without.

If you try to lure your partner in this way, know that you're going to obtain an adaptive agreement rather than real compliance. If you and your partner make this kind of bargain and you feel suspicious, you're probably right to be skeptical.

As for the liar: Don't let someone yank this kind of promise out of you. You're going to feel even worse about yourself if you take the bait.

Extracted Lies often arise with addictions and habitual behaviors, such as drug or alcohol use, gambling, pornography, or extramarital affairs. The partner says, "Tell me you'll never gamble again," and the gambler says, "Okay." Generally, the partner already feels violated, and the exposed liar feels shamed. There's almost no way the liar can refuse the demand. Of course he should agree to stop unhealthy behavior, but it's more like a New Year's resolution than a commitment to change. He may begin thinking, *This is the year I'll finally do it*, and even convince family members that this time it's real, but a few weeks later he's already looking for ways to cheat. And once he feels guilty about cheat-ing, he goes off and has a drink (or spends money on blackjack, or calls a phone sex line) to make himself feel better.

Lies to the Self

Self-deceptions perpetuate the Freedom Unhinged Stage, postpon-ing the moment when the couple has to confront the mess they've cre-ated. The lying partner deceives himself about how his behavior is affecting his partner. "What she doesn't know won't hurt her." Some-one who lies rebelliously and calls it independence is fooling himself about his own fears. "Sure I could tell my spouse about it, but I just don't think I should *have* to." When the other person lies, someone may deceive himself by saying, "This will pass," or "Whatever I do, it won't make any difference," or "I'm sure I'm making too much of things."

With many Freedom Unhinged lies, there's an overriding justification the person gives herself in order to continue lying. The excuse may be pretty weak, but it's enough for the liar to feel comfortable about herself even while building herself a house of cards.

John did this when he told himself that seeing prostitutes was "okay" since there was no emotional attachment involved. The self-justification becomes an ongoing lie that facilitates an ever-increasing number of lies to the partner.

When you hear yourself making these self-justifications, you're probably on thin ice. Common lies include

"Just one more time won't matter."

"It won't be a problem if nobody knows."

"I have enough money to cover it so no one will find out."

"So-and-so got away with it. Why wouldn't I?"

"I've been too good in this marriage. It's time I had some fun."

"Everyone cheats sometimes. People weren't intended to be monogamous."

Getting Caught

John and Sarah finally had their face-off two years into John's affair. While straightening up one day after work, Sarah found a wrapped gift tucked into a drawer in John's office.

The years of denial were finally over, and the next few hours were an emotional torment for Sarah. She felt rage at John and rage at her own stupidity. She felt some relief about having her suspicions confirmed, but she also felt remorse and guilt about her long-held silence. The immediate question was what to do with this discovery?

That evening John came home late, as usual. Sarah put the box on the table, already set for the next morning's breakfast, and didn't say anything. The silence was unbearable, John later recalled. He could hear the kitchen clock tick; it felt as though his time in the house was running out. After a lengthy interval, Sarah said, "You're involved with another woman." By now weary and drained, John simply nodded his head.

Freedom Unhinged is unique among the stages in that there is a showdown. The deceiver becomes ensnared in his own lie—ready or not. This usually happens when the partner finally pushes questioning far enough and decides *not* to accept any more feeble excuses. Some people are relieved to get their comeuppance. They were looking for ways to end the dishonesty and were hoping to salvage the marriage. Or, more likely, they wanted out but wouldn't take responsibility for ending the marriage. Others get caught short. They devoted so much energy to bolstering the lie that they truly didn't know what was left.

Often the one who has been deceptive will continue to hold back some of the truth. She may force her partner to badger her for details. Sometimes this is because the truth is ruthlessly hurtful, and the liar wants to avoid allowing it to escape. Sometimes the liar is reluctant to expose just how low he has stooped in his deception. When the truth is incomplete, the other partner wants to think, *That's it, there's nothing else to learn*, but then more unpleasant information seeps out. Each time this occurs it destabilizes the relationship even further.

Denials

When one partner catches the other in a deception, the liar often simply does what she always does when she's in a bind: She lies and denies all accusations. But lying on top of lies severs every last thread of credibility a person may have. The more someone lies to cover other lies, the harder it will be to pull things back together. At a certain point this becomes worse than the original dishonesty. It makes the other partner feel irrational because it's humiliating to beg for the truth and still not receive the full story. The continued deception makes it that much harder to forgive.

John admitted that he was having an affair, but he continued to hedge about how long it had been going on and how committed he was to the other woman. He would refute Sarah's accusations, saying, "You're just making this stuff up" or "You're imagining things" only to confess later that Sarah had been right. After several rounds of this, Sarah angrily told John that each time she believed what he said and found out otherwise, she felt the full weight of the betrayal all over again.

A Window of Truthful Opportunity

After John finally admitted the truth, he and Sarah went through several months of back and forth discussions, honesty alternating with deception. At Sarah's insistence, John moved out of the house and into a rented apartment. From that safer distance, they had several heartfelt conversations on the telephone. John revealed to Sarah how deeply he had felt rejected by her in the past. Sarah admitted that she had wanted support from John all along but didn't know how to ask. The intimacy of these conversations made them each hopeful and even rekindled tender feelings of the past. But at other times, often when reminded of John's deceit, Sarah would harangue him for what he had done to her. And John would lie, saying the affair was over long before it actually was.

That cycle of deception, exposure, contrition followed by more deception, exposure, contrition ran its sequence too many times for Sarah's taste. She said, "That's it" and filed for divorce.

The period immediately after the truthful revelation is crucial. It's the couple's Rubicon; they have a very brief time in which to decide their next moves. Like any crisis, it presents both opportunity and danger. The opportunity is for one or both partners to undergo major self-examination and make significant changes in their way of relating. Without those changes, the risk of continued lying, hurt, and defensiveness remains. If the partners lapse into old patterns, their chance of surviving as a couple is slim.

When the deceiver continues lying, it's tantamount to ending the relationship. Some people who aren't ready to be truthful tell more lies to cover their bases. But this, they soon realize, rules out other options—like ever being trusted again. Couples who do decide to try honesty face the difficult task of repairing all the damage the deceptions have wrought.

No one should fool themselves about the impact a significant deception has on a marriage: It's huge. Usually, it's not the event itself—the affair, the sex, the drinking—that leaves the deepest scars, but rather the very fact of dishonesty. That's what's so hard to forget. If it can happen once, why not again?

One couple, Eli and Fran, came to us when Eli admitted to having an affair. Through therapy they resolved some issues and said they felt ready to try again. A year later, Eli had another affair, and Fran said good-bye. Eli felt duped. His gripe was, "We worked it out once. Why not now?" Fran said, "We obviously didn't work it out well enough. I won't trust you now." Eli wanted to save the marriage, but he was one affair too late.

What to Do About Those Lies

You're better off not waiting to get caught in an unhinged lie if you have any hope of preserving your marriage. It's preferable to take responsibility up front for the deception. The longer a deception continues, the lower the chances of rebuilding trust. The less responsibility the partner takes, the less likely it is that he will do the difficult work that will be needed to restabilize the relationship.

IF YOU HAVE LIED, ACKNOWLEDGE YOUR PARTNER'S ANGER

The damage inflicted by extreme lies can be repaired. It won't be comfortable. It won't be simple. It won't be quick. This section addresses the partner who wishes to make a sincere attempt to repair and atone for the devastation those lies have wrought.

Where do you start? You start by noting the reasons why you are choosing to undergo the ordeal of rehabilitating your relationship. And it will be an ordeal. The more reasons you can generate, the more motivated you will be. The reasons may stem from the horrible feeling weighing on you for having corrupted a relationship. You have violated your own integrity about how you want to be as a partner, a parent, a human being. You will have to come to terms with the fact that no matter how you were treated by your partner, you are still responsible for your choices and how you carried them out. Justifying what you did because of how you were treated in the past or are treated in the present is only making an excuse and undermining future trust.

Here's an example of what not to say and how you could express the same point more effectively.

What not to say: "The reason I had an affair was because our sex life was practically nonexistent. Plus, I was never taught how to discuss emotional problems when I was growing up so I really couldn't talk to you about this problem."

How to say it: "The affair took place because of a series of small decisions I made that led me to justify having an affair. I repeatedly rationalized that even if I couldn't have sex with you, I shouldn't have to spend the rest of my life feeling deprived of something that is a natural human need. I also rationalized that if there was little emotional connection with the other woman, then the affair wouldn't be that terribly bad. Plus, the thought of trying to talk to you more openly about my sexual frustration was, frankly, overwhelming to me. Rather than go through the painful effort of articulating these feelings, I took the easier way out."

Here are things to keep in mind as you own up:

- *Claiming responsibility for deception is difficult.* It will require a lot of soul-searching on your part, and you will feel growing pains. Know this: Feeling bad for owning up to your responsibility is a good thing. Directly admitting your choices will require eating some humble pie. Such growing pains are necessary if you are to going to come clean.

- *Recognize that the ugly truths that get exposed only represent a part of you, not all of you.* If your partner launches an all-out attack, you don't have to accept everything that is said. You can acknowledge wrongdoing without feeling like you're the lowest life form on earth.

- *Your partner will want to keep exploring the events that occurred.* She will want enough data to make sense out of what happened. This is not to beat you up. You must tolerate this search for truth and not squirm away.

- *There will be anger.* There has been a betrayal with significant implications for your partner. He or she is going to be enraged at you for causing such pain.

- *The thought of unleashing this anger terrifies you.* You don't relish getting an earful of your partner's fury. Perhaps you even lied in the first place because you so feared being the brunt of this anger, but you're going to have to confront the rage if the two of you are going to have any future relationship.

- *Choose a time and place to deal with rancorous feelings.* Don't allow them to seep into every conversation. Unless your partner knows she'll have a set time to air these feelings, she'll take every chance she gets. You may be reluctant (who would look forward to having all that rage unleashed?), but it's amazing how creating a set structure for discussing problems can calm things down. This limitation prevents the anger from spiraling out of control.

    One couple set aside twenty-minute blocks of time twice a week. Another couple decided only to speak about the betrayal in therapy sessions. They laid out specific topics related to how and why the affair took place that they wanted to address in scheduled appointments.

- *Accept that you can't talk your partner into giving up his or her anger and grief.* If you try, it will be perceived as skimming over the offense. He or she will see your attitude as, "We're going to sweep things under the rug and pretend that nothing happened." That's simply not going to fly. Trying to convince your partner not to feel so bad is also akin to inviting a lie. If your partner is a person of high integrity, in order to begin trusting you again, he or she will want to see substantial change. Any backtracking or delaying is going to set you back.

- *Give up any hope that you can appease anger with a quick promise.* Glib promises to be truthful in the future—"I'll never lie to you again"—have no substance. Pledging sincerity at this point is a lie: No matter how impeccable your behavior is from now on, you're not going to remedy the distress. It puts you in a one-down position, which makes deception all the more likely to strike again.

- *Try to understand how you've struck your partner's vulnerable points.* What kinds of situations are likely to reignite this sense of vulnerability? Ask questions about his grief. Developing a truly empathic understanding lowers the likelihood of such a lie occuring again.

- *Your partner is going to expect you to take responsiblity for your deceptive-*

ness. A key step in this direction is offering a full, honest apology. Here's how to assume responsibility without resorting to excuses:

1. admit what you did;
2. expose how you feel about what you did;
3. acknowledge that you recognize the impact the deception had on your partner and why it had that impact. This last part is challenging. To be effective, you have to know your partner better.

Frank was having an extramarital relationship. It wasn't sexual, but he and another woman spent time together and wrote romantic letters to each other. When it came to light, his wife, Jenny, was devastated. It turned out that her father had had multiple affairs, and they had been humiliating to the whole family. Frank had no idea that the notion of infidelity carried this additional psychological baggage for Jenny. In a moment pivotal to mending the marriage, Frank expressed heartfelt sorrow that his behavior seared her in a way that was uniquely unsettling for her.

Some people don't ever want to admit the extent of the damage they've inflicted on their partner. One man compulsively gambled for three years and insisted that it wasn't a problem because he never delved into family accounts. But it *did* impact the family: He was absent frequently and highly distracted around his kids; his wife was weary and resentful.

If, in the process of coming clean, you find yourself impatient that your partner's not getting over it, ask yourself if you really *get* what he is expressing. Feeling sure that you truly empathize with his experience will help lead to forgiveness.

Anticipate your partner's need to see evidence of real change. Facile assurances will be experienced as lies. She's been misled before; she's going to want to witness change with her own eyes before being satisfied that you intend to change.

As part of this, you may have to do things you're reluctant to do, even some you find humiliating. For instance, your partner might ask to see a letter that you write to the other person in which you end the affair. Recognize that there's a reason she wants this and step up to real accountability. Certain situations are going to increase anxiety, such as when you return to the place where you had the affair or when you get a new secretary or boss who is physically attractive.

Be proactive. Try to recognize what your partner wants even before you're in the situation. If you can say, "I know my behavior is such that you may be worried when I'm away on business, so here is my phone number and tentative schedule," you're sending a strong message: "I take responsibility for what I've done, and I have nothing to hide." As another example, a woman who had an affair said to her husband, "You'll see a man's name and a phone number on my bed table. He's a new veterinarian my sister recommended we try." When you can show a capacity for self-awareness and reach out in the spirit of giving rather than contrition, you'll be quicker to put the marriage on firmer ground.

Certain situations will provide opportunities to demonstrate your willingness to change. If, for example, your brand of Unhinging involved rebellious lies, your partner will want to see you act out of responsibility rather than defiance.

IF YOU WERE LIED TO, BE PREPARED TO LISTEN TO THE TRUTH

The truth is revealed, but it's not what you want to hear. In fact, the very thing you've feared—an affair, a bad business situation, something you believed is exposed as a lie—has come to pass. Now what?

The most important point to remember is, *You are not a victim*. You may merit sympathy but not pity. As the story of the treachery unfolds, you'll need to accept that, one way or another, you were a player in this drama, perhaps by inviting lies, or by purposely ignoring what you didn't want to know, or at least by denying to yourself that such a thing could ever happen to you. Many people resist examining their own role in a deception because it's so easy to play the aggrieved party and persecute the other person instead. But it's all part of the narrative that you'll want to understand to move forward.

Decide What Type of Future You Want

After being dealt a tremendous shock, you must ask yourself these questions: *How much do I want to go on? Do I want to try to repair the damage that's been done or would I be better off resolving my grief and moving on?* Recognize that your answers may be changing from day to day and week to week.

When they've been blatantly lied to by someone so close to them, many people make their forgiveness contingent upon a promise. Someone may say, "I'll continue to live with you if you guarantee things will be different from now on." Don't do this. Your partner may immediately agree without recognizing how difficult it will be, and if he does agree to your terms, you won't really believe him.

You need to assess the situation as well as you can. Given what you now know about the relationship and the lies that have been fed to you, do you want to make the effort to reconstruct the marriage? Are *you* willing to change? Do you want to be accountable for any part you played in the current chaos in your marriage? In particular, can you look at your role without thinking that it diminishes the other person's responsibility?

Reject Revenge

Do you want to stay with the other person just as a means of punishing him? Often, the deceived person has felt one-down and unloved for a long time. When the truth is laid bare, the betrayed partner finally feels justified in taking a one-up position and holds on to it tenaciously. It seems to vindicate them for what they've suffered all those years.

Are you willing to loosen your hold on revenge in order to take a hard look at yourself? If you want to punish the other person (give them a little taste of what you've been going through) be up front about it. Sometimes honesty involves being truthful about some negative aspects of yourself, including vengeful feelings. For many people, once they can acknowledge a desire to punish their partner, they're able to move beyond it. Some people, however, want to milk it for all it's worth. Your self-deception is the belief that this will give you power and gratification. It won't.

Acknowledge Your Own Lack of Action

Evaluate your own surprised reaction to your partner's deceptions. Often there were clues that you disregarded.

As an exercise, we ask our clients to write things down and try to re-create the environment in which the deception occurred. Were there indications that something was amiss? Were you conscious of them? Did you approach your partner about them? This is not so you can berate yourself for being duped by lies that should have been obvious. Rather, glancing back and recognizing overlooked hints can make the whole experience *less* scary. It's much less frightening to accept that you missed clues that your mate was lying to you than to think that the entire edifice you had built simply crumbled without warning.

Bill had an affair on the Internet. His wife, Pam, professed complete shock. As we explored in therapy what happened, however, she revealed that he had disappeared into the basement, where they kept their computer, for a couple of hours every night. She had noted this change in his routine but assumed he was trying out new software and, therefore, didn't really question him about it. She acknowledged that she hadn't questioned him because she was conflict avoidant: She didn't think she could handle any upset should she learn that anything suspicious was going on. Now she saw that allowing things to slide carried its own price. After accepting her denial and realizing that she didn't have to let hints slip by her again, Pam did not feel nearly as helpless.

The earlier you can notice lies and bring them to light, the better. You must trust both your intuition and yourself more than you trust your partner. You also need to follow up on your instincts. If you ask your partner a question and the answer seems evasive, ask again.

Don't ask a question unless you really want—and believe you can handle—the answer. After a devastating revelation like an affair, the deceived partner often scrambles to find out what really happened. She may ask questions that will only bring her more pain, like, "Did you really enjoy sex with this other person?" and other sordid details. She may start obsessing about the particulars and rummaging through her own past to find previously overlooked clues.

Don't do this. First of all, you *can't* literally know everything. There's a point beyond which you don't need to know any more. Far from reassuring you, a play-by-play account may make you feel worse. Intimate details may be hard to forget. Ask only for particulars that will help you orient yourself and help you understand what brought this deception about. The details aren't as important as your investigation into your partner's character. What you really want to know is, "How many times have you looked me square in the eye and lied to me?"

To get that answer, one man whose wife had an affair, said to her, "I want to hear the story from your side all the way through. I've heard it in bits and pieces but not enough for me to get a sense of how much you were lying to me and what was motivating those lies."

Moving On

When major lies are revealed, the big questions are, Will your marriage become more honest, or will it collapse under the stress? If you stay together, are you going to revert to old deceptive patterns, or can you transcend them? Crises often shock people out of complacency and call upon new strengths. After the blow-up, there's a sliver of opportunity where all pretense has been stripped away, and you can choose how to cope with the catastrophe. In our experience, couples typically respond in one of two ways:

1. Many couples minimize the gravity of the situation and huddle together, insisting that the crisis was merely an aberration in an otherwise good marriage.
2. Other couples are so overwhelmed with rage that they can't even talk without risking another conflagration.

At this juncture many questions require quick answers: Can we work through this and have any hope of salvaging the marriage? Are we really going to change? Can we break out of untruthful patterns?

When things have come close to being irreparably unhinged, some dire measures are in order. The actions you take must be commensurate with the extent of the lying involved. In our work, we've seen couples discover creative alternatives to divorce. Here are some examples:

After her husband lied about ending an affair, one woman proposed that they seek therapy under the terms of a binding two-year legal agreement that gave her more than fifty percent of their assets if it became clear that he was continuing to lie and deceive her about the affair at any time during that period.

One woman told her husband, who was having an affair, that she would hire a private detective to follow him. This was to reassure her until she developed more trust in him.

After her husband repeatedly lied about finances, one woman proposed that she co-sign all large checks before they could be cashed.

When one husband volunteered to see his mistress less often, his wife initiated a trial separation. She said, "I want to give you time to think about what you want to do. I can't go on this way. It looks like you prefer having contact with her, and I want space to figure out what I want to do."

Sometimes the fact that one partner cannot uphold the terms of agreement brings things to a head. With the proposed legal agreement in which the wife would get more than half of their assests, the husband kept backpedaling and then said "no deal." At least the wife knew that she gave it her best shot, and she did *something* rather than feel like a helpless victim or drive herself crazy wondering whether or not she should trust her partner. Recognizing the severity of the damage, and the extreme responses needed to repair it, will make it unlikely for you to be made to look like a fool.

Occassionally you can catch yourself before the marriage unravels. We were recently approached by a couple teetering on the brink of Freedom Unhinged. The wife had significant health problems, and the husband had done a lot of caretaking in the marriage. Recently, the husband had begun to spend time with another woman. This relationship wasn't consummated, but he could feel it was on the verge of becoming serious. In seeking help, he was saying, "Let's work this out, or decide that we can't. Let's deal with this dilemma honestly." The man knew he was flirting with compromising his integrity, and he didn't want to cross that line. By tackling the issue head-on, he turned a potential deception into an opportunity to explore the truth. Rather than unhinging, the marriage had a chance to become rebracketed, with mutual honesty reinforcing the joints.

10 ✤

Together As Two:
The Compelling
Case for Getting
to the Truth

*L*ies in a marriage often cause wanton destruction. In this next stage, lies can be constructive, but reaching this stage is tough; you don't merely happen into it due to the passage of time. But when you've arrived here, you value your relationship and the honesty that has helped to create it. The marriage, however, remains vulnerable to all the unavoidable challenges of life and with them the possibility of slipping back into old patterns.

Paul and Mary thought about having another child, but when it didn't happen, Mary expressed relief. "Our family is fine now. I don't feel any absence," she said. "Maybe it's better to quit when we're ahead." Paul laughed, noting her earlier desire for another baby: "I thought you wanted every inch of this house filled with kids, and that you were secretly holding out for triplets!"

After the success of her work in Japan, Mary received occasional invitations to consult abroad. She wasn't tempted by any of these offers until asked to do a project in South Africa, a country that had always fascinated her. Even though they had to do the usual shuffling of schedules and responsibilities, this time the trip made barely a ripple in their equanimity. Paul volunteered to cover home base.

Interestingly, given how fraught with tension the matter was in the past, they started to team up professionally a bit more. This time around, Paul felt better able to articulate his concerns when he felt intimidated or diminished by the situation. Any loss of confidence was fleeting. He found he could ask Mary to explain things to him, rather than forgoing help in order to to prove himself, only to be doubly frustrated when he floundered. Now, he could take charge because he felt more adept. Increasingly Paul and Mary could shift roles, allowing one person to be the leader and then the other.

Then Mary's father suffered a stroke. She was devasted to see him so helpless, and Paul felt helpless in seeing Mary so devastated. She made frequent visits to the hospital, about an hour's drive, and often had to rely on Paul to manage household responsibilities. This was difficult, but it was important to Paul to make things easier on Mary without him complaining.

Reconnecting

When two partners are enjoying their own independence, such as in the Freedom to Explore Stage, their level of interaction decreases. They spend less time together; they confide in each other less. For most couples with a strong, loving relationship, devoting most of their energy to separate activities and interests is only satisfying for so long. After doing their own thing for a while, they long to reclaim their intimacy. The drive to create something meaningful beyond their own concerns prompts a renewed move towards one another.

The Together as Two Stage is marked by rekindled togetherness. Both partners share a great deal with each other, often communicating without words. They are daring enough to expose aspects of their internal lives, their fears as well as their strengths. The move between intimacy and independence is no longer so unsettling. There's a sense of being able to venture out and reconvene with ease.

The kinds of shifts that characterize Together as Two include

wanting to spend time together

recognizing just how hard your partner is to replace

having the sense that "we've been through so much together"

feeling that "freedom for the sake of freedom" is hollow

initiating synergistic projects and plans

having the feeling, "Oh, I don't have to do so much all by myself"

realizing that asking your partner for help or support isn't a sign of weakness or inadequacy

With a solid base of honesty beneath you, the relationship feels secure, not the illusory preserve of two people clinging to each other, but a safe haven borne of deep knowledge and trust. You've weathered many challenges, both circumstantial (financial, professional, familial) and in your relationship (disagreements, disillusionments, difficult truths). Each of you has exposed and explored your own psychic shadow. You've been able to expose yourself, and your partner has been able to love you despite your darker sides. You're not afraid of yourself, nor is your partner afraid of you.

This realization boosts your self-respect and self-esteem with the confidence that you can survive tough times. Not that you won't have tough times. Arguments, self-doubts, the usual bumps of life will still arise, but you become like a highly skilled sailor. An able sea hand knows that stormy weather can hit, but he's sure of his ability to detect warning signs or storm clouds, knows when it's serious or not serious, and determines when to head for shore. Like a seafarer respects the fury of nature, you remain aware of the volatility of relationships, but you're not frightened by it now.

At this juncture, starting up another relationship is not even an option. Your marriage is gold to you. You know what it has taken to create it. When challenges arise, you can approach them as a true partnership. You can alternate relying on the other with being relied on. You don't have to feel like you're maintaining the whole show.

Don't even think about casting anchor here until you've put in eight to ten years of marriage. It takes at least that long to survive significant trials: kids, illness, family crises, economic highs and lows. You need to be tested by the distresses of daily life.

Truths Drive More Truths

Together as Two couples enjoy an increased sense of frankness between them. You're not guarding yourselves. Your candor carries its own momentum. Being honest with each other encourages both of you to confront aspects of yourselves; your increased self-awareness amplifies and fortifies the relationship.

There's no lying loophole anymore; you know each other too well to get away with it. Your partner is the ultimate reality check; it's harder to fool yourself. This stage challenges you to grow.

You find that straightforwardness is anything but dull. Each level of revelation and self-disclosure encourages you both to see yourselves in new ways and to move in directions not imagined before. You may explore aspects of your histories previously thought to be too painful; new interests, values, and priorities may emerge.

Some of the truth telling in this stage involves facing your own foibles and defensive reactions. You have a greater understanding of the impact your behavior has on your partner. You're no longer living in a psychological vacuum.

Donna and Saul came to see us because they wanted to improve their relationship. While they enjoyed their independence (Donna was a painter and Saul a professor), they wanted a deeper richness in their relationship.

In the session, they relayed a disagreement they were having about paying their daughter, Tia's, graduate school costs. Saul wanted to pay the entire sum, including living expenses. Donna thought that supplying tuition alone was generous enough. She was concerned that footing the whole bill would undermine Tia's sense of responsibility. We suggested that they each try to speak from the other's perspective so as to understand each other's view. Saul started talking. When he finished speaking from Donna's position, he said, "You've got a point. You're only saying that Tia needs to earn a few thousand dollars, which she can do as a teaching assistant. You're right. It's important for her to work now, too."

This exchange epitomizes Together as Two in that it's not a zero-sum game anymore. You can allow the other person to be right without it taking away from you. It's no longer a competition between who's right or wrong.

What we often see with these couples is an ability to take a retrospective look, and to have a perspective on how their relationship has grown. "In the past, rather than listening to Donna, I would just dismiss what she said and do things my way," Saul said. Now each partner can appreciate what the other brings to the table and be better able to draw on those strengths.

Couples here are ripe for moving forward in their own self-development. Because their lives are so intertwined, any movement on one person's part can create waves for the other. This means no one gets too complacent.

In another session Donna said she wanted to take more responsibility for the family's finances. She said to Saul, "I came into the marriage as a child. I really did want you to take care of me. I didn't want to know what you were doing with the money." Now Saul wondered that if they started discussing money more frequently, would Donna wish he earned a better salary or be disappointed by him in some way?

Sometimes a side of your partner emerges that you *don't* like. In our own case, for example, Pete sometimes thinks he has led too timid a life so he wanted to go skydiving. After two skydives, I really began to express my misgivings. Early widowhood while raising a daughter was not appealing. Pete, meanwhile, found he liked meeting and conquering his fears. Bungee-jumping from bridges with 300-foot drops was next on his list. This created huge conflicts of interest. After several discussions in which we both expressed our concerns, Pete said he could wait until Molly was at least in college. While not perfect, this was a decision we could both live with.

Laying Down Arms

Not many of these couples come to marital therapy. When they do, it's usually because they're struggling with difficult choices, such as how to care for an aging parent, or they are confronting a major life change. Or, like Donna and Saul, when they intuitively feel that their marriage could be better.

We can quickly identify a Together as Two couple by how they talk about conflict. Their stance is open, not defensive. Each can claim a part in a problem without trashing herself; each can make a point without trashing her partner. They will have conflict, but every altercation doesn't cause alarm that the marriage will self-destruct. They've survived disagreements before. They know that this too shall pass.

This is not a stage for complacency nor for cowards. These couples are alive and vibrant, and their honesty upholds this. They don't duck into the jerry-built shelters that lies can provide. The ongoing challenge of truthfulness generates new energy, new ideas, new points of connection, new points of departure.

Yes, they will irritate each other. They will disagree. In fact, the extent of their interdependence ensures that. But though they may clash, they don't hold on to bad feeling for long. They have a few sparks which flicker for a while and pass. Likewise, they may resent some of the things they do for a partner, but that resentment doesn't fester. We're not talking about saints, but people with normal human imperfections who enjoy being with each other and who have learned how to differ without allowing their independence to grow divisive. Each of them is able to grasp the bigger picture.

When they experience a conflict, they can deal with the disagreement in real time. They handle the situation as it is, without dragging old baggage into it. If they're not clear about what their partner is saying, they can ask questions rather than make assumptions. They have confidence in their ability to communicate, so they don't have to play things over and over in their heads first.

Certainly a significant conflict will shake up their marriage. But by the time they arrive in Together as Two, they both have so much in the bank. They've made so many emotional deposits that no one withdrawal will bankrupt them.

Truths of Attraction

Another feature that keeps this stage interesting is that you don't shy away from hot topics anymore, or try to camouflage them with lies. One area of truth that becomes transformed in Together as Two involves attraction to the opposite sex. Before, this may have been a flash point for anxiety. In various stages, one or both partners may have denied attraction, felt shameful about it, or used it to punish the other. By this point, however, you can accept that appreciating the charms of the opposite sex does not necessarily mean flirting with danger.

Nick and Polly have a daughter, Stacey, who's a senior in high school. One evening when Stacey's boyfriend, Chuck, and some friends had paraded through their house en route to a prom, Polly said, "You know, Stacey's boyfriend and his pals seem like good kids. In fact," she winks, "they're quite attractive. I wouldn't mind going out with them myself. I love a man in a tuxedo."

"You mean I'm not your Prince Charming?"

"As a matter of fact, right now Chuck looks a lot better than you do."

Nick pulls his stomach in. "Even after all those sit-ups?"

"Don't tell me you've never had any passing fantasies about any of Stacey's girlfriends."

"Me? Never," he said coyly.

"You'll need more sit-ups!"

"You, too, for the boys."

They both chuckled over the absurd notion of trying to make themselves attractive to eighteen-year-olds.

In Together as Two, when one person says, "So and so is really sexy," it's not a threat because you know he's not going to act on it. You're might even say, "Really, why?" and be intrigued to learn what turns your partner on. Before, you might not have known if the other person would actually pursue the attraction, if it meant they were turned off by you, and what all the ramifications were.

Finding others attractive and being found attractive is pleasurable at any age. It's one of those things that makes us feel vividly alive. You can't expect each other to be visually, socially, or even sexually inert.

One Together as Two couple was discussing evening plans. "I can't make it to the dinner," the wife said, "but a colleague of mine will be there. She's bright and a great conversationalist, and I know you'll enjoy talking to her." The wife's associate and the husband hit it off, and the woman became a good friend to both of them.

When your confidence falters because of an attractive third party, you can express your insecurity to your partner rather than let your uneasiness eat away at you. Aaron told his wife, "Last night I dreamt that you went off with Sam. I thought it wouldn't bother me that you two were teaming up on some projects, but I guess it did."

At this stage, you can bring up difficult topics. As couples recognize how much they value each other, they may talk about the effect adultery would have on their relationship. Rather than making a rule, "Never have an affair," which sounds coercive and robs the partner of offering the gift of fidelity, someone in this stage may say, "I care about you so much that it would be devastating to me if you went out with someone behind my back." There's the understanding that we all have choices.

Often, an attraction to another person *isn't* a desire to break away. But at less forthright stages, the shame, guilt, and subsequent lies about it could intrude and start to poison the marriage. When your mate says, "I'm having fantasies about someone else," what does it say about your marriage? It could be read several different ways: as a warning that your marriage is losing its passion; a sign that your partner feels taken for granted; an indication that your partner feels safe enough to share this with you; an invitation for sex.

This situation is difficult to confront head-on. In earlier stages you may feel that by even *thinking* about, much less articulating, an attraction to another person, you've already betrayed your partner. But if you can discuss what those wayward fantasies mean, you can actually get to know each other better. There's something to be said for sharing your experience and not living in an emotional isolation booth. By this stage, you can talk about such thoughts solely as thoughts without getting mired in apologies and accusations.

Back and Forth Through the Stages

The marital stages aren't fixed. You don't simply reach Together as Two and sit there, as in a pair of comfy chairs. Typically, a Together as Two couple will dip in and out of other stages. Situations will arise, and you will push each other's buttons. A family crisis may challenge a couple for a while. A new venture, a new friendship, a new outlook may take the other partner by surprise. Such instances may revive less-than-productive patterns and give the pair a bit of déjà-vu from earlier in their marriage.

Touching on habits from earlier stages is normal and expected. The difference between then and now is that you can drift into a previous stage without fear of getting marooned there. Maybe there are differences you haven't quite accepted, or a new challenge stretches your ability to cope. The point is not to view a relapse as a failure but rather to mobilize your resources. You now know what it's like to be Together as Two. You know what works for you as a couple and have that as a reference point. This in itself is enough to motivate you to do the necessary work to return to where you were.

As they dealt with the stress of illness in the family, Paul and Mary found themselves on some old terrain. When Mary's father was released from the hospital and was recovering from his stroke, Mary decided that she wanted him to move in with them. She was always close to her father (Paul called her "daddy's girl"), and she couldn't bear the thought of placing him in a nursing home. Paul kept postponing the decision. They had always pledged that when it came to the health and well-being of their aging parents, "We'll do whatever we need to do." But now that he was faced with the situation, Paul wanted to back down. He simply didn't think he could manage having another adult in the house indefinitely.

At first, Paul went into Dark Side of the Honeymoon mode. He pretended Mary's plan didn't bother him. "Of course, it's fine with me," he'd say, even as he found another excuse to avoid putting support bars in the bathroom.

Then they began to reckon with the fact that they each wanted different things. Mary told Paul how, as the only one among her siblings in a position to help, it was important to her to be there for her father. Paul made it clear that while he was fond of Mary's father, he was concerned about the added stress to the family. This set them off on another round of dealing with differences, forcing them to try to accept and reconcile their conflicting concerns.

There were weeks of tension. Paul would agree to have Mary's father move in, and then realize that he was lying. He honestly didn't want that. Meanwhile, Mary devoted all her free time to visiting her father, and she felt the strain.

They continued to hash out the alternatives, however, and finally Paul suggested a new strategy: They would fix up their garage as an apartment for Mary's father. They also agreed to hire some help. This way Paul and Mary wouldn't have to do everything twenty-four hours a day as Paul had feared. And it would still cost less than moving Mary's father in to an assisted-living residence.

This solution brought them back into Together as Two. When they started to address the situation, only two opposing options were considered. Because they could be honest with each other, Paul and Mary were able to stick things out and identify an approach that would work for everyone concerned.

Many couples will be surprised to learn that their marriage will continue to require work. Some differences won't surface until circumstances force them to arise. Sometimes Together as Two type of adjustments—such as sharing more activities or pooling finances—raise new questions about authority and control.

If a couple's truth-telling skills aren't strong, they may be lured back into lying patterns. However, by following the guidelines in this book, you will navigate the treacherous terrain more clearly. The more interdependencies you have, the more capacities will be called upon, and the more you will be summoned to further develop and fine-tune them.

Truths Only You Can Say

You're sitting at the dinner table with your husband, and he's rambling on about an annoying situation at work. He hits upon one particularly vexing encounter with a coworker and describes that person in a way that's astonishingly accurate and utterly devastating, then you look him in the eye and say, "You're a pig." You both laugh.

Even if truthful, this doesn't sound like a terribly profound exchange, but in Together As Two what is said is often less important than the *context*. Here, saying "you're a pig" can be honest but playful rather than hurtful, sarcastic, or disruptive, as it might have been previously. In earlier stages you're *building* a context. At this stage you can *draw upon* it.

Let's look at the admittedly unsubtle and oafish comment "you're a pig." Actually, a great deal is being expressed: Some shared knowledge about the coworker; the fact that your husband, a nice guy by anyone's standards, has a "bite"; the implicit understanding that you appreciate that edge of his and know that it rarely gets directed at you; the playful aspect of you coming right back at his meanness with your own mean comment, which breaks the tension; and on through layers of knowing and experiencing each other's private, hidden places.

There's no one else in the world who could say "you're a pig" to your partner with just the right expression, tone, and inflection. Someone else could try to duplicate it, and it would come out two degrees off center or somehow be forced.

Productive Lies

No one ever completely transcends lies. No one is totally objective about himself, so there will always be self-deception. No one is always clear about everything he wants to say. You can't escape human nature; someone will always find cause to rationalize, distort, minimize, or exaggerate.

The important difference in this stage is that lying to your partner is done in a spirit of generosity, not to avoid conflict or protect yourself. You don't suppress distress. You don't fool yourself. Lying is done out of respect—respect for your partner and the marriage. Often, this isn't even conscious.

Lies take on a new meaning because of your deep caring for and knowledge of your partner. You know the kind of boosting your mate needs to get revved up for a challenging event. You know what's going on beneath the surface. You know that certain gripes aren't worth air-ing, and so *not* speaking up is a sign of acceptance rather than pretense.

Disruptive lies are rare in this stage. You know each other too well for artifice to carry much corrosive power. There's no masking who you are or what's important to you. There's no equivocating to avoid disagreement because you aren't afraid of confrontation. There's no sneaking around because you can abide each other's independence. There's scant deception between you, for you've invested a great deal in honesty. At this point, falsity would feel so inconsistent with the gist of your relationship as to be downright incongruent.

The lies that emerge now come from a special psychological place, from love rather than fear. An all-truth-all-the-time marriage would be too much, like a bright light you couldn't switch off. When you're in Together as Two, any time you fiddle with the truth it's intended to be useful—not merely convenient to you as an individual but constructive for your partner and the relationship.

Loving Lies

A man tells his wife, "I don't mind making dinner tonight." Well, maybe he does mind and would rather have a three-course meal magically appear while he read the newspaper. But the inconvenience to him is minimal compared with the relief his wife will get from knowing dinner will be taken care of so she can attend a lecture after work.

These are the Loving Lies. Marriage partners make maneuvers to please each other throughout the stages. But you can't be in Together as Two unless your partner is there with you. If you're doing all the giving, someone's not being honest. Loving Lies are benign because the degree of sacrifice involved is minor. You're not compromising anything in yourself. You're not giving your last pint of blood. The lie promotes what you value: your marriage and your mate. You don't need to spell out what would ideally suit you at that moment because it's immaterial.

Zach has a sixtieth birthday coming up and is thinking about a party. Not just champagne and a large fluffy cake but the whole shebang: having the kids fly in, renting a space, dining, drinking champagne, and dancing. Maura feels overwhelmed by the idea and isn't wild about putting together this kind of to-do, but she also knows that Zach isn't ordinarily one to make a fuss over himself. This birthday is important to him (she isn't even sure why), and the party will touch him. She may be withholding some small truths, that the party will be a bother for her and that she'd rather commemorate the birthday with a quiet romantic meal. But both her reservations pale in contrast to the larger truth, which is that she wants to honor what's important to him.

Loving-Parent Lies

A defining principle of productive lies is that what you say might not be *exactly* true, but it is *emotionally* true. Think of the way a parent interacts with a child. You look at the little scribble Junior makes on a piece of paper, and you say, "What an incredibly beautiful drawing!" Now it's hardly incredible and barely a drawing, but knowing that doesn't detract from your enthusiasm. On some level you *do* see it as extraordinarily beautiful. You honestly feel it, so it isn't a lie.

Let's say your husband gives a presentation, and you say, "You were great." Maybe he did just fine, but no more. This was a generous lie because what you said may not be accurate, but it is emotionally true. You think "great" rather than "satisfactory" because you can see *underneath* the result and know how he stretched himself to take on the challenge.

Furthermore, suppose his shirt was wrinkled throughout his lecture, and you don't mention it. This is also a generous lie if you felt it didn't serve anyone to point this out, or even if you didn't say anything because you found that imperfection endearing. Such withholding may be different in another stage. You might have kept quiet because you didn't want to argue about it ("Whose job is it to iron my shirts anyway?" or you thought, "Let everyone else know what a slob he is!").

Wink-Wink Lies

Because of the rich context reflected in all your interactions, even *lying* is a way that you two express truths to each other. You and your husband are walking down the street. It's a sunny spring day, and everyone seems newly aware of each other after months of being indoors. You see him glance at a pretty woman—the click of her heels subsiding as she sashays down the block.

"Did you look at that woman?" you ask.

"No, dear, you're the only woman in the whole world who's beautiful to me."

That's a lie (you saw him look), but you smile anyway. By this stage, it's not necessarily the words that matter, but rather the attitude. A woman catches his eye. But you *are* beautiful—and beyond that, irreplaceable—to him, so the look doesn't matter. And there's the context: At this point, he *knows* that you *know* that he *knows* that when he says, "No, dear" he's just blowing smoke. But that's okay. You're on the same wavelength. You know he's not going to leave you because someone momentarily draws his attention.

Keeping Tabs on Lies

Constructive lies are not really lies in the deceitful sense. You may not be telling the whole truth and nothing but the truth in specifics, but when you step back, exchange the zoom lens for a wide-angle model, you're being truthful. You've hammered through the significant things. You have a better sense of what's acceptable in the context of your marriage and where the fabric of it has give.

The same applies to keeping things to yourself. Let's say, for instance, that you minimize the extent of some physical complaint: "Oh, my back isn't bothering me that much." In this stage, the motivation is likely to be, *Talking about it only makes it feel worse; I'm just going to do the best I can with this* rather than *I don't want to say anything because I know he doesn't really care what I'm going through* (a dark-side sentiment) or *Let me suffer—then he'll really be sorry!* (a stalemate response).

Lies that are giving express a high level of truth. You're being honest in that you're talking from your heart. When the man says to his wife, "Sure, I don't mind making dinner," he's speaking from the part of him that sincerely wants her to enjoy her lecture, not the part of him that wants to be left alone to read the newspaper. This is the very gem of the good feeling in marriage.

No one, however, should become lazy about lies. The danger of lies in

'Together as Two is that they may cease to be loving. There's a fine line between humoring someone and making him out to be a fool, between keeping mum out of respect or out of indifference. At any point in a relationship, a couple is vulnerable to falling into a habit of deception.

If you utter an untruth to your partner, check yourself. Are your loving lies really loving? Are you lying in the spirit of giving or in the spirit of making things easy for yourself? When you tell a small fib, are you left with a good feeling—with the knowledge that you are giving to your mate—or with a bad aftertaste?

One way to know if what's uttered between the two of you is a giving lie or something else altogether is to apply the "In the Scheme of Things" test. Let's say your partner disappoints you by arriving late to pick you up for the theater, and you miss the opening scene. When you say, "It's no big deal," are you really feeling that in the scheme of things it's no big deal? Or are you thinking something quite different, like *Yet another instance of his total disregard for me* or *This is the last time he's picking me up late because the next time I will have walked out the door?* Can you be honest with yourself about it?

Living with the Truth

Creating an honest marriage is a matter of attitude, not technique. Even at this stage, unraveling deeper truths and disagreeing about significant things can be nerve-wracking. To move beyond dicey issues, you need to have built an orientation of trust and commitment. You can't have one foot in and one foot out *and* keep pushing yourself to be ever more truthful and ever more intimate.

When we see a couple who have weathered some marital catastrophe (one partner has an affair or survives bankruptcy without the other person getting unglued over it) we ask, "How did you surmount this?" We want to keep learning how these couples utilize their strengths and capacities. Usually somewhere in the answer is something like, "Because I'm committed to making this work," or "I knew we would find a way."

The attitude "I want to make our relationship work" is different from "I want *my partner* to make this work." You have to honestly mean it. We've seen many couples who mechanically follow advice about how to listen and respond to each other. When they do it that way, nothing changes. Another couple with similar problems will really *get it*. These couples perform the minor miracle of seeing the world through each other's eyes, and things profoundly shift as a result.

Likewise, telling and hearing difficult truths is a kind of high-wire act. If you're shaky going into it, you're going to have trouble maintaining your balance. You need to tell yourself things like:

"I want to do what I can do to make this work."

"I'm not going to deny what I feel."

"I'm going to hang in there."

"Setbacks don't have to be permanent."

"I can keep pushing for resolution even if I'm scared."

"This may be painful now, but there's long-term gain. I have to keep the big picture in mind."

Truth telling also has to be ongoing. Though it makes great theater, you can't create enduring intimacy with one grand burst of awareness or confession, nor can you have one brilliant illuminating insight and expect automatic change. The power of such moments leads you to see your situation differently and more accurately; you're no longer wandering in the swamps. But *sustained honesty* requires *sustained effort*.

The Tasks of Marriage

We all know that a good marriage involves work, but what does that mean? In our experience, most people take this to mean that they should simply do more of what they're already doing. Submissive people think they should submit more; narcissistic people believe they should think more about themselves.

When you're in Together as Two, you know when the going gets tough, the tough get honest. Lying and evading is the easy way out; honesty takes effort. For one person, putting effort into the relationship means speaking up when feeling fragile. For another, it means listening to a partner rather than bulldozing. What is easy for one person may be a challenge for the other.

Usually those aspects of ourselves that we try to conceal—our personal demons—do shade how we come across. We like to believe that what we lock away won't affect us. Actually, it's like a radioactive leak: Most of the time it does.

For many people, the hardest thing to say to a spouse is "I'm angry at you." They may feel it; they may communicate it obliquely, but they won't admit to it. The anger strikes too close to those taboo emotions. This may frustrate the other person because the anger is intuited but never confirmed.

For someone who bottles up anger, a marital task would be to learn how to express it. On the first try, it may come out clumsily and not very nicely. This is largely because you haven't had experience in talking about it. Because it's been long-hidden, the anger is bound to burst out in an awkward way. When it provokes tension or an all-out rupture, you have two choices: (1) Say, "I'll never do that again," or (2) ask, "What can I learn from this? Can I express this more compassionately?"

If you persist, you're ripe for change. When your partner doesn't recoil from your darker feelings it kickstarts your own acceptance of yourself, and your own self-acceptance helps you to create a stronger bond.

By the Together as Two Stage, you can say to your partner, "It terrifies me to say this, but I have to tell you that I'm furious with you." The other person breathes a sigh of relief because your words are congruent with what you portray. Finally, the anger is out there! At that moment, you and your partner are on the way to a special kind of synergy, primed for the type of healing only couples can give each other.

Because marriage is so interdependent, the growth potential is enormous—not by pleading or demanding, nor sitting at a drawing board, but through the models of integrity you provide for each other. You can't develop intimacy without involving and evolving yourself. Both people are going to enter into the marriage with some rough edges. Those jagged borders are what you need to polish in order to grow.

When you've reached Together as Two, you've been immersed in the dark crypt of your psyche. You've been together long enough so that your partner will activate your most forbidden feelings and impulses.

It's only a question of whether you express it. There are many people walking around with the idea that they're not very acceptable. Married partners offer each other the chance to exorcise these demons. You don't generate growth, intimacy, or maturity from being polite to each other for fifty years.

The Expanding Truth

Honesty is multifaceted. There is no "simple truth" when it comes to a person's emotional life. Let's say you're finally going to tell your partner the truth: "I'm angry at you." Fine. But that's only one part of the truth. By expressing your anger, you haven't cleared the air once and for all. You've simply opened the door to deeper truths.

In the earlier stages, perhaps "I'm angry at you" is as far as you can go. Later on you may be able to say, "When I'm angry at you like this, I feel some hurt, some pain, and a twinge of regret over how I treat you when I'm angry. I want to tell you how I contribute to the problem and what I appreciate about you."

Communicating in an open way involves risk. Being accountable for your own shortcomings requires confronting humiliation. When you say, "What else are you feeling along with the anger?" you don't know what else you may hear. Usually there's some vulnerability beneath. What you find in the "what else" is usually buried in the crypt: the frustration, fear, disappointment, and stifled hopes. Asking and then answering the "what else" launches the journey inward. The dominant feeling or behavior is often only the coping mechanism, the top layer. When people reach Together as Two, they've been able to explore the "what else," creating stronger bonds and promoting healing. You have the belief, "My partner is genuinely interested in me." You get a more in-depth, full-spectrum version of one another.

Speaking and listening in this way is an acquired skill. Once you can do that, the rich get richer. It becomes easier to describe your experience. You won't run from yourself or your partner. You will have a broader frame of reference for what your partner tells you. It will be easier to focus on the issue at hand, rather than facing a backlog of untended feelings.

Sharing Nonverbal Truths

Much of what intimate couples share goes unarticulated. This next exercise helps couples deepen their connection by requiring their collaboration on a visual expression of their dreams and ideas.

Here's how it works: Collect about forty or fifty magazines, particularly those with plenty of pictures. Then go to your local office-supply store and get a large poster board and a glue stick. Armed with poster board, glue, and a pair of scissors, throw these magazines on the floor and start making a collage. Cut out photos, words, drawings, anything that captures your mutual or individual interests, values, strengths, or aspirations, like snapshots of different aspects of your personalities. Make the collage fun and visually interesting to you and hang it somewhere where you will see it often. It can serve as a powerful visual reminder and stimulus to help keep you on track for fun, interesting, and rewarding activities to do separately or together.

You must experience a lot of truth telling to reach this stage. Inspired truths don't come from a formula, but they don't come from magic either. They come from plowing the ground ahead of time. They come from comprehensive thinking about your partner and who he is. The exact truthful words can't be prescribed. All we can do as therapists is set the foundation for people to make their own unique, divine shifts.

As for telling your truths, we have presented ways to think about it. We have given you a framework for understanding marriage and what the truths at a given stage might be. We believe this: As you move along in your marriage, you will come to a place where you will bring all your knowledge of your partner to the conversation, and you will say just the right thing, at just the right time, in just the right way. You will risk it, and your partner will "get it" and pick up on all the nuances and subtleties, and it will happen faster than the speed of light. Your partner will say, "You're right!" and the two of you will hug each other because you both know that you've found each other again.

11 ✱

Truth:
A User's Guide

*B*y now you've learned that truthfulness is the beating heart of a thriving marriage. Lies keep a relationship stuck. They prevent couples from living up to their possibilities, creating barriers to happiness and growth as they accumulate over the years.

Throughout this book we've offered snapshots—almost like still frames from a moving picture—of marriages at different stages and discussed how both honesty and deception have figured into them. We've explored ways to get "unstuck," using truthfulness to dissolve any blockages so that trust and good feeling can reign freely again.

For this final chapter, we've pulled together many themes from the book and created a "user's manual" for truth telling in marriage. This will include the steps necessary for when you're stating a difficult truth, as well as how to cope when you're on the receiving end. These suggestions apply to situations encountered throughout all of the marital stages.

Nine Steps to Telling the Truth

Here's a couple that we'll follow through the truth-telling process. Tina and Tom met when they were both students at a large Midwestern university and married soon after graduation. They both come from religious, church-going families. In their five years of marriage, they have been busy starting their careers and buying and fixing up a house. Tina has always faked orgasm when they make love; she's beginning to feel she wants to speak up about it.

STEP 1: MAKE THE DECISION TO BE TRUTHFUL

Tina recognizes that sex is becoming more boring for her and longs to feel more pleasure. She wrestles with the thought of mentioning this to Tom. She doesn't want to hurt his feelings, but the pretense has worn thin. She hates feeling like a phony.

Tina decides that she will tell Tom the truth because, she concludes, there's a chance that they'll be able to change their sexual routine. If she doesn't tell him, she's only going to become more and more frustrated.

STEP 2: DECIDE WHAT YOU WANT TO HAPPEN

Knowing what you want helps to formulate your approach and what you say. Tina hopes that telling Tom the truth will allow her to

a. not feel like a phony anymore
b. make changes to improve their sex life
c. feel less angry

STEP 3: EXPLORE YOUR OWN AVOIDANCE

It's important to try to understand what led to the deception. Tina recognizes that, because of the way she was brought up, talking about sex is uncomfortable for her. She has also been reluctant to say anything that might hurt or humiliate Tom. She started faking orgasms because she wanted him to feel that he was a good lover even when she felt completely apathetic. Admitting that she was faking would have defeated the purpose. And so on it went.

A key component of Step 3 is understanding your own ambivalence. You can ask yourself, "Is there a part of me that doesn't want to change?" Understanding your own doubts will help clarify your resolve.

Tina realized, ironically, that faking orgasm eased some of her anxieties about sex: If she knew she was faking orgasm, she didn't have to worry about whether or not she would actually have one. Also, a "yawn" of a sex life meant that they wouldn't have sex very often. Though that wasn't necessarily a good thing, it did feel predictable and safe.

STEP 4: SET A TIME AND PLACE

You want to create a situation conducive to your partner hearing your message and sensing the compassion you bring to it. It would be best for Tina to bring up the topic when Tom isn't tired or otherwise preoccupied, such as when they are taking a walk or when they're sitting comfortably in front of a fire.

Bad times would be right as Tom is walking out the door or the instant he comes home, weary with jet lag, from a business trip. Be sensitive to anything your partner may be dealing with that might make your truth an unnecessary burden. If there's illness in the family or serious trouble at work, postpone the discussion.

With significant or surprising truths, the setting is important. Choose a time and place that's comfortable and where you're not going to be interrupted. We've heard men, in particular, suggest going for a walk or talking while working in their garage or woodshed.

Sometimes meeting in a public place, like a restaurant, is a good idea. The neutral backdrop can calm things down. If you're revealing some major news—say, you've decided to end the marriage—you'd want to do it in a public setting where you'll be surrounded by others, especially if there's any history of abuse in the relationship. Because of the private, sensitive nature of the topic, however, this would *not* be appropriate for Tina. In her case, choosing a social, public setting would be akin to broadcasting their sexual problems around town.

Step 5: Don't Be Passive Aggressive

In choosing a setting, make sure you don't mislead your partner about what's coming. For instance, don't invite your mate out for a romantic dinner when you're about to announce that the marriage is over. Similarly, for Tina to approach Tom in a negligee, or otherwise pick a sexually charged situation in which to tell him about faking orgasms, would be thoughtless and cruel.

There are definitely ways to reveal truths that *don't* make things easier. One woman hid the fact that she was pregnant from her husband because she knew he didn't want another child. She finally enlightened him by leaving a voice mail message at work when she was away. This was playing hardball because she'd waited past the first trimester before giving him a chance to respond.

It's also not wise to wait for a time and place to choose *you*. Some people are so passive about truth telling that their mates have to chase after them. For instance, we've seen people conceal the fact that they were heavily in debt until the local utility cut off the heat and electricity. It's also common for people to leave clues around and wait to be caught in an affair, or for women to stop using birth control and not tell their partner until they're pregnant.

Tina would be passive aggressive if she started avoiding sex altogether to force Tom into asking *her* questions. This way Tina would be denying responsibility for her own indirectness, and it would cause Tom to feel angry and distant.

Step 6: Plan What You Will Say or Do

Nobody would go on a four-day hike through the jungle without planning ahead. Yet people invariably launch into an explosive conversation with no forethought and then wonder why it was a disaster.

A little preparation can avoid a lot of grief. You can say to yourself, "My partner will probably get defensive. When am I most likely to cave in? When am I most likely to counterattack?" Refrain from speaking in a moment of anger. Do enough preparation, either mentally or by writing it down, so that you aren't impulsive.

STEP 7: START THE CONVERSATION

Tina says something like: "Tom, I want to talk to you about something difficult. It's kind of scary for me to talk about it. I know you may think I'm blaming you. Could you do your best to listen without feeling like I'm attacking you or that it's your fault?"

Give a warning that you're going to say some things that may be difficult to hear. Ask your partner to listen to you all the way through, assuring him that you'll respond to him afterward.

You can alert him to what he might feel about the topic so he's less likely to be caught off guard and can steady himself. This also demonstrates that you take his feelings seriously.

If your partner *isn't* ready to talk, ask when he might be.

STEP 8: TAKE RESPONSIBILITY FOR WHAT YOU'VE DONE

Tina might say, "I want you to know that I've only been pretending to have orgasms. I know I've given you some mixed signals over the years. I gave the impression that I was wowed by your lovemaking so as not to make you feel bad, but I've been faking it. I'm bringing this up so that we can do something to change our physical relationship so that it works for both of us."

During this part of the process it's important to do the following things:

- Acknowledge that what you say might seem like a 180-degree turn.
- Resist demanding an immediate response. Sometimes the truth teller wants reassurance from the other person that everything's still okay. For instance, Tina might say, "But I still want to know that you find me physically attractive and that this won't change any of your feelings about me." That's asking for reassurance when your partner wants time to register what you've said.
- Avoid defensive patterns. Some people blame the other or make up excuses even as they speak. This is your moment to come clean. Do it right.
- Be open. You must be receptive to knowing more about yourself than when you started. This openness allows you to be a good

truthteller. Tina could say, "I should have told you sooner. I've been rationalizing that I've been doing this for you, so you'd think I was satisfied, but I know I have my hang-ups and inhibitions. Sex isn't an easy thing for me. I don't know why I let it continue for so long. I guess I was just too afraid to say anything."

- Take responsibility for what has stopped you from revealing the truth earlier. If Tina was afraid to let Tom see that she didn't feel comfortable talking about sex, she can say it.

- Describe your own struggles with telling the truth. This helps your partner understand what's happened in the context of your relationship. It will help him or her to see that your sentiments haven't simply appeared out of nowhere. Tina says, "I know I should have told you sooner. I was hoping the situation would magically fix itself. It seemed easier to fake. Sometimes I was afraid of getting too carried away so I wanted to get it over with so I wouldn't feel afraid."

- Be sensitive to your partner's reaction but don't use every hint of distress as a reason to bail out too soon. For example: Tom looks at Tina with sad eyes and says, "You've been what?" She says, "Uh, you know I must have faked it only about one or two times. It's no big deal, just something I felt like telling you." End of truthtelling. End of any chance for change.

  Here's another way Tina could handle it: Tom looks at Tina with sad eyes and says, "You've been what?" She says, "For me not to tell you would be to demean you and me even more. I finally realized that by bringing it out in the open we could find a way to have a better physical relationship and enjoy each other more."

STEP 9: AN OPTION: DO IT IN WRITING

Particularly when the truth involves some sensitive material, it may be helpful to write your partner a letter. The process of writing can clarify what you want to communicate. Another benefit is that by writing it down you know you will hold your audience all the way through. When you just spontaneously talk, you encounter a lot of verbal interference. The truthteller is put in a position to defend himself. Even in a psychotherapist's office, whoever's hearing the truth will start rising out of the chair. Nobody puts down a letter to rant and rave the way they would with the person standing there. And while you can write a rough draft, you can't do a rough cut for the live version.

When you commit your thoughts to paper, tell your partner the ambivalence you feel about telling the truth. Tina could write: "I have talked myself out of this before because I always said it wasn't the right time," or "I've felt too ashamed to admit this even to myself," or "This is why it's been hard for me." Self-disclosure softens the impact. A letter can be a catapult for understanding, giving your partner a larger context for what's been going on. It can also help your *own* understanding because you can practice formulating your thoughts. You never actually have to give the letter to your partner.

Expressing your viewpoint isn't simply a ploy to get your partner on your side. Imagine if you said, "I lied to you and don't know why." That will not inspire confidence. If you explain what you've experienced, your partner will have more to hold on to as he or she tries to understand what's going on.

Most people do feel more comfortable expressing themselves in person, but you may find it helpful to tell your partner *and* have a written version. Your mate can ask, "What do you mean by this?" and you'll have something to refer to. If you're simply speaking and he says, "What do you mean by that?" you may dissolve into gibberish and watch your good intentions dissipate.

Say Tina had a really defensive and ugly initial response from Tom. "No woman ever says something like that to me!" Rather than drop it altogether, Tina could write down her thoughts to keep the issue alive until she feels they could deal with it.

Dealing with Shame and Guilt

Part of the capacity to tell the truth comes from an ability to handle shame and guilt. Sometimes people keep things to themselves because they know what the truth would do to their partner. This is guilt. Others remain silent because of what they're going to feel about themselves. This is shame.

For Tina, the dominant, conscious feeling was "I don't want to hurt Tom." But there was another side to the guilt: She wasn't able to ask for what she wanted sexually. She felt bad about being too demanding, wanting more than Tom gave her, and taking too long to have orgasms in general. She will have to reckon with her guilt and shame if she wants to feel engaged sexually.

You may feel badly about the truths you reveal as well as issues that underlie those truths. This comes with the territory. On the other hand, you don't have to feel ashamed about truths you're not remorseful about. Often, when one person is seeking more independence or asserts her need for integrity in a way that inconveniences the other, the mate will try to wrangle some repentance out of her.

In one couple, Nate believes that they should be together absolutely every spare moment, but Bettina cherishes her solitude. When Bettina told Nate that she wanted to take off for a few days by herself, Nate said, "I can't believe you're even asking me for that!" Bettina wasn't doing anything sneaky, and she didn't feel guilty. In this case, a free conscience suggested that she was on a good path and didn't have to get pulled into Nate's game.

Finding Ways to Calm Yourself

Mountain climbers know that, as they reach the top of the peak, they don't think very clearly although they believe that they do. It's the same thing in a high-stress conversation with your mate. Under any threat, physical or psychological, people automatically take shallow breaths, which means your brain is not getting as much oxygen. You're now primed to *react* as opposed to *think*. Increasing your ability to both think and feel at the same time will go a long way in helping you interrupt some nasty argument cycles after they have begun.

Breathing deeply with a complete exhalation will help your mind remain clearer. You can think of your partner's verbal attacks as a reflection of his or her pain. The attack only represents one aspect of your partner's response while another part is acute pain. It might prove worthwhile to understand that pain. You can ask a question like, "How has that been a problem for you?" Asking a few questions may slow your partner down so that he doesn't merely react, and it may help you regain your bearings. Recap what you hear, and both of you will slow down even more.

One of the hallmarks of a high-anxiety discussion is that you don't feel secure or "grounded." If you are standing during the argument, you can increase your sense of emotional balance by pressing one foot more firmly on the floor. If you are sitting down, place both feet on the floor and let yourself become conscious of the back of the chair, feeling its support. While sitting in your chair, rub one or both knees with your hand. Rubbing your knees may sound foolish, but it is actually quite effective in helping you think more clearly under stress. One other quick physiological exercise that will help calm you is to blink your eyes slowly and focus on relaxing the muscles around your eyebrows and forehead.

Though simple, these techniques may be hard to remember when you're feeling under threat. Write them down on an index card to have for reference when you feel tension well up in your head or stomach.

USE HUMOR

Of all the ways couples communicate, humor is the most private and idiosyncratic, the most unique to your relationship. When you laugh together, you share in an intimate way. With humor, you get a visceral reminder of the bond you have. In its essence, humor involves the ability to see things from a different angle. This helps you put things in perspective: In the long run things will be fine.

Humor, however, is a touchy thing. A person who's upset, for example, is unlikely to enjoy a joke. Also, humor can be a way of deflecting the truth. It's impossible to prescribe just how any one couple can "do" humor effectively, but it can create relief and confirm your emotional connection.

Sometimes Ellyn will communicate something to me in a serious way. I'll say, "Underneath all those fancy words, what do you really want to say to me?" And she'll say, "I think you're a dolt." I find that tremendously funny. Some people would get ticked off, but I think, *Aha! Now I know what she means.* Dolt is such a blunt, evocative, even silly word, but I get the point. And she's usually right. When her criticism is delivered in a preaching manner, I find it difficult to take. But if I can laugh at what she says, I can laugh at myself.

If Tina and Tom reach a place where they can laugh about what they're dealing with, they'll know they've survived the toughest part. They'll know that sex is not such a loaded issue for them.

How to Hear the Truth

In order to invite candor and be able to hear what your partner is telling you, you must be certain that what you discover isn't all personal. It's going to be hard for Tom to hear that Tina has been faking sexual pleasure, but ultimately this reflects truths about Tina, not him. He needs to see it that way; otherwise, he's going to become defensive or devastated.

However, an element of the truth may be about you, reflecting how the two of you interact. Perhaps Tina has had a hard time getting Tom to listen to her about other issues. This falls into the history of the deception and can be examined as part of the process of change.

Even when, intellectually, you know someone else's truths aren't about your inherent worth as a person, it can be hard to deal with emotionally. How can you stay in a difficult conversation without feeling attacked? Here are some things you can say to yourself to preserve your equilibrium when hearing a difficult truth:

1. "I'm glad that my partner is being honest with me."
2. "Even if I don't like what I'm hearing right now, if I listen, there's a better chance we'll be able to work this out."
3. "Take a deep breath and keep listening. Take it slow."
4. "I'll have the chance to digest this later at my leisure and see it as part of the larger picture."
5. "Remember, this is not about me. What can I ask my partner so that he can see what this is about for him?"
6. "There must be a reason my partner felt that she couldn't be honest before now. I need to stay open-minded so I can hear what that is."

For example, Tom can focus on the fact that Tina has done something difficult in bringing up this topic, and that having this in the open means that they can take steps to improve their sex life, which he has probably sensed in some way wasn't quite working.

Psychological background music to avoid includes the following kinds of thinking:

1. "I don't deserve this."
2. "What a jerk. I don't have to listen to this."
3. "Wait until I get my turn."
4. "My partner is nothing but a stupid liar."
5. "What my partner is saying isn't true, and I can ignore it."
6. "It's all my partner's fault."

Tom would be moving in a negative direction if he took this as a personal affront and focused on the messenger rather than the message.

TOUGHEN UP

Being a good listener—a listener who invites the truth—requires a certain level of self-esteem. In turn, listening to the truth *builds* self-esteem. When you know you can manage a lot, you will have more self-confidence and less to fear.

Let's see how Tom struggles with his self-esteem after hearing Tina's truth. At first he thinks, *How can I be so stupid? How can I not have picked up on this? I must be a terrible lover, or an awfully self-centered husband.*

Then he reins in the negative thinking. *Wait a minute. This is not just about me. What is Tina trying to tell me? Now that I think of it, there were times we made love when I wondered whether she was really into it. Sometimes I wondered whether she liked sex. I wonder what the story is.*

If Tom had left the conversation feeling like the victim without being curious about Tina's situation, he would have walked away carrying more responsibility than he needed to. He would have assumed that her feigning orgasm was entirely his fault and that any improvement depended on him becoming a kind of superlover. As a result, sex would become a testing ground for him and lose all its pleasure and playfulness.

Many people have the distorted notion that revealing anything negative will weaken the relationship. But what's kept secret *can* hurt. If Tina hadn't talked to Tom—or if Tom couldn't hear Tina—Tina probably would have retreated from sex more and more, and they would have become increasingly estranged.

Here's another example from a couple we've worked with.

Mara gives singing lessons in her home and sometimes gets paid in cash. In one counseling session, Jason, her husband, said, "I've suspected for a long time that she hides this extra money and spends it, and that has led me to not trust her."

I (ELLYN): "Have you ever asked her?"
JASON: "No. I knew we would just fight about it."

I encouraged Jason to ask Mara directly right then and there.

JASON: "Mara, do you get paid in cash sometimes?"
MARA: "Yes."
JASON: "Do you spend that money?"
MARA: "Usually I put it in a box on my dresser, and I use it to buy things for the kids. I do this because, when we talk about getting toys and little extras for the kids, we fight. So it's just easier to do it myself."

Through this conversation, Mara sees that her fiscal strategy had an effect on Jason. And when Mara says, "I use it to buy things for the kids," Jason learns just how much his frugality has affected her.

As long as Jason remained in the dark, he didn't trust Mara and felt resentful about the fact that every cent he earned went into family funds while she had some discretionary spending. He also felt bad about himself for lacking the gumption to bring it up. This was not the kind of situation that created warm feelings.

People avoid discovering the truth because they're afraid of the initial hit: "What if I find out that she is spending that money on frivolous things? What does that say about her? What does that say about me?" But the things you avoid keep you fearful and hobble the relationship. When you can initiate the conversation and openly listen to what your partner reveals, both you and the relationship build backbone.

LISTEN ACCURATELY

There is such a thing as listening deceptively. Many people listen to confirm negative views of themselves and their partners. For example, Tom might think, *Tina's really trying to tell me that she doesn't love me. Or that she wants to have an affair. Or that I'm a bad lover. I wonder what's wrong with me. Do I smell?*

Here is how to keep your ears sharp:

Listen all the way through.

Ask questions for clarification.

Don't assume the worst about your partner.

Don't rush to premature decisions or solutions

Try to hear what your partner tells you through what you know about him rather than what you think based on yourself. For example, Tom can be open to the possibility that there may be other things (Tina's own doubts or guilts) getting in the way, even though he might never have experienced such inhibitions himself.

LISTEN MORE THAN HALFWAY

Listening halfway can be as bad as telling half the story. Some people hear a bit and then shut themselves off. Others play the Lie Invitee and hold out for the answer they want to hear whether or not it's given freely. When this occurs, you don't see the whole picture. Your partner doesn't have the relief of knowing that she's spoken the truth and been heard. The unspoken part sits in that precarious limbo between acknowledged and untouched.

Imagine if Tom merely said, "Oh, you fake orgasms" and never asked any questions beyond that. How comfortable do you think Tina would feel? How comfortable do you think sex would be?

BE AN INVESTIGATIVE REPORTER

The model Ellyn often uses for being a good listener is an investigative journalist. You must be dispassionate and make connections, keeping your eye out for the bigger story as it emerges. You want to ask effective questions.

Often the truth-telling partner doesn't have all his motivations clearly understood or stated; he won't have thought things through to the point that he can divulge the complete story. You bring out the best in a partner when you can have a conversation that helps him process difficult things out loud.

For example, I recall one evening when I noticed it was growing dark outside and suddenly became worried because Molly was still out. I yelled to Pete to go pick her up without explaining why. He accused me of being bossy. "Why didn't you just tell me at the time that you were scared instead of ordering me around?" I said, "I just didn't know then. The situation was too sudden, and I thought it warranted quick action. I was reacting in the moment. I didn't want Molly walking home in the dark." When Pete started to see that I wasn't dominating or manipulating him purposely but rather that my awareness simply hadn't gelled, the tension diminished.

It's invaluable to have a partner who can really listen to you and help you make sense of your inner world. Finding room for that in your marriage is a gift for you and your partner. Frequently, this necessary process of working things through aloud gets stalled. The listening partner says, "You're not being straight with me," or "You've been hiding your feelings." The speaking partner starts defending herself and isn't able to explore the thought.

ASK HIGH CALIBER QUESTIONS

A good question

1. doesn't contain any references to you, the listener, but focuses strictly on the truthteller
2. elicits the feelings and motivations of the speaker

3. reflects the complexity of the issue at hand
4. demonstrates that you can accept the truth

A bad question is defensive, self-referential, blaming, and places the person asking the question in a victim position (as in, "How can you do this to me?" or "Don't you care how *I* feel?") Poor questions also carry the implication that the truth is designed to punish.

Some good questions for Tom to ask would be

"How is faking orgasm a problem for you?"

"When you pretend, what do you conclude about yourself?"

"When you feel you want more stimulation from me, what makes it so hard to tell me in the moment?"

LISTEN COMPASSIONATELY

Compassionate listening often involves recognizing the truth *beneath* the truth. With Tom and Tina, a truth beneath the truth was Tina's discomfort with sexual expression and being explicit about what she wanted in bed. Another one of her fears was feeling a loss of control when sexual feelings became intense.

If you're open to discovery about yourself and your partner, you may find out that you don't need to be afraid of the truth. For example, Tom may long have wondered, in a subliminal kind of way, whether he was really satisfying Tina. Now he has the chance to know her and bring more zest to their lovemaking. Even if he decides to change his sexual style, it doesn't mean that he was ever a "bad" lover.

Some truths may seem devastating at the time, but once you have some distance they may actually bring the two of you closer. You may think that you'll fall apart if your partner says anything critical of you or what you do. But the ability to elicit some of those truths can strengthen a relationship as you learn more about your partner and about your own fortitude.

If you expect a revelation to be horrible, you're likely to hear it as horrible. Instead, you can say, "Maybe this won't be so terrible. Maybe this doesn't suggest horrible things about me or the relationship."

RECAP SKILLS

One useful skill is being able to recap what the other person has said. While your partner is speaking, periodically repeat back what she is telling you, emphasizing the emotional content and piecing together important themes. For example, Tom can say, "It sounds like you were afraid of my reaction."

This accomplishes several things. It

1. keeps the two of you on the same track;
2. the other person get a clear picture ("It's not that I was afraid, I just didn't want to cause you to feel bad");
3. helps the other person feel understood more deeply;
4. demonstrates that you understand him or her.

The Whole Truth Won't Come at Once

Don't expect that everything will be tied in a neat bow after a single truth-telling session. It will take more than one conversation for important material to emerge. The truth will unfold; you will each make more discoveries. As this happens, you build truth, confidence, and collaboration.

Here's what might happen in Tina and Tom's first round.

TINA: "I've been faking orgasms for the past two years."
TOM: "Why haven't you told me before?"
TINA: "I was afraid I'd hurt you."

After Tom has had a chance to think about it, they have a second conversation.

TOM: "What did you think I'd do if you told me?"
TINA: "I was afraid you'd be angry and not want to do anything to make things better."

Notice how Tom's questions refer to himself. For that reason, these first two conversations didn't take them very far into Tina's truths. Now see what happens in the third conversation.

TOM: "Have you had orgasms with anyone else? Does it scare you?"
TINA: "Actually, I've always been kind of shy about being sexual. Sometimes I wonder if I'm turning off because I want to."

If, during their first two exchanges, Tom really understood that the situation wasn't about him and therefore wasn't feeling defensive, he would have had these questions available to him earlier. Note, however, that even after several conversations, they have not even addressed what to do to improve the situation. The entire process can take you a long time—and to places that neither of you expected to go.

Truth: The Pain-versus-Gain Equation

All the suggestions in the world won't lead to a more honest marriage. You have to seek honesty on an ongoing basis. A part of your brain, however, will always be doing a cost-benefit analysis on whether or not to reveal more. You can ask yourself what it might "cost" you to continue concealing vital aspects of yourself. For example, how much will it affect your self-respect? How will it affect your credibility with your children? How will it affect your ability to trust others? Since we tend to ascribe our own level of honesty to others, the more you conceal the more you will suspect that others are hiding things as well.

Questions to test the benefits of telling the truth could be, Will it increase my self-respect? Could it strengthen my relationship with my partner even though there may be some short-term pain? Would it make it easier to teach my children to be more honest? Will I sleep better at night?

Suppose Tina encounters a snag on her way to telling the truth. She expects to be alone with Tom that evening but surprise houseguests arrive. She may be tempted to say, "Forget it. This is too nerve-wracking. I want to go back to Plan A, which is keeping everything to myself."

I'd ask her to make a list in two columns (the pain-gain equation): the pain of feeling chronically frustrated and of being aware that she's misleading Tom versus the potential gains of remaking her sexual life with him and not feeling phony anymore. By making this list she confronts herself with why she's telling the truth. The formula creates, and then reinforces, her commitment.

For Mary, the pain of being open with Paul and possibly losing him was outweighed by the joy she anticipated from having a child. The path of least resistance—going along and hoping Paul would change his mind—would carry the high cost of giving up the chance to have children and resenting Paul for it. That price was too high for her.

John and Sarah, whose unceasing deceptions took them all the way to Freedom Unhinged, chose differently. Each of them was sufficiently petrified of voicing discontent that they were willing to endure the nip of a frostbitten marriage. Might things have been otherwise had either of them considered the pain versus the gain? Might they have maneuvered themselves into some sort of thaw? Perhaps.

In every significant endeavor, you are going to encounter obstacles, from people around you and from yourself. When the pain-gain ratio is your reference point, you won't collapse when you confront a hurdle; you'll be able to hold on to your commitment. And once you have the commitment—when what you've resolved has become so integral to you that you no longer waver—you finally see transformation in how you are with your partner and how you believe in yourself. Many couples struggle with that commitment. No one does it in one giant step. Many couples never get there but rather hover around the margins of possibility, wary of taking the risk.

We can only apportion a certain amount of our psychic energy to change. The effort serves a weeding-out function. It's a good thing we have some kind of filter; otherwise, we'd all be psychological contortionists. But we want to be able to push past that resistance when the potential rewards are great. The rewards of telling the truth, couples like Paul and Mary learn, include greater individual emotional fortitude and a stronger marriage.

Don't Expect Miracles with the Truth

We're not going to lie to you. Honesty is risky. Treacherous, even. Sometimes your partner will feel pain; sometimes you will experience pain: the pain of uncertainty, the pain of acknowledging what a lie has wrought, the pain of the desire to be honest on one hand and to conceal the truth on the other.

Sure truth can hurt. That's why you've avoided it. But if the truth is told with positive intent and from a standpoint of compassion, then you and your partner can work through those very rough spots.

Nor is truthfulness a panacea. It would be nice to say that on the other side of every lie you will find Nirvana. That would give you courage and make the awkwardness of telling the truth a minor trial on the way to Happily Ever After. But the outcome is unpredictable, and the benefits may be a long time in coming.

Laurel learned that the "gain" from telling the truth didn't come immediately upon unburdening herself (as she had hoped), but only after some hard work spent addressing the problem she had so carefully concealed from her husband, Ron. At an individual therapy session that she had specifically requested, Laurel told me (Pete) that she was bulimic. She was terribly ashamed and kept it hidden from Ron—limiting her bingeing and purging to when she was alone in the house—because she was sure he would be appalled. But she could see that this strategy had its own costs. "I want to be rid of this secret already," she said. "It's making me feel trapped. I spend my time trying to figure out how to spend time away from Ron, but it's really me I want to get away from, not him."

We agreed that she would tell Ron at their next session together. In a labored confession, Laurel told Ron that she had struggled with bulimia for years, ever since her parents started fighting, and she felt it was her job to make everything seem "normal."

After Laurel explained herself, the room was silent. The ticking of the clock, suddenly quite audible, seemed slowed by half. Ron was the first to speak. "I'm really glad you told me, honey, and I feel better and closer to you for sharing it with me. I really feel for what you're going through."

Laurel's reaction, which she was only able to articulate later, was this: "I was relieved that he didn't turn away in disgust. But now that the worry has dissipated, I have to deal with the problem of the bulimia."

Telling the truth does not in itself provide the solution. Here's the paradox we've often found: When you reveal vulnerabilities about yourself, your partner will usually feel closer to you, more understanding of you, and more accepting of you; however, you, who have done the revealing, may not necessarily feel closer to your partner. You get a reprieve, but you're still faced with the reality of what you've hidden. The surge of relief is fleeting.

The payoff comes later when you tackle the situation head-on. Now that the secret's out, the work is different. You're no longer putting all your energy into hiding the bulimia, the debt, the drug problem, the frustration in the marriage, or whatever you were withholding, but rather are addressing the problem directly.

People often say, "Don't you feel better now that you've said it?" The answer is generally "Yes, but. . . ." If it felt good to divulge whatever weighed on you, no one would keep secrets in the first place. The knowledge that once you spill it you have to start dealing with it acts as a kind of break.

So temper your expectations. Things are not going to be instantly clearer, immediately better. When the truth is out in the open, you will both have a better sense of what you're dealing with. That's worth a lot. But the truth doesn't always set us free. If often forces us to confront ourselves at a different level.

Compassion: The Key Ingredient

The basic formulas for truth telling are

1. Truth + Compassion = Growth
2. Truth − Compassion = Pain

People can be ruthless with the truth. They emphasize the virtue of "getting it all out" and ignore the fact that what they say may be hurtful to their partner. If this were the case with Tina, for example, she might have said something like "I never had trouble with any *other* lovers," or "I thought I'd get excited once I knew you better."

We've heard people say brutal things to each other under the guise of "telling the truth." Honesty isn't an excuse to lash out at someone. Comments like "you're fat" or "I hate everything you do" are simply unnecessary. They may feel true at that particular moment, but they do nothing to promote understanding.

Nor are such vicious rantings so "truthful." When someone becomes angry and explodes at a partner by saying, "You're thoughtless," "You never listen to me," etc., they aren't exercising honesty. The truth is about a person's own feelings, not the relative awfulness of his or her partner. "I think you're a rotten jerk" is not a revelation that leads to any growth.

Occasionally someone will simply blurt out something because of anxiety. But sometimes this is a form of vindictiveness. The verbal outburst has the effect of getting back at the partner. It's important to reflect upon that part of yourself that sometimes wants to hurt your partner. When you can be compassionate and accepting of the part of you that wants to get even, you can be more accepting of your partner as well. This will enable you to address vengeful feelings in a constructive way rather than continuing to fire off a barrage that could have long-standing consequences.

You can also strive to understand the part of you that doesn't want to be vindictive but that simply feels the hurt. It may take some effort to figure out the source of hurt feelings. One question you can ask yourself is, "What vulnerable spot has this discussion touched?" The response will give you some strong clues about the nature of your hurt. You can then decide whether or not to express this to your partner. If you do choose to expose some of your more sensitive feelings, you can ask for the chance to redo the discussion with your pain in mind.

When you have a difficult truth to disclose, use consideration. Don't speak impulsively. Don't do the verbal equivalent of a hit-and-run. Our general rule is, Don't say something harsh unless you're willing to stick around and take responsibility for what you've said. In our view, part of telling the truth is helping the other person handle what you're going to tell him. That's where the real compassion comes in.

HAVE COMPASSION FOR YOURSELF

When we talk about compassion, we include compassion for yourself. It's hard to be more compassionate with your partner than you are with yourself. If you're someone who habitually trashes yourself, you'll have a hard time letting your partner get a peek at your vulnerabilities, which would help her to see your point of view. When you can maintain compassion for yourself, it will come across to your partner.

This is much more than a technique. It's an attitude of empathy and courage. If you can appreciate yourself and your own struggles with the truth, you will be much more sensitive to what is going on between you and your partner in the process of truth telling. Being generous to yourself frees you to feel concern for your partner. You will be able to express the impact a lie or secret has had. You're less likely to be attacking, impatient, or dismissive of what your partner's experiencing. You will be able to speculate about how the truth will affect him. Whatever you say will be easier to accept. But if you try to contrive this awareness, your partner will see through it immediately.

The Case Against Telling the Truth

There are times when speaking the truth is not the best choice. Unfortunately, you won't always know when this is the case.

We can say this: If you're not going to make the effort to repair any real damage that may occur, think twice before telling the whole truth. If you're revealing hurtful things to your partner just to get them off your chest, don't fool yourself that you're "just being honest" and not being hostile.

The two main reasons that people choose to spare a partner and keep truths to themselves are

1. Someone is planning to leave the relationship and feels that telling the truth will serve no useful purpose.
2. Someone has been less than honest and decides to do something about it before speaking up to the partner.

For example, someone starts distancing himself sexually because he thinks his partner is fat. Rather than say to the partner, "I think you're fat," he may seek professional help to understand why his lover's weight is a turn-off to him and figure out how to express this.

Any significant truth telling or revealing any major deception is going to create some fallout. Most damage can be repaired if you're willing to do it. But if you're not going to repair the spoilage, you probably shouldn't set off the grenade.

Making amends often means more than simply talking about it. If, for example, you reveal that you've been hiding funds, part of making good on the truth is going to involve being accountable for your money. (See Freedom Unhinged for examples of healing after significant lies on page 190.)

Sometimes the truth is well stated, but the couple cannot tolerate what has been exposed. At this point, professional counseling would be advisable.

The Case for Truth Telling

If we haven't convinced you yet, consider this: In telling the truth, you're creating your own model of marriage, and there is no one type of good, healthy marriage. With honesty, you can do things that aren't considered the norm, like traveling separately, managing your own money, or being open about sexual fantasies. You may not embrace convention but discover instead what's right for you. Your truth-built version may well be more solid than marriages where people don't test themselves. It will be a marriage based neither on shared anxiety nor an automatic acceptance of cultural scripts, but on who you are and what's important to you.

As a final exercise, create an image of the marriage you would like to have. When people think of what they want from marriage, they often focus on how they want the *other* person to be. It's all very well to set goals for your partner—e.g., "I want to marry someone generous and kind"—and another to set them for yourself.

Knowing what you now do about truthfulness and the stages of marriage, try to come up with a vision of how *you* want to be in your marriage. In this picture, try to incorporate the kinds of truths you will tell. Get a palpable appreciation of the satisfaction and pride you'll feel in maintaining your integrity and resisting the temptation to withhold certain aspects of yourself. Try to project into the future the closeness you'll be capable of when you know you can be honest with compassion. Let your imagination create for you the marriage to which you can aspire.

Author's Note

*B*ecause we have always been interested in couples helping other couples, we are interested in hearing from you with examples or incidents from your relationships. Let us know when you have been successful in forging through a difficult truth or when you have regretted not telling the truth. We want to know how lies have affected your relationship.

If you have a situation you are willing to share with us, please write to us at:

The Couples Institute
445 Burgess Drive
Menlo Park, California 94025
650-327-5915
or E-mail us at
Peter Pearson ptpphd@AOL.com
Ellyn Bader drebdr@AOL.com

Contact us at the above if you would like information on our workshops for couples.

Acknowledgments ✖

A child requires two different biological parents to bring it into the world. We deeply appreciate the "biological parents" of this book, Meg Schneider and Lynn Sonberg, who conceived the idea and were the driving force to create this book. Truly, if it weren't for them, this book would never have been born.

We also thank our writer, Judith D. Schwartz, who spent countless hours interviewing us and writing and polishing this work. Judith was remarkably quick in her ability to take our verbal concepts and turn them into an organized whole. Her touch is everywhere throughout this book.

We also appreciate the enthusiastic support of Lara Asher, our editor at St. Martin's Press. We could always count on her optimism and confidence in the value of our ideas. A special thanks to James Belser who did such a wonderful job as copyeditor. And thanks also to Laura Yorke, who first believed in the potential of this book.

Lastly, we thank Lois Nissman and Lorraine Calta. Without their administrative help on the home front for the past year, The Couples Institute would never have run so smoothly.

About the Authors ❋

Ellyn Bader, Ph.D. and **Peter Pearson, Ph.D.** are internationally recognized experts on couples therapy and cofounders and directors of The Couples Institute in Menlo Park, California. They maintain an active lecture and workshop schedule for couples and professionals, and they have appeared on a variety of radio talk shows. The California Association of Marriage and Family Therapists gave the Clark Vincent Award to their previous book, *In Quest of the Mythical Mate*, for its outstanding contribution to the field of marital therapy.

Both have very active professional careers: Bader serves as president of the International Transactional Analysis Association; Pearson is a consulting professor at Stanford University. Their many one-, two-, and five-day couples groups and workshops are enthusiastically received by participants.

They have been married since 1982 and have three daughters. They live in Menlo Park, California.

Judith D. Schwartz is a widely published magazine writer, and author of *The Mother Puzzle*. She specializes in writing about psychology and holds Masters degrees in Counseling Psychology and Journalism. She lives in Bennington, Vermont, with her husband, Tony Eprile, and their son, Brendan.